300 YEARS OF BEER

300

YEARS OF BEER

AN ILLUSTRATED
HISTORY OF BREWING
IN MANITOBA

Bill Wright & Dave Craig

GREAT PLAINS
PUBLICATIONS

Great Plains Publications
345-955 Portage Avenue
Winnipeg, MB R3G 0P9
www.greatplains.mb.ca

Great Plains Publications gratefully acknowledges the financial support provided for its publishing program by the Government of Canada through the Canada Book Fund; the Canada Council for the Arts; the Province of Manitoba through the Book Publishing Tax Credit and the Book Publisher Marketing Assistance Program; and the Manitoba Arts Council.

Design & Typography by Relish New Brand Experience
Printed in Canada by Friesens

Library and Archives Canada Cataloguing in Publication

Wright, Bill, 1959-
    300 years of beer : an illustrated history of brewing in Manitoba / Bill Wright.

ISBN 978-1-926531-71-7

    1. Brewing--Manitoba--History. 2. Beer--Manitoba--History.
3. Advertising--Beer--Manitoba--History--Pictorial works. 4. Beer
labels--Manitoba--History--Pictorial works. 5. Beer bottles--
Manitoba--History--Pictorial works. I. Great Plains Publications
II. Title. III. Title: Three hundred years of beer.

TP573.C3W75 2013   338.4'766342097127   C2012-908064-0

ENVIRONMENTAL BENEFITS STATEMENT

Great Plains Publications saved the following resources by printing the pages of this book on chlorine free paper made with 10% post-consumer waste.

TREES	WATER	ENERGY	SOLID WASTE	GREENHOUSE GASES
3	**1,589**	**1**	**106**	**293**
FULLY GROWN	GALLONS	MILLION BTUs	POUNDS	POUNDS

Environmental impact estimates were made using the Environmental Paper Network Paper Calculator 3.2. For more information visit www.papercalculator.org.

MIX
Paper from
responsible sources
FSC® C016245
FSC
www.fsc.org

To our wives, Irene Craig and Patricia Thornhill.
Thank You for your love, patience and support.

A Streamlined Brewery Products van delivering barrels to the St. James Hotel – 1939: Incorporated in 1936, Brewery Products handled deliveries for Drewry's, Shea's, Pelissier's and Kiewel Breweries.

TABLE OF CONTENTS

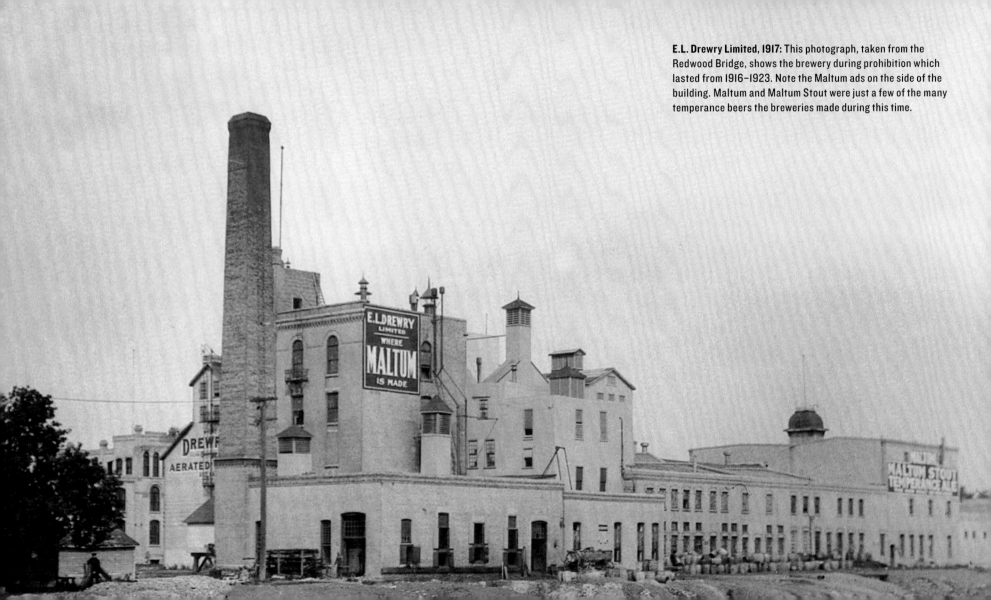

E.L. Drewry Limited, 1917: This photograph, taken from the Redwood Bridge, shows the brewery during prohibition which lasted from 1916–1923. Note the Maltum ads on the side of the building. Maltum and Maltum Stout were just a few of the many temperance beers the breweries made during this time.

PREFACE

Brandon Brewing
Co. Premier Porter
Quart Bottle

I had no idea what I was in for! When I first met the guys from the Great White North Brewerianists, I thought a beer collecting club was a cool hobby but not necessarily for me. Granted, I considered beer a part of my heritage. After all, my father had worked for Carling's and I was pushing 30 years of service with a local beer distributor. But collecting beer cans and signs didn't really appeal to me—until I met Dave Craig. Dave had the biggest label collection I had ever seen and that impressed the heck out of me. But what impressed me even more is Dave's not just a collector, he's a historian too.

My fascination with Manitoba's brewing history goes back to when I was a kid growing up in Brandon. I first became aware of the existence of old breweries when my Dad took me to the Carling's warehouse in Brandon. The building had been the bottleshop and shipping floor for the Brandon Brewing Company in the early part of the 20th century. As soon as I discovered the old dusty bottle washing equipment in the basement I was hooked. I couldn't have been more

than ten years old. I did the odd reading but there wasn't much information out there when it came to brewing in Manitoba, so I put it behind me.

Dave Craig has been collecting beer labels since the late 1950's and is an early member of the Keystone Breweriana Collector's Club. This club later morphed into the Great White North Brewerianssts and Dave has spent the last 30 years collecting information and writing stories for the club newsletter. When I first laid my eyes on

Pelissier's new bottle shop, 1950.

300 YEARS OF BEER—AN ILLUSTRATED HISTORY OF BREWING IN MANITOBA

Dave's collection of articles I knew the club had something special. After getting to know some of the other members and seeing the amazing collection of local memorabilia they had amassed I had to ask Dave the big question—did he ever consider writing a book? His reply was yes and no. He said he had thought about it, but never seriously considered it. This is when I put my foot in my mouth and said, "Well, I'll do it!"

Was I out of my mind? I had never written anything in my life! I was confident on one thing; the material was too good to let sit in someone's basement. I had some experience as an amateur photographer and in photo-restoration and with Dave as co-author we spent the next five years putting this monster together. But we can't take all the credit. There are others in the club who were invaluable to us and this is their book as much as ours.

Before any club member stepped into a library or archive there was one man that had gone before. Norm Gorman was an amateur historian and in the late 1970's he scoured the archives of local libraries and documented every piece of brewery history he could find. The result was a self published book called "A list of Manitoba Breweries and Their Locations." Norm's book was a stepping stone for more research and although I hadn't discovered it until I started this project, other club members had used it extensively.

Former club member Leo Hryhoruk has compiled binders of material over the years and has sniffed out old newspaper ads like a veritable hound dog. Much of the material on the pioneer breweries we owe to Leo. Thanks Leo for inviting me into your home and museum. The late Richard Sweet of Saskatoon was a true collector and historian in his own right. Richard was legendary for his research into the history of Canada's brewing industry and his research material is now with the University of Saskatchewan.

Another collector from Saskatchewan we are grateful to is George Chopping. Looking like he just stepped out of Bill Cody's Wild West Show, George is infamous for his museum and pioneer village just outside of Whitewood, Saskatchewan. His book "Bottles of the Canadian Prairies" was a bible for many bottle collectors and George lent his story and pictures of Brandon's Empire Brewery for this publication.

There are beer collectors across the country we would like to thank. Loren Newman has been the editor and publisher of the Canadian Brewerianist since its inception. The CB is Canada's national magazine on breweriana collecting and Loren's contribution to our book has certainly improved it. Portions of the story on Labatt's coming to Manitoba first appeared in the CB as well as his articles on Labatt's Blue and Captain Blue and his Blue Bomber. Frank Mrazik of Montreal and Lawrence Sherk from Toronto are two of Canada's premier label collectors and they lent some of their rare labels for us to show.

Was I out of my mind? I had never written anything in my life! I was confident on one thing; the material was too good to let sit in someone's basement.

EDWARD L. DREWRY

With research material provided by Dave Craig our friend Scott Bryant of Hamilton, Ontario also made a valuable contribution with his story and photographs of Pelissier's Brewery. Scott is the great-great grandson of brewery founder Henri Pelissier. We thank microbrewing pioneer Frank Appleton for giving us his personal perspective on Manitoba's first brewpub. We extend our appreciation to the staff of the Archives of Manitoba, City of Winnipeg Archives, Western Canada Pictorial Index, Manitoba Hotel Association, University of Manitoba Archives and Special Collections, Manitoba Historical Society, St. Paul's College, Winnipeg Free Press, Nellie Swart at Labatt Breweries of Canada and Labatt Breweries, Manitoba.

Local collectors from the Great White North are the true heart and soul of our project. Their memorabilia is what makes this book eye candy for history buffs and beer lovers alike. To Phil, Bruce, Randy and Wayne, thank you for your generosity. And to Dave Craig, thank you for your trust and great friendship.

Of course, all the former brewery workers, their families, salesmen and owners have also been a great help to us and although we can't name everyone, our heartfelt thanks go out to them. Unfortunately, many of those people have passed away in the five years it took to write this book. One of them was my father, Bob Wright. No one liked their beer better than dear old dad.

—Bill Wright

I think Bill has pretty well covered everything. You will see lots of pictures in this book. There are many more that could not be used due to space limitations. If any readers have old beer related items we would love to photograph them for our club archives. I would like to say thanks to Russ Gourluck for connecting us with Great Plains Publications and to publisher Gregg Shilliday for going all out for us by doing colour printing throughout this book. Thanks to Bill Wright for taking my notes and adding more research to make this final effort so great. Without your belief in our work this book would not have been possible.

Finally I want to say thank you to my wife Irene. She has endured my collecting bug and as she says "clutter" for many years. My two daughters, Brenda and Debbie, who despite growing up in a house full of beer signs, glasses and other beer collectibles and still do not drink beer themselves. Thank you for listening to me about being careful around my stuff.

—Dave Craig

Shea's Beer Made Winnipeg Boom: That is the inscription written on the side of the gigantic storage tank on the left. In this L.B. Foote photograph workman relax during the construction of additional buildings to the McDonagh & and Shea plant.

INTRODUCTION

There is an empty lot at the foot of the Redwood Bridge. As it sits waiting for future development, its rich history slowly fades from memory. The corner of Main Street and Redwood Avenue was once the symbolic centre of a proud and storied industry which dates back before the province was born. Beer was made at this site for over one hundred and twenty years. There were other great establishments in Manitoba besides the brewery on Redwood and Main. Throughout our history beer was brewed in some fashion or another in almost every corner of the province, including on Hudson Bay 300 years ago!

As Manitoba grew and prospered our breweries provided a place for thousands of men and a few women to work, raise families and help build a province. Malting companies, cardboard manufacturers and the hotel industry were also huge beneficiaries. Hardly anyone was untouched by its wide scope. Brewing beer became big business and in the process it made a select few wealthy. They in turn, gave back to the community through generous acts of philanthropy and public service. Countless others lost money in failed ventures when they discovered how difficult it was to break into the business.

The industry had its detractors too! It came under fire from the temperance movement and survived Prohibition when many wished the breweries would shut down for good. In the 1950's the government liquor commission was held accountable for the huge profits breweries were making. Beer companies and their owners were always good fodder for the headlines.

This book takes us back to a time when beer barons like E.L Drewry and Patrick Shea were household names. Their past is our past and for the first time ever we can look back at this colourful history through rare photographs and advertising items and discover what our province was like in its early years.

Although Labatt and Molson's closed their breweries here in the 1990's, they didn't take their business with them. Most beer is shipped in from other provinces and today there are more choices for the beer drinker than ever before. More importantly, thanks to a few brave entrepreneurs, we still have local products we can embrace as our own. No one knows for sure what lies ahead for Manitoba's modest brewing scene, but one thing is for certain; it will never be as it was.

York Factory

The first permanent brewery in what eventually became the province of Manitoba was at York Factory. The longtime head-quarters of the HBC in North America, York Factory lies on the banks of the Hayes River, 100 kilometres south of Churchill. In 1694, ninety-two years before John Molson began brewing his beer, York Factory was operating a small brewery. It ran spo-radically for over 100 years. William Clarke was the first brewer, but his tenure was cut short. The French captured the fort in 1694, the same year brewing began. They drove 53 men out into the bush to survive the winter on their own. Twenty-five men were left come spring, only to be taken to France as prisoners. Whether brewer William Clarke was among them isn't known.

PIONEERS
THE ORIGINAL MICROBREWERIES

This replica of the Nonsuch was commissioned by the Hudson's Bay Company in 1970 and has been on public display at the Manitoba Museum since 1973.

When looking back on Canada's brewing past, historians invariably start with the colony of New France. After a few individual attempts to brew beer in the early 1600's, the first successful commercial brewery is credited to civil servant Jean Talon and his effort to bring some economic stability to the young colony in 1667. His undertaking was short lived and by the time John Molson began his brewing empire in 1786, many other breweries in Quebec had come and gone.

However, beer was being brewed in parts of the vast frontier that lie to the west. In the outposts of the Hudson's Bay Company, small brewing operations supplemented the diets of company employees and eased the boredom of living in such isolation. In fact, brewing began before the Hudson's Bay Company was formed. Although explorers Henry Hudson and Thomas Button were here before, credit for very first brew ever made in the Northwest goes to the Captain of the *Nonsuch*; Zachariah Gillam.

In September of 1668, two years before the founding of the Hudson's Bay Company, Gillam landed his little ship the *Nonsuch* on the shores of Hudson Bay at the mouth of the Rupert River. Funded by a syndicate that later became the HBC, the expedition founded Fort Rupert. The fort and the river were named after one of the syndicate's backers—the prominent noblemen, Prince Rupert, who later became the first governor of the HBC. The crew cleared the land and built a stockade and small house. It's here that they brewed beer for the winter. They buried kegs of strong beer in the ground to keep from freezing and saved it for the voyage back the following spring. Small beer was also made for the men while they wintered. "Small" refers to the alcohol content. After the beer is brewed, the spent barley was used again, to brew another lot of beer. There wouldn't be enough fermentable sugars left, making the second brew weak in taste, body and alcohol (a seventeenth century "light" beer.)

THE STONE FORT BREWERY – LOWER FORT GARRY

The centre of development in Rupert's Land was the Red River settlement and by the late 1830's the population had grown to more than 4,000 inhabitants. Undoubtedly, some of the inhabitants had a thirst for beer. There was no established brewery at that time but local individuals were supplying the market anyway. In 1837, the Council of Assiniboia felt compelled to pass a resolution banning the sale of beer to the Indians with a fine of 20 shillings for the offence. To satisfy the needs of the growing population and to suppress the illicit trade, a proper brewery needed to be built.

After the devastating flood at Upper Fort Garry in 1826, HBC Governor Sir George Simpson decided to build another fort on higher ground north of the St. Andrews Rapids. Upper Fort Garry was rebuilt in 1835 and regardless of the fact that it was the centre of administration for the HBC, an industrial area to the south of the lower fort was developed. The area included lime kilns (they reduced limestone for use as mortar and whitewash), a grist mill, sawmill, bakeshops and in 1845 a brewery. Simpson wanted to build a distillery and brewery earlier, but the HBC head office in London was opposed to the plan; as was the local clergy. Lower Fort Garry was locally known as the Stone Fort, and so the brewery was aptly named.

In June of 1846, 337 officers and men, along with 17 wives and children, were sent to the Fort. The troops were the Royal First Warwickshire of Foot. They were there to protect British interests in the threat of war between the British and the

Chronic shortages of barley for malt caused brewing to be done on an irregular basis.

United States. Their arrival brought great prosperity to the area. Governor Simpson ordered 2,000 bushels of barley converted to beer for use of the troops but since there was a shortage of grain that year they were rationed to just one pint a day.

Typical of pioneer living in the mid 1800's, the struggle to supply the staples of life was a constant challenge, as was running a brewery. Chronic shortages of barley for malt caused brewing to be done on an irregular basis. The other main ingredient for beer was hops and a fair quantity was supplied by the settlers. In fact, 700 pounds were purchased by the company in 1860. Later the industry relied on the higher quality hops imported from Wisconsin, Oregon and Germany.

The brewery operated until the 1870's and was demolished in 1880. By then there were many other breweries competing for the market.

Lower Fort Garry, 1869. The Stone Fort Brewery was nestled beside a creek south of the main fort. Brewing began in 1846.

"JUST CALL ME WHISKEY"

St. Paul's Parish was created in 1880 by an act of the Manitoba Legislature. Starting in 1839, the Hudson's Bay Company granted to their retired employees river lots in this area. These men served in the more menial work of the fur trade. Many had taken Aboriginal wives or were descendents of these unions and by 1856 there were 584 inhabitants in the area. The settlement was called Middlechurch. This is where the brewing industry separate from the HBC began.

If you're going to make a living in the liquor trade, it's best to have a name that advertises what you sell. For Whiskey Tom and Whiskey Jack, the name says it all. Well, not quite everything. Not only did both these men own distilleries, they also ran their own brewery. Their real names were Celestin Thomas and Henri Joachim and the two are regarded as true brewing pioneers in Manitoba.

Henri Joachim (pronounced Yokum) was born in Belgium in 1822 and trained as a brewer. He worked in St. Paul, Minnesota in 1857 before making his way north to Red River where he built his brewery and distillery in 1859. Located on the corner of Drury Avenue and Main Street the distillery portion was converted to an inn in 1870 and called the Six Mile Inn and Brewery because of its proximity to Upper Fort Garry. Many breweries in those early days ran a public house for their customers to imbibe in. His business was also close to Thomas's brewery on Grassmere Creek and the two became bitter rivals.

Whiskey Jack lived up to his name in more ways than one. He developed a reputation as drinker and trouble maker, which ultimately lead to the Council of Assiniboia refusing to renew his liquor license in 1868. In the days before the creation of the province of Manitoba, the Council ruled the roost. Created by the HBC to govern the territory, members were not elected, but appointed by the company. Representatives of both the Protestant and Roman Catholic clergy (including Bishop Tache) sat on Council; as well as businessmen and former HBC factors and traders. The liquor trade was caught between the Council's desire for order and its thirst for the taxes booze provided. Being a direct competitor to the Stone Fort Brewery didn't help Joachim's cause.

The Council's days ended in 1870 with Manitoba's entry into confederation and Whiskey Jack was back in business. But his health was failing and he tried selling the brewery in 1872 with-

> Whiskey Jack lived up to his name in more ways than one. He developed a reputation as drinker and trouble maker, which ultimately lead to the Council of Assiniboia refusing to renew his liquor license in 1868.

out much luck. He leased the building to George Miller from 1874 to 1877. Joachim finally sold out to Charles De Cayes in 1881 and the name was changed to the Kildonan Brewery. By then poor old Whiskey Jack's reputation was still intact

Brewery of Henri Joachim, Middlechurch – 1859

George Miller's St. Paul's Parish Brewery: Nor'Wester ad, 1874

PIONEERS—The Original Microbreweri

with evidence from a newspaper report in 1879. Described as "boozy as usual" the paper recounts Joachim driving into the back of Rev. Fortim's buggy, demoralizing it to the extent of $8.00.

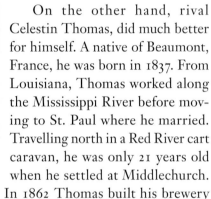

On the other hand, rival Celestin Thomas, did much better for himself. A native of Beaumont, France, he was born in 1837. From Louisiana, Thomas worked along the Mississippi River before moving to St. Paul where he married. Travelling north in a Red River cart caravan, he was only 21 years old when he settled at Middlechurch.

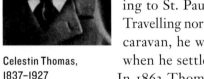
Celestin Thomas, 1837–1927

In 1862 Thomas built his brewery alongside a brook now known as Grassmere Creek Drain. The brewery was locally referred to as the Grassmere Brewery.

Whiskey Thomas was a celebrated character in the early days of Manitoba's history. A trail running to Stony Mountain, built by the men of Kildonan, was named after the brewer. Norm Gorman in his book "A List of Manitoba Breweries" states that Thomas was an exceptional salesman and gave the Stone Fort Brewery a run for their money because in addition to

The Davis Hotel was previously owned by "Dutch" George Emmerling in the 1860's. Emmerling was the brother in-law of Celestin Thomas.

By 1873, it was quite obvious the area around the forks of the Red and Assiniboine Rivers had become the commercial centre for the settlement.

---

manufacturing his own beer and spirits, he imported both. However, they weren't complete adversaries as evidence shows Thomas did some brewing for the HBC in 1866.

Thomas also had an allegiance to a key figure in the hotel business that was emerging near the forks. His brother in-law was none other than "Dutch" George Emmerling. Emmerling arrived at Red River with Thomas in 1859 and built the Emmerling Hotel (later to become the Davis Hotel) just north of the Red and Assiniboine Trails. He later bought another hotel across the street. This was the Royal Hotel, Winnipeg's first when it was built by Henry McKinney in

1859. Emmerling, an American annexationist, sold out and moved back to the States in disgust when Manitoba became a Province in 1870. By then Thomas was well established in the colony and ready to move his business to where the action was.

By 1873, it was quite obvious the area around the forks of the Red and Assiniboine Rivers had become the commercial centre for the settlement. Whiskey Thomas moved his brewery to a new a location along Colony Creek. He named it the Winnipeg Brewery and the impact of this move lasted for a hundred years.

James Spence

BURNELL, SPENCE & CO.

At the same time the two "Whiskey's" were plying their trade, there were other breweries operating with just as colourful reputations. When Whiskey Thomas moved his plant to Colony Creek it wasn't the first brewery in the area. That distinction goes to James Spence. A former cooper with the HBC, Spence formed a partnership with John Burnell in 1868 and built a brewery on land he owned west of Colony Creek. The business was known as the Burnell, Spence Brewery but was often referred to as the Maryland Brewery. Its fate was sealed in 1873 when it failed to meet federal government standards, an unfortunate repercussion of Manitoba's entry into confederation. But alas, James Spence can still be remembered for the street that's named in his honour.

CHARLES GARRETT

Another notable character was American Charles Garrett. He ran a distillery and brewery sometime between 1860 to 1868. The hotel keeper, lawyer, doctor and stump orator was a notable critic of the HBC. As a result, the St. Boniface business that bore his name suffered when the Council of Assiniboia suspended his distillery license. He also opposed the provisional government of Louis Riel and in 1869 this brought him a heap of trouble. He was taken prisoner by the Metis after helping defend the house of John Shultz. Held for 66 days he was forced to leave the country after his release, (he later returned). John Galbraith and Henry Smith's luck wasn't much better when they leased and operated the plant from 1870 to 1872. They left for British Columbia after the renewal of their brewing license was also refused.

> [Garrett] was taken prisoner by the Metis after helping defend the house of John Shultz.

BOTTLED ALE AND PORTER,

ALSO

SMITH & GALBRAITH'S CELEBRATED BEER ALWAYS ON DRAUGHT.

LARKIN BROTHERS

And then there were the Larkin Brothers. In 1873, George and Joseph Larkin erected a brewery on the banks of the Red River at the end of Post Office Street (now called Lombard). A small newspaper ad reported; "*the brewery was turning out a fine article of beer. In warm or any other weather we would recommend its use as a healthy beverage in preference to any kind of spirits*." Contrary to the ad, the Larkin's brew failed to take the newly incorporated city by storm and in 1875 the property was seized by the sheriff. But that didn't discourage the brothers from trying again. They immediately packed up their families and moved to Moorhead, Minnesota. The town newspaper welcomed the businessmen with a column extolling their good judgment and business ability. But the *Manitoba Free Press* knew better and wrote that citizens in the village of Moorhead should get their money in advance of any business transaction. This comment turned out to be prophetic. The Larkin's managed to build their brewery, but the brothers made a major error. They began brewing ale rather than lager which the local Americans preferred. To make matters worse the ale they produced was of questionable quality. Within a year the Larkin Brothers were forced to end their careers in brewing when they faced foreclosure in 1876. The brewery lived on and off under new management but struggled to survive. It burned to the ground in 1901.

REDWOOD BREWERY, Winnipeg — River water being now unfit for drinking, the undersigned would recommend their splendid Ale and Beer, now in fine condition, either in bottles or casks of 5, 10, 15, 20, and 30 gallons.

HERCHMER & BATKINS
Brewers and Maltsters

☞ Leave orders with Samuel West agent Sinclair Street; or at McKenny's hardware Store; or with Reynolds & Steele, Wrights Block   a17.111

Redwood Brewery ad – Manitoba Free Press, 1874

REDWOOD BREWERY

This tiny brewery started by Herchmer and Batkin would still be brewing beer over a century later. Founded in 1872, the brewery barely had a chance at first. The grasshopper scourge of 1875 resulted in financial disaster for the firm and the plant remained idle until E.L. Drewry leased it in 1877. Drewry built it up to be one of the most successful businesses in the city. As for Col. Lawrence William Herchmer, his future took an interesting turn. In 1876, he was appointed Indian agent at Birtle, Manitoba and was successful enough to become inspector of

- -

Drewry built it up to be one of the most successful businesses in the city.

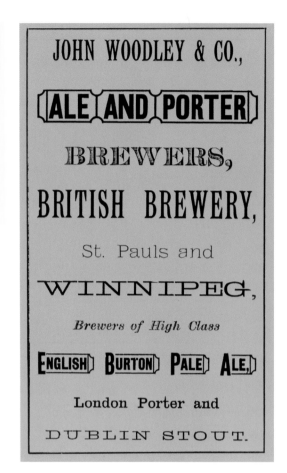

JOHN WOODLEY & CO.,

ALE AND PORTER

BREWERS,

BRITISH BREWERY,

St. Pauls and

WINNIPEG,

Brewers of High Class

ENGLISH BURTON PALE ALE,

London Porter and

DUBLIN STOUT.

British Brewery ad – Henderson Directory, 1883

Indian Agencies for the North-West Territories in 1885. A year later he became commissioner of the North West Mounted Police. At the time the Territories were under Prohibition and were to stay dry. Ironically, it became the former brewery owners' duty to keep it that way.

Pioneer Brewer John F. Woodley

The catch phrase "Have Beer, Will Travel" would be an appropriate calling card for John Woodley. He brought his talents from England and managed to have his hand in five different breweries in three corners of the province. Before arriving in Winnipeg, Woodley worked as a brewer for Bass & Co in England. He brought with him high standards and great ambition. He promised quality before quantity, but lasting success eluded him. He bought the Kildonan Brewery in 1883 and renamed it the British Brewery, but that same year he was off to the boom town of Emerson. He became part owner of the Union Brewery and then the Emerson Brewery. Unfortunately by 1885 the boom had faded and a growing temperance movement in the area was taking hold. The equipment from the defunct Emerson Brewery was shipped to Brandon where Woodley became a pioneer in the brewing industry of that city.

THE BREWERIES OF SILVER HEIGHTS

Silver Heights today is known for the subdivision that began in the late 1940's, but the name itself was well known as far back as the 1830's. Named for the silver hued foliage that grew on the high ground, the area gave refuge to many escaping the rising waters of 1826 and 1852. Deer Lodge was here; it was the home of the Honourable James MacKay. His mansion became a favourite hotel and later a veteran's hospital. There was a large log house built by John Rowand, Jr. who worked for the Hudson's Bay Company. It was also called Silver Heights and later served as Government House for the first Lieutenant-Governor of the province. And of course, there was a brewery.

THE ASSINIBOINE BREWERY CO.

WILL PAY

60 CENTS CASH

FOR

GOOD CLEAN BARLEY

DELIVERED AT THE BREWERY AT

SILVER HEIGHTS.

275-278

ROBT. STRANG,
Manager.

Manitoba Brewery Co.

SEED BARLEY to be given out to Farmers. For terms and particulars apply to Mr. ROBERT TAIT, St. James's, or Dr. BIRD, Winnipeg.

ALEX. BEGG,
Secretary.

MANITOBA BREWERY CO. LTD, 1871–1874
ASSINIBOINE BREWERY CO. 1875–1881
SILVER HEIGHTS BREWERY 1881–1883

Built on land purchased from John Rowand south of Portage Road near Truro Creek, the Manitoba Brewery Co. was established by a few prominent local businessmen such as Alexander Begg, Andrew Bannatyne and James Hargrave. It was the prototypical pioneer brewery. The timbers were oak and imported from St. Paul. Insulated with clay mixed with chopped straw, the plant consisted of three buildings. The brew house was 90 feet long by 30 feet and 20 feet high, the second building held the kiln, drying floor and malt house. A third smaller building was used for steaming barrels. Many breweries of the day employed their own cooper to build and repair barrels or they may have relied on a local cooper. The well was located in the cellar and had a peculiar phenomenon attached it. The level of the water rose when the wind blew from the north and receded if the wind was from the south. There was speculation the well was connected in some subterranean manner to Lake Winnipeg.

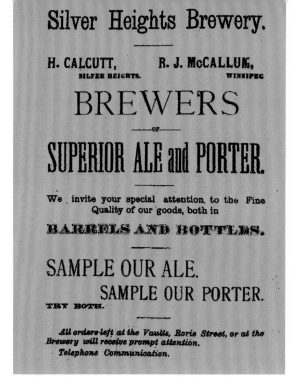

Brewer Henry Calcutt arrived from Peterborough Ontario in 1881 and took possession of the Assiniboine Brewery. With partner Robert Tait, the name was changed to the Silver Heights Brewery. His brewery burned to the ground on May, 18 1883. Calcutt also owned a bottling shop at 151 Kennedy Street that later became the South End Brewery.

The brewery wasn't a success. One problem was the distance from town. The dray wagons full of heavy barrels had almost five miles of bad roads to travel and frequently got stuck in the mud. When it closed on April 1, 1874 it still had not collected from all its shareholders. But this didn't deter some of the original shareholders from trying again. After a brief eight months operating as the Livingston Distillery, the buildings were bought at public auction and the name changed to the Assiniboine Brewing and Distilling Co. They soon dropped the distilling part of the business in 1875.

THE BREWERIES OF EMERSON

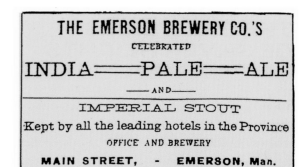

It was called the Gateway to the West and in the late 1870's Emerson was indeed the major entry point for settlers travelling to the west. Part of an area called the Gateway Cities (Emerson, West Lynne, St Vincent and Pembina) the town was founded by Thomas Carney and William Fairbanks in 1874 and named after Fairbank's favourite author, Ralph Waldo Emerson. Before the CPR arrived in Winnipeg in 1881, travel to Manitoba was a difficult task. Most preferred entering from the south through the U.S. where steamers, railway and river boats were the mode of transportation. In 1878 a railway was completed from Pembina to St Boniface and by 1883 Emerson grew to such a size that it is said to have nearly 10,000 people. The town built a bridge over the Red River to tie it to a future branch line of the railway. All those thirsty inhabitants began to attract the attention of a few Winnipeg brewers and George Raywood was the first to set up shop.

Raywood was a brewing nomad. During his career he worked in or owned at least ten different breweries. He first worked for Celestin Thomas in Middlechurch before becoming a partner in the Manitoba Brewery Co. at Silver Heights. He made the rounds of other Winnipeg breweries including a short stint with Herchmer & Batkin and their Redwood Brewery. In 1881, he operated the Brewer's Arms Hotel and opened the West Lynne Brewery — the first local brewery on the Canadian side of the border. In predictable fashion George Raywood sold his interest in the brewery in 1882 and moved to Victoria, BC to start the pattern all over again.

There were only two brewery sites in Emerson/West Lynne. They just kept changing names and it's doubtful anyone ever made money on the ventures. John Woodley bought Raywood's old plant. He renamed it the Union Brewery before selling it and starting the Emerson Brewing Co. on Main Street. By 1885, his brewery closed and Woodley moved to Brandon. Pembina had their breweries too. E.L. Drewry operated one from 1875 to 1877. Raywood's old friend Whiskey Thomas tried his hand on the American side in 1882, but this venture lasted a few years before he reluctantly returned to the Winnipeg Brewery.

As hard as these fellows tried they may have well stayed in Winnipeg. Their timing was just too late. In 1881, the CPR arrived in Winnipeg and later the branch line the town was promised failed to materialize. In 1884, Emerson went bankrupt. The temperance movement was beginning to take hold in rural Manitoba and John Woodley found himself defending the liquor industry at several local meetings held by Rev. Quinn. A petition to council endorsing the closure of liquor outlets began and so the town was left with two idle breweries. Those breweries never opened again and today Emerson is a quiet little border town of 700 inhabitants and a fascinating past.

> As hard as these fellows tried they may have well stayed in Winnipeg. Their timing was just too late.

Ad: Southern Manitoba Times, 1885

THE PORTAGE BREWING COMPANY

HAVE constantly on hand

Ales and Porters,

IN CASKS AND BOTTLES.

Orders by mail and telegraph promptly attended to.

W. J. SOUCH,
Manager.

PORTAGE LA PRAIRIE, NEEPAWA AND MINNEDOSA

While Winnipeg may have been a hotbed for brewing in the province during the early 1880's, there was a demand for beer in places other than the big city. The very first brewery west of Winnipeg was near a small town east of Portage la Prairie. The High Bluff Brewery was owned by Alexander Didiers and may have been operating as early as 1868. It was short lived and by 1879, Portage la Prairie became the main supplier of beer in the area.

From 1879 until 1893, when he left for Edmonton to establish a series of breweries there, his plants operated under a string of different names and numerous owners.

Manitoba's early brewing past is not complete without mentioning Thomas Cairns. With restless ambition and a fistful of stubbornness, he built three breweries in Portage, none with lasting success. From 1879 until 1893, when he left for Edmonton to establish a series of breweries there, his plants operated under a string of different names and numerous owners. His time in Portage was filled with controversy. Whether it was battling his rivals over stealing each other's kegs, accused of selling beer to Indians or taking a Revenue Department inspector to court for slander, Cairns time in Portage was anything but dull.

THE PORTAGE BREWERY
1879–1884
PORTAGE BREWING CO.
1884–1885
MANITOBA BREWING & MALTING CO. 1885–1891
BELL MEYER BREWING & MALTING 1891–1892
BELL & CRADDOCK 1892–1892

Thomas Cairns got the ball rolling when he built his first brewery at the extreme end of Main Street (Third Street N.E.) in 1879. In 1882, he sold his plant to build another in the east end of the town. The Portage Brewery was operated by Goldie & Co. from 1882 until 1884 when it went into receivership.

GOLDIE & CO.

BREWERS AND MALSTERS.

Portage Brewery,

PORTAGE LA PRAIRIE.

Ale and Porter in Wood and Bottles.

Orders by Mail and Wire Promptly Attended to.

The Commercial, 1883

North-West
BREWERY.

THE UNDERSIGNED HAS

Opened a Brewery,

— AT —

PORTAGE LA PRAIRIE

— AND IS NOW BREWING A —

Good, Wholesome Beer,

— WHICH WILL BE SOLD BY THE —

Barrel, the Keg, or in Bottles !

BOTTLED ALE AND PORTER ALWAYS ON HAND.

FAMILIES SUPPLIED

without delay on receipt of order.

THOS. CAIRNS,

PROPRIETOR.

sep3—y

Minnedosa, Manitoba, 1887

NORTH WEST BREWERY
1882–1893

After selling his first brewery in 1882, Cairns immediately opened a new brewery on the east side of town near Fort la Reine. Known as the East End Brewery this venture lasted less than a year before he built the North West Brewery near the Hudson Bay Company Fort. Cairns brewing interest in Portage la Prairie ended when the North West Brewery was destroyed by fire in 1893.

It seems strange then to discover he didn't drink his own product.

SPRING HILL BREWERY,
MINNEDOSA 1886–1894

William Sheriff and Charles Davies were former employees of the Portage Brewing Co. when they established their own brewery in Minnedosa in 1886. The partners were granted a ten year tax exemption to build a brewery near a spring on the north side of town. Sheriff was an experienced brewer, having worked for breweries in Buffalo, NY, Carling's in London, Ontario and even served a stint with E.L. Drewry. It seems strange then to discover he didn't drink his own product. Apparently, the beer was good, but Sheriff preferred a brand from a different brewery. Davies had his quirkiness too. Charlie, as he was called, would rather give his horse a pail of beer to drink than water from a nearby well. The local children used to chase the delivery wagon just to see the staggering horse.

By 1888, business was so good they stopped advertising and tried to keep up with the enormous demand for their product. Just as things were at their peak, the brewery burned down in 1889. William Sheriff left for Vancouver and Davies continued on with new partners in a smaller building in town. By the time Davies had his new location up and running, the town reneged on their tax deal and his good luck came to an end. In 1894, Davies decided to visit relatives in England and while there his business turned sour. He failed to report his annual federal returns and his brewing license was promptly cancelled. Charles Davies died while still in England and his brewery was closed for good.

NEEPAWA BREWING CO.
1894–1896

After the death of Charles Davies, his business partners sold the interests of the Spring Hill Brewery to James A. Currie and the equipment was moved to the quaint town of Neepawa. Of all the places to build a brewery, Neepawa should have been the last location one would choose to set up shop. By 1894, the municipality had for some time been under local option. This meant that any municipality could vote itself dry under the Canadian Temperance Act of 1878. However, this could not keep a brewery out of town as licenses were granted by the federal government. Remarkably, regardless of the citizens'

opposition, a license was granted to the brewery and beer began to flow that same year. Legally, sales could only be made outside of the municipal boundaries, but as is often the case, the rules were difficult to enforce.

In November of 1894, a tragic event occurred that only strengthened the towns resolve to drive James Currie and his brewery out of town. While visiting the plant in the late hours of the night, a perfectly sober Harry Armstrong stumbled into a brewing vat while trying to navigate his way through a steam filled room. Severely scalding himself, Armstrong later died of his injuries. This spurned on the town folk and finally, after a petition of 400, the matter was reviewed by Ottawa. In 1896, the brewery was finally closed when the government refused to renew its license.

And so this was the end of small time brewery operations in rural Manitoba. As Winnipeg and Brandon grew to prominence, the brewing industry grew along with them. A handful of men became rich by turning Manitoba barley into golden beer. An English-born Minnesota brewer named E.L. Drewry was one of them.

A handful of men became rich by turning Manitoba barley into golden beer.

Spring Hill Brewery, Minnedosa, 1887

E.L. Drewry spared no expense when it came to advertising, as proof shows with this calendar illustration from 1899. The full colour painting has soldiers enjoying Drewry's Refined Ale before heading off to the Boer War. Refined Ale was one of the brewery's stalwart brands and was produced until the late 1950's.

DREWRY'S

THE GIANT ON REDWOOD

It might seem an easy task to sell beer in a frontier town filled with young men with nothing better to do than drink. But brewing good beer was more difficult than it appeared. There were a number of local businessmen trying to do just that by the time E.L. Drewry first paddled his canoe from the town of Emerson to Winnipeg in 1875. Two years later he returned and from that time forward until he retired in the early 1920's, Drewry was to become one of Winnipeg's wealthiest and most well-respected citizens. Why he succeeded where others failed was a testament to the type of man he was and where he came from.

E.L. Drewry first came to Winnipeg in 1875 to check out the prospects of the newly established city. He later boasted of making the trip by canoe all the way from Emerson, MB. This is an early photo of the Redwood Brewery on the banks of the Red River.

St. Paul, Minnesota in the 1860's was much like its northern Canadian cousin, Winnipeg. Situated on the banks of the legendary Mississippi River, the community became an important trading centre and a destination for settlers heading west. With the laying of the first railway tracks beginning in the late 1850's, booming St. Paul was an ideal location for Edward Drewry Sr. to set up shop.

Ed Sr. was a brewer from Newport, Wales, who left London and ventured on his own for the new world in 1859. Ed's wife Caroline had died the same year leaving two little boys without a mother. In 1860 Ed and a financial partner opened the Drewry & Scotten Brewery in St. Paul (later known as the North Star Brewery.)

In November of 1860, nine-year-old Edward Jr. and younger brother Frederick set sail for America. Their voyage began aboard the sailing-steamship Vigo, arriving in New York three weeks later. After a brief stay at the posh Astor House on Fifth Avenue, Edward innocently proclaimed it to be "a swell place to stay at the time." They arrived in St. Paul on Christmas Eve 1860. In the next few years Ed Sr.'s business continued to evolve and by 1867 he owned his own brewery on South Payne Avenue.

Right: An early label from Edward Drewry's St. Paul, Minnesota brewery. The senior Drewry was a brewer in London before immigrating to America in 1859. Edward Junior's brewing education was culled from his father's business and by the time he moved North to Winnipeg he had a solid background to draw from.

Below: He continued to serve a role as V. P. in his father's brewery well into the 1890's.

Born on February 6, 1851 in London, England, Edward Lancaster Drewry Jr. grew up within the surroundings of a working brewery and soaked up all the knowledge it had to offer. After attending public schools, Drewry completed courses at Dixon's Business College. With this groundwork he joined his father's company to learn every branch of the enterprise. In 1872, he set out on his own for Chicago, but the Windy City beer market was too well established for his independent goals. Edward resumed working for his father and with his family's increasing status within the community, he married Eliza Starkey, daughter of Captain James Starkey. A prominent member of the first Minnesota Legislature, Starkey was also a soldier in the U.S. Calvary, fighting Indians in the battle at Rum River. His many career accomplishments included establishing a sewer department for the city of St. Paul.

From running a saw mill, acting as contractor for the Lake Superior & Mississippi Railroad and working as Commissioner for Anoka County, the Captain's public service and private enterprise made a lasting impression on his young son-in-law.

Shortly after his marriage to Eliza (Lile) on August 5, 1874, Edward Jr. decided once again strike out on his own. In 1875, with the blessing of his father, and a wife and baby in tow, he arrived in Fort Pembina, Dakota Territory. There Edward managed a small brewing business owned by Nathan Myrich, of St. Paul, Minnesota. He stayed on for two years, but after spring floods damaged the small plant, Drewry decided that this was not where the west would be won. Having previously travelled to Winnipeg in 1875 to seek out future prospects, Edward realized the potential of the young city suited his growing ambitions. The move was a relief to his wife Lile, who felt nervous in the raucous town of Pembina. Little did she know her next destination would soon be referred to as "the wickedest place in the Dominion." Maybe so, but it was the perfect place for the type of product her husband was planning to sell.

Edward Lancaster Drewry Jr.

MANUFACTURERS OF INDIA PALE ALE. EXTRA PORTER & STOUT. GINGER ALE. BIRCH BEER. CHAMPAGNE CIDER. SODA & MINERAL WATERS. FLAVORING EXTRACTS AND SYRUPS.

DREWRY Brewing & Carbonated Beverages MALT & CARBONATED Bottling Co.

ESTABLISHED 1860. TRADE MARK.

INCORPORATED 1890. TRADE MARK.

DEALERS IN GUINESS' STOUT. MURPHY STOUT. ALFRED & SONS PALE ALE. MILWAUKEE BOTTLED BEER. JOHN BEGGS, LONDON SARSAPARILLA. HOWE & CAMPBELLS. BELFAST GINGER ALE. CALIFORNIA ORANGE. PEAR & PEACH CIDER.

E. DREWRY, Pres.
E. L. DREWRY, V. Pres.
A. W. DREWRY, Sec. & Treas.

702 TO 710 PAYNE AVE.

St. Paul, Minn. May 8 1892

E.L DREWRY'S
REDWOOD BREWERY

Arriving in Winnipeg on May 11, 1877 the Drewrys lodged at a hotel on the corner of Fort and Graham Avenue.

The proprietor of the hotel was evidently an honest man because he said to father, "You are young and just starting out in business and you will have to have a horse and I will sell you one for a dollar", so Father bought it. In due course the hotelman said, "Hadn't you better look at it." So out to the stable they went, and the horse was dead. Father had bought a dead horse. However the hotelman was an honest man and said to Father, "Young man never buy anything unseen, you must know what you are paying for." Father said which advice he always tried to remember. – C.E. Drewry, excerpt from the booklet "Redwood"

It's safe to say by the time the young 26-year-old took possession of the Redwood Brewery, he indeed knew what he was paying for. In fact, Drewry only leased the operation until 1881 when he finally purchased the brewery and surrounding four acres. Idle for a year and in disrepair, it took hard work to overcome the hardships its former owners experienced. Edward's 16-year-old half-brother George (Ed Sr. remarried in 1860) made the trip north to assist and soon the brewery was up and running again.

Situated alongside the Red River in the Parish of St. John, the brewery consisted of one main building and a smaller one which served as the family home. Trade would be slow the first year, with business chiefly handled by two men and one horse (obviously not the dead one mentioned above). In addition to delivering the product from the brewery, the horse supplied the power for pumping water and grinding of the malt. From these humble beginnings the business grew by leaps and bounds. By 1879, Drewry had been adding to the brewery yearly and made a decision that would have a profound impact on the future growth of his company.

From these humble beginnings the business grew by leaps and bounds.

Label facsimile: 1878

Edward L. Drewry's

EXTRA PORTER.

Brewed from the best Malt and Hops, expressly for Bottling, and highly recommended by Physicians.

REDWOOD BREWERY, WINNIPEG.

Canadian beer drinkers in the 1800's had few choices as to what type of beer they could consume. Ale was the dominate style since the French and British first settled in Canada. This soon changed with the growing popularity of lager in the United States. Beginning in the 1840's German brewers began importing a new method for brewing beer. This new style of beer, often referred to as scientific lager brewing, had its origins in central Europe in the 1820's, and was finally perfected in the Bohemian city of Pilsen, hence the name Pilsner, a style of pale lager. Because of the large influx of German brewers into the American Mid-West and especially Milwaukee, by the 1870's lager was the dominate brew.

Premium Lager Beer label, 1879: Perhaps the oldest surviving Manitoba label, this was the first lager beer to be made in the province.

CANADIAN PILSENER LAGER

THE FINEST BEER ON THE MARKET

Golden Key Brand
AERATED WATERS
AND FLAVORING EXTRACTS.

Imperial Table Sauces and India Chutney.

EDWARD. L. DREWRY, IMPORTER AND MANUFACTURER, WINNIPEG.

Major changes in the brewing process were required to brew lager. A bottom fermenting yeast is used as opposed to top fermenting with ales. Lager yeasts require an extended fermentation period over ales, but more importantly bottom fermenting yeasts work at significantly cooler temperatures. In order to brew lager, breweries needed to invest in larger storage cellars. In Drewry's case, he had a head start.

"Mr. Drewry, has a chunk of ice in his brewery, 25 feet by 35 feet and six feet thick. It forms the roof of his cellar and makes it probably the coolest spot in the city."– Manitoba Free Press, June 2, 1877

With a small storage cellar already in place, Drewry had lager beer on the market by June, 1879. In November of that same year he won diplomas from exhibitions in both Toronto and Ottawa; proof that he was a quick study in this new beer-making process. It was vital for his brewery to be the first to brew lager in Manitoba. In fact he successfully curtailed the Milwaukee imports that were moving into the local market. In the language of the day, Drewry was quoted as saying "it was against the true interest of the country to send money away which there is every probability might be kept at home." This early success set the stage for the 1880's and the imminent growth that followed.

A building boom began at the Redwood Brewery. A four and one half storey malt house was built for $9,000 and included a 10 foot stone basement which was used as a germinating floor. Unlike today where breweries buy their malt, most breweries in the 1880's malted their own barley. Drewry's expansion and business opportunities continued. He purchased property in Emerson, Manitoba and the Railroad Hotel in St. Boniface. By 1881, Winnipeg boasted of having forty hotels. With further expansion on the way, Drewry needed help managing the business and so the most logical choice would be his own brother, Frederick.

Frederick William Drewry was born in 1855 and like his older brother learned the brewing business the same way—by working in his father's brewery. He arrived from St. Paul in 1881 and established the soft drink and soda water end of the business. In 1880, Drewry acquired Thomas and Ward Bottling and when Frederick arrived, the Manitoba Soda Water Works was

The "Golden Key Brand Aerated Waters" became an instant success with Frederick Drewry as manager.

Frederick W. Drewry

also purchased and relocated to the Redwood plant. A new division was created and an elegant name was chosen. The "Golden Key Brand Aerated Waters" became an instant success with Frederick Drewry as manager.

The years 1882 – 1883 saw further expansion to the plant; among the additions were new icehouse vaults. It would seem this would be enough to keep any man content with the business at hand, but Drewry was much more zealous than that. In 1883 he threw his hat into politics.

Perhaps he was spurred on by Winnipeg's annexation of St. John where he lived, for now he was a citizen of the city he so fervently believed in. When criticized about building a business so far from the town limits he declared, "If Winnipeg grows to the extent I believe it will, my location will be handy enough. If the town doesn't grow, then I might as well be out of the way as in it for my business will be a failure anyway."

The brewery as it looked in 1884: A river boat can be seen steaming by the plant. The boats would moor at St. Johns Park next to the brewery and once a year employees would ferry to Frazier's Grove for the company picnic.

Malthouse extension in the foreground, late 1890's: Typical of most breweries of the era, Drewry malted his own barley. In January of 1929, this building was destroyed in a spectacular fire causing $60,000 damage to the malthouse and several offices. Firemen fought the blaze in 30 below weather and high winds, saving the rest of the complex from being destroyed. The windmill in the background, erected in 1888, was the largest in Manitoba when it was built.

Like many of Winnipeg's prominent businessmen, Drewry was elected to city council. The new Alderman showed his penchant for state of the art technologies by advocating the introduction of street lighting—but not without some resistance from city council. After some debate it was agreed to give the scheme a try and Winnipeg's first street lamp was installed on the corner of Pritchard and Main. Other innovations Drewry initiated included block pavement for streets and improvements to the city's fire alarm system. At the time the system was operated by the city but with unsatisfactory results. Drewry was instrumental in turning the operation over to Bell Telephone.

After many accomplishments, he resigned in October owing to pressure of his business and declined the nomination for Mayor in 1885. In 1896, he surprisingly jumped back into the political arena to represent Winnipeg North for the Manitoba Legislature. An ardent Conservative,

he enjoyed a close relationship with Premier John Norquay. He often had a horse and buggy waiting outside the old Legislative Building in the wee hours of the morning to drive the Premier to his residence on Argyle Street. The election would be a testament to his popularity, since his majority was double that given to any other member. But in the end, the rabble rousing game of provincial politics was a poor fit for Mr. Drewry's calm, soft spoken nature. He served until 1889 and did not seek re-election despite the party's urging to run for a seat in the House of Commons.

This didn't mark an end to his public service. He was more at home as chairman of the first parks board which was established in 1891. Many parts of Winnipeg were described as "flat, and featureless; a treeless prairie." His vision of a city with "lungs and breathing spaces for its workers" would serve the city well into its

future. Within the first year, four parks were developed; St. John's Park next to his brewery, Fort Rouge Park, Central Park and Victoria Park, the latter lost when the land was sold to Winnipeg Hydro for its downtown steam plant. His efforts were so appreciated, that every year on his birthday he received a bouquet of flowers from the board.

The Redwood Brewery began expanding outside of the Winnipeg market in the late 1880's. Rail lines were moving further west and Drewry began shipping beer to the North-West Territories (now Saskatchewan and Alberta). Although the Territories were governed by federal law and under Prohibition, beer and wine could be shipped for personal use with a permit. By 1886, the brewery shipped its first beer to British Columbia. Expansion of a different sort took place in 1891 when Drewry bought the Empire Brewery on Osborne Street. After one year he moved operations over to his Redwood plant and it became the Redwood & Empire Breweries. The year 1891 marked the first time he brewed one million barrels of beer. In 1893 Drewry also won three medals at the Chicago World's Fair.

A practical man as well as a deep thinker, Drewry was often ahead of the times. Today we

Although the Territories were governed by federal law and under Prohibition, beer and wine could be shipped for personal use with a permit. By 1886, the brewery shipped its first beer to British Columbia.

think buying locally as being "green", but Drewry always supported local industry. "I always operate my business," he once said, "on the principle that it is better to purchase my requirements in Winnipeg if possible." He always bought from local sources if the price was not more than 10 percent higher than elsewhere. According to Drewry, the farther away money was spent, the longer it would take to make its way back.

Active in local real estate, he owned land on both sides of the Red River near his brewery as well as in Deer Lodge. His farm on the east side of the river in Elmwood later became Glenwood Crescent. Drewry actually reduced the size of his property with one generous act going towards the building of Winnipeg's oldest bridge. The city wanted to build a bridge over the Red River at St John's Avenue. Drewry's daughter, Mrs. Gertrude Code, and her brother Charles, happened to live on St. John's. Along with the objections of other residents, the Drewry siblings were able to persuade their father to donate land used as a road into the brewery. The city accepted the gift on the terms that Drewry would not have to pay frontage taxes on the Redwood Avenue approach to the Bridge. Always willing to compromise, the deal was good for the brewery too; it made for easy access to Elmwood on the other side of the river.

FOOTE.

Winnipeg Board of Trade delegates in front of the little log house that started it all, 1931: E.L. Drewry served as Vice-President in 1897; later Frederick Drewry became President.

there including the Hon. Alfred Boyd and Col. William Herchmer. In 1873-74 Redwood became the home of Mr. Batkin when he was operating the original Redwood Brewery with Herchmer. Finally it became the home for the Drewry family. Three of their children would be born there, including Charles.

It wasn't long before the family relocated to something more fitting of a successful brewery owner. Redwood No. 2 was built on the other side of this expanding property. The little log house was later occupied by the Boy Scouts (free of charge) after the First World War. After that it became a paint shop and finally a museum model of a Red River Settlement house. By the 1940's it had been demolished.

THE FIRST REDWOOD

Today in the City of Winnipeg, the name Redwood may bring to mind the plight of the neighbourhood and street that shares its name. Or it might remind residents of an old bridge many wish replaced with something more modern. Back in the late nineteenth century, Redwood was more famous for the brewery and the little house it was named for.

Redwood House was built by William Inkster, brother of Sheriff Colin Inkster, another of Winnipeg's pioneers and whom Inkster

Boulevard is named after. In 1916 Colin wrote to Charles Drewry describing how the house was built in 1857 and finished the same year, an extraordinary achievement in those old slow moving days. He recalled that the house was named Redwood, simply because the roof was painted red—the only one of that colour in the settlement at that time. The Inkster's lived in the house until 1869. The next occupant was the Hon. Thomas Howard, Manitoba's Provincial Secretary. State functions were given inside the house during those first humble years of Manitoba's existence. Others would live

Redwood House

REDWOOD NO. 2

The 22-room home facing Main Street may not have looked like the grand mansions that many of Winnipeg's millionaires would later build, but for the 1880's it was state of the art! It was built for F.W. Drewry and his future bride Augusta (Gussie) Kiefer in 1880. An interesting aspect of Fred's life was that he closely followed in his older brother's footsteps. Like Edward, he apprenticed at his father's brewery, married the daughter of a St. Paul politician and travelled north to Canada to make his fortune. Sadly, he never had the large family his older brother enjoyed. After moving to Winnipeg in 1881 Gussie became ill. Fred and his bride left for California hoping the warmer weather would benefit her health. Gussie died April 17, 1885 and Fred returned to live with his brother's family.

The Drewrys' moved to the house in 1884 and filled it with life for 40 years. E.L. was always in step with the times so the house was the first in Winnipeg to be wired for electric lights. He was also an early adopter of the telephone, the house having two, one a direct line to the brewery. Drewry's pride and joy was his 1902 Waverley; the first electric car in Winnipeg. Electric cars were particularly popular with the wealthy—they didn't much care for the noise and fumes from early motor cars.

The family's private life was filled with social affairs and sports, Charles being the most athletic one. Not only was the house close to the brewery, it was right next door to the other important pillar in Drewry's life. He was a devout Christian

and an early supporter of St. John's Anglican Church. Life was not exclusive to home and brewery. Drewry spent winters in California and travelled to Egypt in 1902. In 1914, E.L. bought a large tract of land in Havana, Cuba. He expected it to double in value within six months. One of his most treasured places was the family cottage at Bay Point on Coney Island near Kenora. He was one of the first of many well-to-do families that built summer homes in the area.

All good things must come to an end. A few years after Lile died E.L. moved out of Redwood to live with his daughter, Gertrude Code. True to form, Fred followed suit and the two brothers lived together until Fred's passing in 1927. In 1941 the home was converted into a nursing home and ten years later 1149½ Main Street was demolished. Once the hub of Winnipeg's social life, the site became the first location for Community Chev-Olds—a popular local car dealership.

Redwood No. 2: Located on the north-west side of the 7 acre brewery property, the Main Street house was torn down in 1951 to make way for a car dealership.

Mr. Drewry and his wife Lile driving Winnipeg's first electric car, a 1902 Waverley.

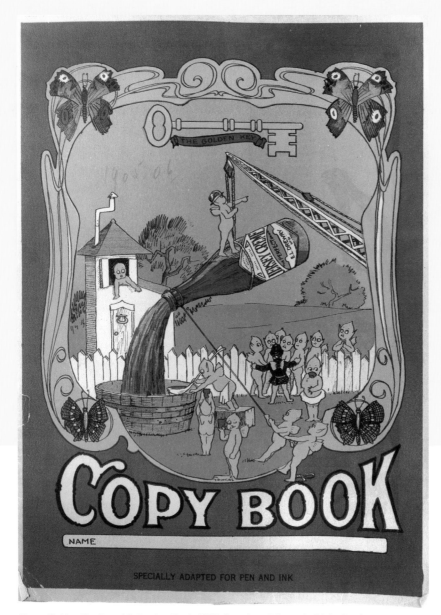

A pair of ink blotters from the turn of the century: A popular form of advertising in the first half of the century, these are very highly prized and sought after collectibles. The felt lined flip side of the card was used to absorb the excess ink from the tips of fountain pens. The advent of the ballpoint pen in the late 1940's brought an end to these colourful little billboards.

Above: Golden Key Brand Colouring Book, 1905: Beer for adults, soft drinks for the kiddies, Drewry had his market covered. Jersey Crème was just one of a large line of soft drinks available.

Right: Watch Fob, early 1900's: Another example of the type of advertising lost when the item itself fell out of fashion.

Workingman's
Tonic

DREWRY'S
REDWOOD
LAGER

The beer that is always
pure and wholesme.
Ask for it.

E. L. DREWRY, Manfr
WINNIPEG

REDWOOD FACTORIES 1897–1911

The dawn of the new century saw even more growth for the brewery, now under the name Redwood Factories. The change in name came with the business branching out into flavouring extracts, table sauces and glassware. Warehouses in Portage la Prairie, Brandon and the Pas were established and in 1903, a branch warehouse was built in Regina. Drewy's market reached from Port Arthur, Ontario to the Pacific coast and as the brewery moved into the 20th century it became as modern and complete as any on the continent.

Moving from being a pioneer businessman to a leading member of the business elite, Drewry immersed himself into the financial and social fabric of the community. Drewry and his sons were generous benefactors to many of Manitoba's social causes. The list of organizations he was involved with was as long as his arm and he wasn't content with just being a figure head. He served as president of the Board of Trade and president of the Winnipeg General Hospital. In 1907 he helped initiate the building of the Tuberculosis Sanatorium in Ninette. An active sportsman himself, he was also a founding member of the Winnipeg Rifle Club and supported amateur sport throughout the province.

In 1910 the Winnipeg Telegram compiled a list of millionaires the city had produced. The list numbered nineteen and of course E. L. Drewry was one of them. By then "E.L.", as everyone referred to him, had become as successful and well known as one could be in Manitoba. But an approaching storm soon threaten his business and the industry he had laboured at for over for 30 years.

FARMER'S ADVOCATE
AND HOME JOURNAL
Western Canada's Agricultural Weekly

REGISTERED IN ACCORDANCE WITH THE COPYRIGHT ACT, 1875

VOL. LV — Winnipeg, Canada, August 18, 1920 — No. 1456

Henry Connor 071 dec 20

Maltum
REGISTERED

BEER

"On Ever...

The pleasures of Dancing and all c...
tions are made much more enjoyable w...
Maltum Beer is served. Try it...

Order by the case from your grocer, druggist or con...

E. L. DREWRY, LIMITED :: ...

137

MALTUM

E.L. Drewry Ltd. 1916

A very creative use of the Drewry sales team to promote the Maltum brand: Squint your eyes if you don't see the illusion.

"HOPUM" IS A NUTRITIOUS NON-INTOXICATING BEVERAGE STIMULATING & REFRESHING FOR USE BY YOUNG OR OLD AT ALL SEASONS OF THE YEAR.

SHOULD BE KEPT IN A COOL PLACE

HOPUM
REGISTERED TRADE MARK

AN EXCELLENT TONIC CONTAINING MANY OF THE RESTORATIVE PROPERTIES OF ORDINARY PALE ALE OR STOUT COMBINED WITH THE FRAGRANT AND APPETIZING PRINCIPALS OF THE FINEST ENGLISH HOPS

ABSOLUTELY NON-INTOXICATING

MALTUM CO. LTD
WINNIPEG·MANITOBA·CANADA·

Far Left: Maltum ad from the Farmers Advocate and Home Journal, 1920: Around this period Maltum ads regularly appeared on the front covers of this Winnipeg based magazine. No cover story, just a big Drewry ad.

Left: Hopum label, 1910

Below: The Maltum Co. Limited was formed in 1910 to tap into the new market for temperance beers. Originally formed to distance itself from the brewery business, the Maltum name soon fell under the E.L. Drewry banner.

MALTUM CO., LIMITED.
MANUFACTURERS OF
MALTUM, (REGISTERED) HOP BEER, HOPUM, (REGISTERED) ETC.
ALL ABSOLUTELY NON-INTOXICATING TEMPERANCE BEERS

MALTUM CO., LIMITED
TEMPERANCE MALT BEER
WINNIPEG

E.L DREWRY, LIMITED
1913–1924

In the uncertain times leading up to Prohibition it was imperative to Mr. Drewry that he have all his soldiers in place. In 1913, the family business was re-organized and the name changed to E.L. Drewry, Limited. The temperance movement had been a threat to Canada's breweries since Parliament passed the Canadian Temperance Act; better known as the Scott Act in 1878. This legislation allowed for any city or municipality to vote itself dry and would be the foundation for Canada's Prohibition.

As the campaign for total abstinence grew in the period before the war, Drewry began offering products that fit the atmosphere of the times. As early as 1910 they began selling a product called "Maltum" under the company name "The Maltum Co." This may have been an attempt to create some distance from the brewery business. It was the beginning of what would be known as "Temperance Beers" or beers with alcohol content no more than two percent. Maltum was a non-alcoholic brew to be enjoyed by everyone, even nursing moms! In the days before "truth in advertising," manufacturers could make claims about the health giving properties of their beverages without regulation.

As the Temperance forces grew stronger and gained political clout, E.L. became so concerned, he wrote a letter to the Prime Minister in 1911 declaring that if Prohibition came into effect, the government must compensate brewers for the loss of their livelihood. In spite of his fears, Manitoba voted in favour of Prohibition and on June 1, 1916,

NURSING MOTHERS

will find a daily glass or two of MALTUM STOUT of greatest benefit. Brewed from caramelized malt, it is a valuable blood making and strengthening tonic.

MALTUM STOUT

REGISTERED

aside from its healthful nourishing properties is a delicious drink—one which every member of the family will enjoy. It is pure, wholesome, positively non-intoxicating.

Put up in quarts, pints, or in casks.

Order from your grocer or dealer in your town, or direct from

E. L. DREWRY, LIMITED - Winnipeg, Man.

One can only imagine a mother nursing her child while quaffing a bottle of Maltum Stout.

We must try and make the best of it."

As devastating as this would appear for the brewery, there were a number of important factors which were in Drewry's favour. With the "Golden Key Brand" they had an established soft drink and soda water division in place, in addition to the temperance beers they were selling. More significantly, with the network of branch warehouses in other provinces, they could take advantage of loopholes between the federal and provincial laws. The sale and consumption of beer was under provincial jurisdiction while production was under federal. Therefore Drewrys, and other Manitoba breweries, were able to export their beer to other provinces and vice versa.

it took effect. However, Drewry tried to take it all in stride. Charles, in his book about Redwood, reflects on his father being opposed to all kinds of bitterness. "When Prohibition came into law and the bottom seemed to fall out of everything he had built up, he did not hold it against the government who carried out the wishes of the people. Inwardly he no doubt felt, that all his life's work should end up this way. All he said was; "if the majority of the people want it this way, it is their privilege to have it.

In the days before "truth in advertising," manufacturers could make claims about the health giving properties of their beverages without regulation.

Left: Drewry's parade floats were always a sight to behold. In past years floats were constructed with wooden beer cases for a particular theme. In this photo they decided to make the entire display a beer case which included 24 giant replica beer bottles. Who knows how they were made but one thing is obvious; you couldn't return them for a refund.

Below: The brewery in the mid 1920's looking east from Main Street: Originally built as stables in 1910, the building on the right served as the company garage. Above the garage were offices and a room for holding large community social functions including the company Christmas parties. Also important to the community was the area in the foreground. In the 1930's it was called "Drewry's Park" and hosted softball games in the summer. At Christmas time the brewery transformed the park into a winter wonderland of lights and ornamental decorations. A full time groundskeeper was employed to tend to it all. Redwood Avenue is to the right.

By the time Prohibition ended in 1923, E.L was 72 years old. He had accomplished more in his life time than most people could ever imagine. His business had survived when many of his Canadian counterparts fell to the wayside, and he did it all while maintaining the high moral standards he tried to live by. In 1924 The Manitoba Free Press stated that other breweries had suffered heavily from Prohibition and Drewry more so, as the head of the company had stated, for adhering steadfastly to a policy of obeying the law.

In 1924 with his business intact, it was announced that E.L. would retire and stock of the company would be transferred to a syndicate, with the firm of Armstrong and Black conducting the deal. The new company would be known as "The Drewrys Limited" with Charles taking over from his father as president. His tenure would be short, lasting until 1925. At the age of 48 he left the business he had been around since birth.

E.L. performed one last generous deed before giving up the company he had built from a two man operation, into a business which employed hundreds of people over the years. In 1921 he decided upon retirement, to distribute a certain amount of shares to employees of one year or more. The amount given varied and depended on the position and level of responsibility of each employee. His workers respected the old man and weren't keen to see him retire. Pragmatic to the end, Drewry reasoned his gift might give his employees an incentive to keep the new company successful after he was gone.

On November 2, 1940, Edward L. Drewry died at the home of Mrs. A. Code. He had lived with his daughter at No. 3, St. Johns Avenue for the last 15 years, his wife having passed away in 1922. At the age of 89 he was one of Winnipeg's last remaining pioneers. Not only had he witnessed the city's growth, he was part of its fabric for three quarters of a century. The only reminders we have of him are tucked away in two of the city's parks his vision helped create. For a man who gave so much, it's unfortunate we have so little to remember him by.

With the passing of the torch, Drewrys Ltd. was now in the hands of another skilled businessman. George Montegu Black was born in Halifax, Nova Scotia in 1875. His father, George Anderson Black had been employed with the Hudson's Bay Company before moving to Winnipeg. Black was an established businessman and a partner with the real estate and insurance company of Armstrong and Black. This was the same firm that brokered the sale of Drewrys and by 1925, Black had become president of the brewery. For George Black this was the beginning of his family's assent into national prominence and

Edward L. Drewry was inducted into the Citizens Hall of Fame in 2005. The Hall of Fame is located in Assiniboine Park. Drewry's contribution to the city is also remembered with a plaque in St John's Park and a walkway in the park is called Drewry Lane. Mr. Drewry was the original owner of the land adjacent to the brewery.

notoriety. G.M Black and his son George Jr. were soon to become important names in Canadian business, but it was his grandson Conrad who would make the family name a household word.

Winnipeg Industrial Trade Exhibit, 1909: Every year the Drewry display at the Winnipeg Industrial Exhibition proved to be the one of the most attractive sights of the fair. A wall to wall array of all the products the brewery produced, each year the displays would be more elaborate than the previous one.

Special Old Style German Bräu ink blotter: With the outbreak of WWI and the heavy anti-German sentiment it brought, Mr. Drewry was forced to take this brand off the market. Many of the mugs advertising it had the words German Bräu ground off. "Bräu" in German means beer.

The Mettlach mug made in Germany: Mettlach was the best known name among the manufacturers of old beer steins.

Good Company Anywhere Anytime

ESTABLISHED 1877

Soft Drinks were an important part of many local breweries and helped to pad their bottom line. Government rules stipulated that soft drinks had to be manufactured separate from the brewery buildings. The Golden Key Brand was introduced in the early 1880's. The brand is named after the gold skeleton key used to lock the door to the little red roofed house the brewery was named after. The soft drink business helped save the company from being another casualty of prohibition.

Below: Ginger Beer Crock Bottle

Soft drink label – 1911

Soft drink fleet, 1940: Drewrys soft drink line remained a strong part of the business in the 1940's but no longer went under the Golden Key Brand name. Drewrys Dry Ginger Ale was its most popular brand.

THE DREWRYS LTD.
WINNIPEG, MAN.

MOOSE JAW BREWING CO. LTD.
MOOSE JAW, SASK.

PREMIER BREWING CO. LTD.
BRANDON, MAN.

THE HUB CITY BREWING CO. LTD.
SASKATOON, SASK.

PLANTS OWNED BY

WESTERN BREWERIES LIMITED

Above: Promotional Serving Tray

Right: **Old Cabin Ale label and ad, 1930's:** It might not be obvious at first glance, but this label is made to look like the end-cut of a log.

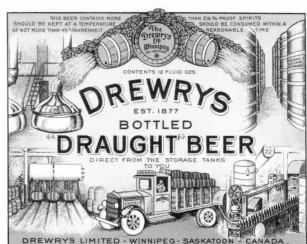

Label c. 1930's: Drewrys had draught in bottles long before the trend became popular in the 1980's.

THE DREWRYS LIMITED

With George Black at the helm, Drewrys celebrated its 50th year in business in 1927. To commemorate their Jubilee Anniversary, the company introduced Standard Lager, a brand that eventually outlived its creators and the establishment itself. For the time being, the brewery at Redwood and Main was about to enter into a new era for the brewing industry. Consolidation would soon become the name of the game. In Quebec, National Breweries Limited was formed in 1909 as a holding company for a number of breweries in that province. As this became the new trend, George Black began planning for the future growth of his company and envisioned an expansion to the west as the first stage. In 1925, the Brandon Brewing Co. was bought and became the Premier Brewing Co. During that same year, the Moose Jaw Brewery was also acquired. Western Breweries Limited—a holding company created to control the assets of four breweries in Manitoba and Saskatchewan—was incorporated in 1927.

- -

CBL through Western Canada Breweries Limited owned and operated Drewrys in Winnipeg and Saskatoon as well as the Blue Label Brewery in Regina and Vancouver Breweries in Vancouver.

The late 1940's was the beginning of the end for the Drewry name in Canada. In next few years the business changed hands again and the leadership moved from George M. Black to his son George Jr. How this played out was unusual and rather ironic.

As a chartered accountant George Black Jr. served as comptroller for Western Breweries Limited in the late 1930's. During the war he was on staff for the Department of National Air Defence as well as Executive Vice-President of Canadian Propellers. With this experience he caught the eye of E.P. Taylor who's Canadian Breweries Limited (CBL) had a dominate position in Ontario and Quebec. One of its holdings, Carlings, would soon be a familiar name in Western Canada. In 1945 Black became Executive Assistant to the President of CBL.

Meanwhile, after fifty years as a businessman, George Sr. retired when Western Breweries Limited was taken over by Brewers & Distillers of Vancouver in 1949. Like big fish swallowing little fish both those companies fell into the grips of Canadian Breweries. In 1950, the Vancouver firm was renamed Western Canada Breweries Limited—just in time for George Black Jr. to became president of CBL. From the back door and on his own merit, he was able to move into the same position of power as his father previously held; perhaps more so, as he was now in charge of the vast holdings of Canadian Breweries. It must have made George Sr. proud.

With this, the stage was set. CBL through Western Canada Breweries Limited owned and operated Drewrys in Winnipeg and Saskatoon as well as the Blue Label Brewery in Regina and Vancouver Breweries in Vancouver. The Blue

George M. Black

Label Brewery became the first plant in western Canada to produce a Carling product. That product was Carling Black Label. For a few years the Drewry brand continued to be sold in Manitoba. However, the die had been cast and the remainder of the 1950's saw the beginning of the end for the local home grown breweries as we had known them.

E.L. DREWRY:
FIRST IN CANADA TO ADOPT THE CROWN CORK SEAL

Today we take for granted the everyday household items we use; never giving a second thought to the impact it has on our lives. The invention of the crown cork seal—or the bottle cap as we know it today—undoubtedly brings convenience to our lives. But back in the 1890's it revolutionized the bottling industry. Before the 1870's bottled beer was not widely sold. Most beer was only available in wooden kegs of various sizes and consumed in saloons or bought directly from the brewery. Beer bottles of the time were larger than today. One type was the Growler, a jug style container holding up to 1.89 litres of beer and was meant for home consumption, (it's doubtful growlers were used in Manitoba since no examples have been found.) Glass technology improved by the 1870's and bottles were now able to withstand the high pressure beer exerted on them without being too heavy. In Manitoba, the Redwood Brewery and the Assiniboine Brewery ran ads offering beer in bottles or casks. The problems with these early bottles were how to seal them. Most bottles of the time had blob top necks and used lightning stoppers, but these were cumbersome and labour intensive to fill.

In 1892 William Painter, an American from Baltimore, Maryland, devised a closure system that didn't leak or allow pressure to escape. This was a metal crown with the underside lined in cork. Before he could sell it he had to prove it would work. He persuaded the American Brewing Co. of Baltimore to fill several hundred cases and use his crown. Then he was able to get a shipping company to use the cases as ballast. When the ship returned some months later, all the bottles were still full. Despite this, it was not an immediate success. Bottlers had to be convinced to buy new bottles and bottling machinery. But E.L. Drewry had no problem buying into this new idea. In December, 1893 he was the first to introduce the "Crown Cork" stopper in Canada. Now, with a reliable and inexpensive method of sealing bottles, breweries could establish efficient bottling lines and make beer drinking more convenient for its customers.

William Painter's Crown Cork and Seal Company is still around today, now called Crown Holdings, Inc. The bottle cap hasn't changed much over the years. In the early 1960's, plastic replaced the cork liner and the number of teeth is now 21—down from the original 24. However, the biggest change of all arrived with the twist-off cap. Labatt's was first in Canada to introduce this in 1984.

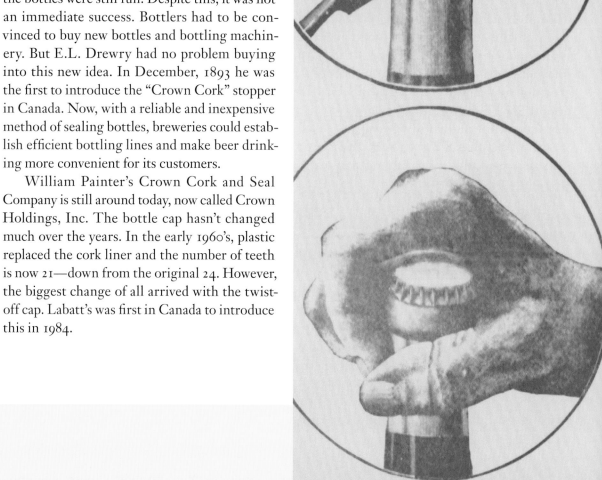

It was easy to use the new Crown Cork and Seal, as this period illustration shows.

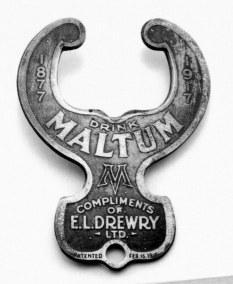

Most openers were not packaged in folders like this Pelissier's Brewery giveaway.

With the invention of the bottle cap, openers were devised and with them a whole new way of advertising products. A cheap and compact form of promotion, bottle openers came in endless shapes and sizes, from wall mount types to small key chain openers.

The Drewry's Limited fish shaped key chain opener is a great example of the different designs available. Manufacturers held patents for certain shapes and breweries could order these with their name stamped onto the opener. Because of its unique shape, the E.L. Drewry Maltum opener is often referred to as the muscle man.

Sometimes bottle openers served dual purposes like the combination can and bottle opener pictured above. The distinct shape of this type of opener may be the inspiration for the term "Church Key" since they resembled the shape of skeleton keys used to open old churches.

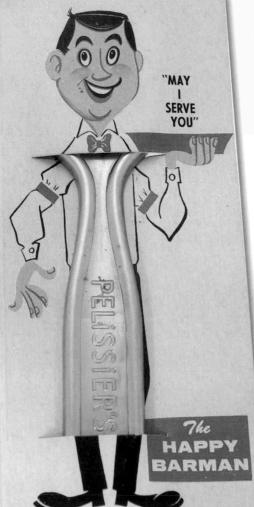

MOST good things like this opener are basic in design.

Service and quality are two basics in the grand design of customer satisfaction and acceptance.

Please accept this memento of the occasion with our compliments.

FREE HOME DELIVERY AND PICK-UP SERVICE

Phone 775-8207

"MAY I SERVE YOU"

The **HAPPY BARMAN**

Edward Drewry Sr.

DREWRY'S AMERICAN CONNECTION

When Ed Drewry Sr. established his brewery back in 1860, it's doubtful he imagined how widespread the Drewry name would become. Nor could his sons realize how important their decision was to move north. Ed Sr.'s brewery faltered during Prohibition, but it was the son's legacy that carried the name right up to the 1990's.

Drewry founded the North Star Brewery in 1860 with fellow Englishman George Scotten. The brewery, located at the foot of Dayton's Bluff near Phalen Creek, was the one of a few that brewed ale in a time when the popularity of lager was sweeping over the Midwest. Perhaps this is why Drewry never achieved the level of success his two sons later enjoyed. By 1864 Scotten sold out and was replaced by L.B. Greig. Now under the name of the Northwestern Brewery, the partnership lasted three years before Drewry went out on his own and relocated to Payne Avenue. This new location was next door to the huge Theo Hamm Brewery on Minnehaha Avenue. In the shadow of Hamm's, Drewry and Son's operated as a brewery until it became a casualty of Prohibition. Edward Jr. served on the board of directors of the St. Paul plant and step brothers Arthur, Harry and Richard also held various positions. On December 16, 1926 Ed Sr. died at the ripe old age of 97. He had been working at his desk only a few days earlier. The firm had turned to producing soft drinks by then

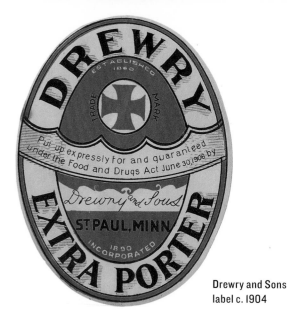

Drewry and Sons label c. 1904

and in 1932 Drewrys Limited of Winnipeg took over operation of the company.

Taking control of the St. Paul plant was the first step in a plan George M. Black devised to move into the U.S. market. In 1932, Drewrys Limited announced they would open a plant in the Chicago district as soon as congress repealed Prohibition. The St. Paul location was to be part of their brewing plan but that never transpired. Black was convinced that Roosevelt would be elected and the sale of beer would soon be permitted again. He wanted to be the first to brew Canadian ale in America and tap into the thirsty market that was waiting to be satisfied.

It soon became evident that an American company needed to be formed and so Drewrys Ltd. U.S.A. was incorporated. After abandoning the idea of opening its own plant, Drewrys first U.S. brewed beer was produced in 1933 under

> In 1932, Drewrys Limited announced they would open a plant in the Chicago district as soon as congress repealed Prohibition.

contract by the Sterling Brewing Co. of Evansville, Indiana. Roosevelt received the first case of Drewrys Canadian Ale brewed in the United States.

The importance of the brands Canadian heritage was illustrated by the ever present Mountie on all its labels. So too was the slogan "First brewed in Canada in 1877, now brewed in the U.S.A." As the brewery grew and established its own consumer base, the Mounties role in advertising lessened and by the 1960's was only a small part of the label graphics.

Early in 1936, the Canadian connection was severed when the assets of Drewrys Ltd U.S.A. was sold to a group of American investors and the Muessel Brewery in South Bend, Indiana was bought for production. With a solid local management base in hand, Drewrys popularity grew and the company expanded by taking over breweries in the Midwest and the eastern seaboard. At their peak Drewrys was rated one of the top ten breweries in the U.S. In 1965 Drewrys merged into the Associated Brewing Company of Detroit.

By the 1970's, regional breweries began to lose sales to the larger nationwide companies such as Anheuser-Busch. Associated Brewing Company began to cut their losses and

> With a solid local management base in hand, Drewrys popularity grew and the company expanded by taking over breweries in the Midwest and the eastern seaboard.

the Drewrys plant in South Bend was sold to G. Heileman Brewing of LaCrosse, Wisconsin in 1972. That same year Heileman closed the South Bend plant but continued to produce Drewrys at their Evansville Brewery (the former Sterling plant—what goes around comes around). The plant later became the Evansville Brewing Co. and this is where the brand finally drew its last breath. When the brewery closed in the late 1990's the Drewry name ended its association with beer after a run of more than 130 years.

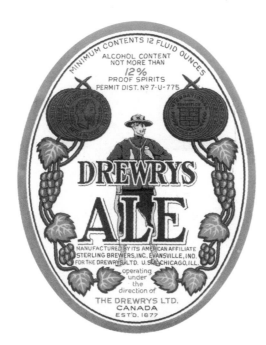

Drewrys Ltd. U.S.A. Label - 1933. Similar in design to Drewrys Dry Ginger Ale, the Mountie was a reflection of the brand's Canadian heritage.

BRANDON
THE WHEAT CITY AND BARLEY TOO!

If Dugald McVicar had his way, beer drinkers in western Manitoba might have been drinking Grand Valley Ale instead of Brandon Lager. Back in 1881, the CPR planned to make the village of Grand Valley a divisional point for the brand new railway. Mr. McVicar's property sat smack dab in the middle of their plans and he should have enjoyed a nice profit for himself. Unfortunately he made the mistake of taking on the CPR and its Chief Engineer, General Thomas Lafayette Rosser.

When the pioneer settler tried to hold out for more money, Rosser would have none of it and decided Grand Valley was to have no depot and no town for that matter. He chose the next best place, which was two miles west on the opposite side of the Assiniboine River. Grand Valley quickly died, but Brandon soon blossomed.

Settlers, businessmen and land speculators alike flocked to the area. They came before permanent structures could be built, so a tent town quickly rose in its place. Brandon grew at such a pace that it never attained the status of a village or town. The city was officially incorporated May 30, 1882. Three years later the first of the city's breweries was built.

A depiction of Brandon in 1888 with the city's very first brewery built next to the banks of the Assiniboine River: The brewery changed its name from the Brandon Brewing & Bottling Co. to the Spring Brewery in 1887.

BRANDON BREWING & BOTTLING CO. 1885–1887
SPRING BREWERY 1887–1889
THE BRANDON BREWERY 1889–1891

Sometimes the task of unravelling history can be a frustrating affair. Buried deep in newspapers and public archives lie information that may be vague or convoluted. Brandon's brewing history is a prime example. There were three breweries with variations of the same name. Two of these breweries were at the same location—but operated a few years apart. The players in this saga moved around from one brewery to another and at different stages in time. Just to confuse things even more, two men named Ferguson operated a brewery—but not the same one. The first of these two Ferguson's started it all in 1885 when he built the Brandon Brewing and Bottling Co.

William Ferguson

William Ferguson was the owner of a wholesale distributor that dealt with wines and spirits and built the brewery to enhance his business. Before building began, he shipped in railcars full of ale and porter from the Dominion Brewery in Toronto and from Labatt's in London. The growing town needed a brewery to quench its thirst, but after going before city council to ask for a fifteen-year tax exemption, he was met with stern protests from the local temperance society. Thirst prevailed and Ferguson was granted a seven year exemption.

The brewery sat squeezed in between the railway tracks and the river near the foot of the First Street Bridge. It was the first of two breweries built in this vicinity.

In 1887, Ferguson sold his brewery to a familiar face in the province's brewing community. John F. Woodley purchased the brewery with partner Joseph Neumeyer. Woodley had just arrived in Brandon after failing to succeed in Emerson. Always moving to where the action was, this was the third city in the province where he owned a brewery. Given his track record for success, Woodley must have been a persuasive man, as he was never short of investors willing to gamble on his behalf.

The name was changed to the Spring Brewery; appropriate, since they were tapping into an underground water source. Beers such

THE BREWERY,
BRANDON.
NUMEYER & PARES
Late Brandon Brewing Company,
BREWERS OF THE CELEBRATED
INDIA PALE ALE,
IMPERIAL STOUT,
NOTED - - XX - - PORTER,
IN CASKS OR BOTTLES
Telephone Connection.

This ad ran in the Brandon Times – 1888

WOODLEY & NEUMEYER,
LATE BRANDON BREWING COMPANY,
SPRING BREWERY,
BRANDON, MANITOBA.
Brewers of the Celebrated India Pale Ale, Imperial Stout,
Noted XX Porter, in Casks or Bottles.
Also HARVEST BEER, at Rock Bottom Prices

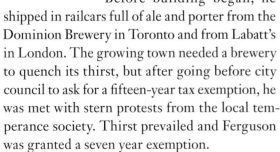

Spring Brewery Ad, Brandon Mail – 1887

an IPA, Imperial Stout, and XX Porter became available in bottles and casks (kegs). They also brewed a special Harvest Beer which they sold at "rock bottom" prices.

In 1888, the brewery changed back to its original name but with a slight variation. Now known as the Brandon Brewery, its fate was short lived. In the fall of 1888, Woodley left the firm to manage the new Crown Brewery across the river. This left Neumeyer and another partner named William Pares to carry on. Pares, an Englishman had joined the brewery in 1887 after trying his hand as a farmer in Ontario. As the salesman for the brewery, he traveled all over western Manitoba, but after the partnership ended in 1891, he returned to England.

The Crown Brewery was built in 1888 on the North Hill west of what is now known as Kirkcaldy Heights. Costing $4000, the building was perched on the slope of the hill near a spring that flowed out from the ground. The brewing equipment came from Woodley's former brewery in Emerson.

John Woodley was a restless soul. After getting involved in one brewery, within a year or two he'd move on to the next. After leasing the Crown Brewery for two years and becoming part owner in 1890, he made his exit in 1891. This was the end of the line for Woodley in the beer business. He settled for working as an accountant in 1892. The new buyer was his former partner, Joseph Neumeyer.

Neumeyer was in dire need a new brewery—the Brandon Brewery's water supply had failed and this new location proved to be reliable. In these early years the brewery was a primitive operation. A writer of the day described the premises as inadequate and consisting of just "three old tubs and a flat cooler." The business needed an infusion of capital. Wolfgang Kohler had been a partner since 1889, but when he left to start his own brewery in 1895, the Crown Brewery shut its doors. The Crown name was later used for a Winnipeg brewery in 1908.

Situated on the side of Brandon's North Hill, the Crown Brewery drew its water from an underground spring. This spring still provided water for the taking long after the brewery was forgotten.

CROWN BREWERY BRANDON

FINE ALES . .

EXTRA PORTER

Only the Finest Quality of Ale and Porter turned out by this Brewery.

JOSEPH NEUMEYER, PROP.

After sittling idle for a few years the Crown Brewery became the Empire Brewing Company in 1899.

Bottling Room at the North Hill location.

Above: **Mash Tub**

Right: **Wash Room**

THE EMPIRE BREWING CO. 1899–1931

After the Crown Brewery lay idle for four years it was finally rescued by local businessmen Isaac Robinson and R. G. MacDonald. They immediately modernized the equipment and doubled the capacity—but it wasn't enough. If they wanted to see their business grow beyond the turn of the century, bigger changes had to be made.

_____

Even after the company was bought by the Canadian Brewing Corporation in 1928 and then closed in 1931, the buildings remained a local landmark.

In most cases, cities grow outward from their centre. Not in Brandon's case. It has always sported a strange lopsided look to it—the majority of its growth spread south of downtown. The Assiniboine proved to be the major impediment to growth north of the river. Because of this fact, and in order to take advantage of newly installed sewer and water lines, Robinson moved his brewery from the North Hill to the south side of the river in 1903. The location he chose was First Street and Pacific Avenue, just south of the former Spring Brewery. That same year, new partners came on board and by 1906, a bigger brewery was built.

Isaac Robinson later left the brewery and went on to a distinguished business career. He was a founding member of the Brandon Club and later resided at Villa Louise, one of Brandon's most prestigious residences of the city's bygone era.

By 1908, the Empire Brewery Company finally began to enjoy the success its owners had planned and the plant at the foot of the First Street Bridge became an important part of Brandon's economy. Even after the company was bought by the Canadian Brewing Corporation in 1928 and then closed in 1931, the buildings remained a local landmark. Although the Bell Bottling Company used the soft drink portion of the plant for many years, it was the unsightly scrap yard that dominated the site into 1960's and 70's that older Brandonites will remember the most. Today the area has been completely cleared. The scrap yard is gone, replaced with a bike path. Now young cyclists can ride by an empty field, oblivious to the rich history that once lived on that corner one hundred years before.

Pre-Prohibition bottles: Empire Lager 22 oz. - Empire Ale 24oz. - Bulldog Stout 11 oz.

"Preferred wherever it is known"

Distributed in Winnipeg by

Douglas and **King Limited**

Phone ~ 88 442

Empire Ale ad – 1929

This piece of advertising art may have hung on the wall of some smoky pre-prohibition saloon.

Two labels from Empire's soft drink division.

Empire float display in front of brewery at First & Pacific

LIFE AT THE EMPIRE

About 1907, Cyril Taylor left Croydon, England and came to Canada to work on a farm. He was called back to England after the death of his father and when he returned to Canada in 1912, he found employment at the Empire Brewing Company in Brandon, Manitoba. In the 1970's Cyril was interviewed by George Chopping for his book "Bottles of the Canadian Prairies". George has graciously allowed us to reprint segments of his interview for this book.

Isaac Owens was a scrap-iron dealer in Brandon. He would go around the city collecting bottles to bring back to the brewery and on some occasions, 150 to 200 dozen bottles were collected. One of Cyril's first jobs in the brewery was sorting bottles. Sometimes, they were returned in wooden kegs with no packing around them and he recalls that while retrieving bottles from the bottom of the barrel, he accidently scratched his head on the nails. He'd have to count the bottles and discard any that had cracks, chips, or were oily. Once a year the bottles were sorted into clear and amber. They were then smashed and loaded onto a boxcar which would be sent to Dominion Glass in Medicine Hat to be re-melted and made into new bottles. The brewery would order new bottles from the glass manufacturing company and they would arrive packed neck to neck three feet deep on the floor of the railroad car.

Barrels were not only used for draught beer back then and Cyril commented that he used to pack the kegs with pint beer bottles and straw.

His next job was washing bottles in the bottling room. The pay was $2.00 for a 12 to 16 hour day. There were two other employees who used to wash and clean out the wooden kegs. They would use a wire and curl it at one end to hold a candle and then insert it into the bung hole of the keg to see if any foreign matter was in it, or if any of the pitch had been shaken loose while it had been in transportation.

Barrels were a big part of breweries in the old days. The stays and the hoops for the beer kegs would come in bundles and the cooper would have to assemble them. Barrels were not only used for draught beer back then and Cyril commented that he used to pack the kegs with pint beer bottles and straw. Each barrel could hold 10 to 12 dozen each.

The company had two teams of horses, one delivering beer daily to the sixteen hotels and the other hauling to the railroad. A single dray delivered to the pop stores. Sometimes there would be from 20 to 30 barrels stacked 3 high on a dray wagon. One of the drivers recalled delivering to the Gladstone area. He hit one hell of a bump and lost three kegs of beer. After realizing they were gone he went back in the dark that night and tried to find them— but with no success, (Perhaps a lucky farmer stumbled upon them and not believing his good fortune, stumbled for sometime thereafter.)

Empire labels from
the 1920's

Once the plant was closed down after the provincial police caught the employees drinking after hours. The company was forced to pour 30,000 gallons of beer down the drain. Taylor remembers a driver, Mr. Lee Hintz had 12 cases of beer, and since the place was being locked up he just automatically took it home. General Kirkcaldy used to drink at the Empire Road (a little trail east of the brewery), and on this account the plant was only closed down for a couple of weeks.

There were always someone in the plant making bets and one day Mr. Butch Deitrich made a bet that he could drink two 24 oz. bottles of beer without stopping. The way he went about it was by lying down on his back and swallowing the contents of the two bottles together. The beer was over 9% but he still won the bet.

When visiting the brewery, there was a keg with a pump on it and anyone coming to the factory could help themselves. The most common visitors were the railroad men because the tracks ran beside the brewery. They would come and ask for a drink of water on a warm day. Sometimes, up to 2 or 3 kegs would go in a single day.

The spent grain from the mash was never thrown away. The experimental farm would send wagons to pick up the mash to feed the cattle and the reports were the cows would produce more and better milk. Some of the mash was fed to

the dray horses while the rest would go to local farmers—a practice that's still in use today.

Coca-Cola was bottled at the Empire in the early 1920's during the lean years of Prohibition. It was shipped in big black 36 gallon kegs along with labels and crown caps. Taylor remembers there was just the right amount of caps and labels for the amount of syrup shipped.

At Christmas time the company gave out $5.00 gold pieces to employees and a case of pop for the kids right up until the First World War.

The good times ended when the company closed on September 15, 1931. Everyone was given one a free keg of beer for each one bought. When the plant was sold, tenders were let out and it was sold to none other than Isaac Owens, the scrap-iron dealer. The price: a paltry sum of $675.00.

The most common visitors were the railroad men because the tracks ran beside the brewery. They would come and ask for a drink of water on a warm day. Sometimes, up to 2 or 3 kegs would go in a single day.

The Empire Brewing Co., Ltd.
BRANDON (Phone 2643) MANITOBA

CITY PRICE LIST
IN EFFECT JANUARY 24th, 1927.

EMPIRE ALE, STOUT { Per Case } ...$4.20
LAGER, PORTER { 2 Doz. Pts. }
OLD ENGLISH STYLE ALE, 2 Doz. Pts. ...$5.20
Refund Empties, 30c per doz. Bottles Pints.

Ale, Beer and Stout in Kegs
ONE-EIGHTH KEGS, NET ...$3.25
QUARTER KEGS, NET ...$6.50

SOFT DRINKS
BELFAST GINGER ALE   STRAWBERRY SODA
DRY GINGER ALE   APPLE CIDER
BIRCH BEER   CHERRY SOUR
BREWED GINGER BEER   LEMON SOUR
ROOT BEER   LEMON SQUASH
CLUB SODA   LIME SQUASH
CREAM SODA   ORANGE SQUASH
     RASPBERRY SODA
SMALL BOTTLES, PER CASE, 2 DOZ. ...$1.85
LARGE BOTTLES, PER CASE, 2 DOZ. ...$2.30
Refund Empties, $1.00 Per Case.

CIDERS
APPLE   ORANGE   LEMON   GRAPE
LOGANBERRY   CHERRY   RASPBERRY
         STRAWBERRY
IN JARS, PER GALLON ...$ .75
IN KEGS, 5 GALLONS ...$4.50
IN KEGS, 10 GALLONS ...$8.00

REFUND EMPTIES
1 Gallon Jar ...$ .25
5 Gallon Kegs ...$2.00
10 Gallon Kegs ...$3.00

SYPHONS OF SODA WATER, PER DOZ. ...$15.00
Refund on Empties, $12.00 Per Dozen.
DISTILLED WATER, PER GALLON ...25c

OUR SPECIALS
ORANGE SQUASH | LEMON SOUR | APPLE CIDER
     BREWED GINGER BEER

According to this 1927 price list, a 24 case of beer was $4.20, but a quarter keg cost as little as $6.50.

THE BRANDON BREWING CO. LTD. 1902–1925

It's fitting that we end our story with the other man named Ferguson. The last of Brandon's brewing legacy to use the city's namesake was started by Alexander Ferguson, Henry Maley and his brother Edward. Ferguson was already operating a soda works business at the time while Maley was a city alderman until 1905.

Hiring a competent brewer is always one of the most important tasks when starting a new brewery and Ferguson found himself an ideal candidate. William Schwartz had come from the esteemed Toronto brewery, Reinhart & Co. He also worked for the famous Miller family in Wisconsin. Even with this great deal of experience, he tried and failed when he established the first Lake of the Woods Brewery in Rat Portage, (now called Kenora). It only lasted two years. With the Brandon Brewing Company, he could concentrate solely on making good beer. Unfortunately he wasn't given much time before disaster struck.

In 1902, newspaper reports boasted of a new brewery being built. Designed by Chicago architect Bernard Barthel, who specialized in breweries, all the fancy work on the façade was dispensed with in the design; the result was a substantial building at a moderate cost. But even though it was filled with state of the art equipment there was a major mistake in the design—it was made of wood.

Whether drying barley malt in the kiln or heating the brew kettles, the process of making beer at the turn of the century required wood

An illustration of the first Brandon Brewing Company building before the Christmas day fire of 1905.

or coal burning fires. With the constant threat of fire at hand and a long history of burned down breweries to learn from, most new breweries built after 1900 were of brick construction. Resting on a stone foundation and rising three stories high, Brandon's newest brewery was of wood frame construction—leaving it vulnerable to the red menace. Of course the inevitable happened.

With the constant threat of fire at hand and a long history of burned down breweries to learn from, most new breweries built after 1900 were of brick construction.

On Christmas day 1905, the two-year-old brewery burned to the ground. The fire started in the boiler room and was so advanced that by the time the fire brigade traveled the mile or more distance, nothing could be done. Situated

Stock advertising sign for Premier Lager. The brewery later changed their name based on the "Premier" product line.

on the north hill of the city the brewery was outside of the water district, further condemning its fate.

The loss was estimated at $100,000, and with only $20,000 insurance coverage, the task of rebuilding was daunting. Regardless, a new brewery was to be built and just as in the story of the three little pigs, this new one would be made of brick.

A rather exaggerated view of the second plant at 1401 Assiniboine Avenue

Located on the south side of the river at 1401 Assiniboine Avenue, the new building was finished in 1906 with a stone and brick heating plant. Additions were later added and the business flourished until Prohibition reared its ugly head.

For Henry Maley this proved to be devastating. In 1912, Maley had just built a stately home on the north-west corner of Victoria Avenue and Sixteenth Street for the princely sum of $12,000. With the pressure of Prohibition leaning heavy on Maley's brewing business it's believed they ceased production in 1919 after running afoul of the Manitoba Temperance Act. The company was caught shipping full-strength beer to a customer in Moosomin, Saskatchewan, which was legal. What wasn't legal is shipping it back to an address just one block away from the brewery. The company was slapped with a $250 penalty. In 1917, Maley's dream home was foreclosed on and sold to another prominent figure in Brandon's history; Dr J.S. McDiarmid. Today the ornate

Tudor style mansion still stands as testament to Brandon's great economic boom.

After repeal of Prohibition the company was purchased by a Winnipeg syndicate and re-organized with new owners which included G.M. Black and future chairman of the board for Shea's brewery, Col. Arthur Sullivan. In a strange sort of postscript, the syndicate had to obtain permission from Anna Ferguson, widow of Alexander, for the word "The" in the name as she held the rights.

In 1936, the buildings became Brewery Product's distribution warehouse for Drewry's, Shea's, Kiewel's and Pelissier's and later for Carling and Labatt's until it closed in 1974.

PREMIER BREWING CO. LTD.
1925–1930

A little over a year after The Brandon Brewing Company was re-incorporated in 1924, the name was changed to Premier Brewing Co. in August of 1925, (to reflect the name of the "Premier" product line of beers the company was now producing.) The name change wasn't enough to save the company from the fate of consolidation. In 1928, the plant became part of George M. Black's Western Breweries Ltd. and a year later was closed for good.

In 1936, the buildings became Brewery Product's distribution warehouse for Drewry's, Shea's, Kiewel's and Pelissier's and later for Carling and Labatt's until it closed in 1974. Unfortunately the brewhouse, having lost its purpose, was torn down in the 1930's.

Three Premier Brands: High Life, Three Castle Stock Ale and Double Diamond Ale

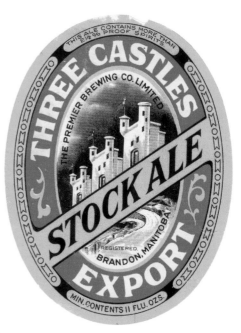

Sitting idyllically on the banks of Colony Creek,
the brewery that Celestin Thomas began in 1873
was still brewing beer a century later. Painting by
artist and Brewerianist George Vine.

BOULEVARD OF DREAMS

THE BREWERIES OF OSBORNE STREET

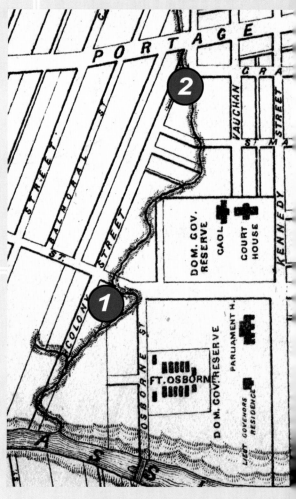

In 1884 Colony Creek had two breweries on the edge of its banks; The Winnipeg Brewing & Malting Co. (1) Blackwood Bros. (2)

Names change — streets, roads, avenues; as a city grows, new streets are built and older ones renamed. Streets mysteriously morph from one name to another. A perfect example of this is Osborne Street in Winnipeg. Depending on where you are, the name changes several times without making a single right angle turn. The same can be said of Winnipeg's brewing past. Depending on what period of history you choose, breweries changed hands and names, but the location stays the same. This especially applies to Osborne Street. In a comparatively short stretch of one street there were more breweries than in any other part of the city. One reason for this is a long-forgotten stream called Colony Creek.

Colony Creek was once the western boundary for the Hudson's Bay Reserve — a parcel of land the company was allowed to keep after surrendering Rupert's Land to the Canadian Government in 1869. The creek began its short journey near Balmoral Street and Qu' Appelle Avenue; notorious as the city's first brothel district. Long since filled in, it ran a zigzag course south down present day Memorial Boulevard and Osborne Street. It's here in 1873 that Celestin Thomas built his new brewery. For $800 he purchased one acre of land on the banks of the creek at the end of Broadway. The stream served as a source for water and ice but it wasn't long before the brewery was forced to draw from a well. Winnipeg was expanding and with no proper sewer system, the creek eventually became a dumping ground. The only visible reminder of the little tributary is the slight dip in Broadway right next to Great West Life.

THE WINNIPEG BREWERY

The brewery stood on the banks of the creek in relative isolation until the 1880's. Thomas had taken in his old friend George Raywood as partner. Just as Winnipeg was about to experience a building boom, the veteran brewer turned his back on the young city and headed south for another town with high hopes. In 1881, after operating the plant for eight years, he sold out and moved to Pembina in the Dakota Territory. Brewers were flocking to the area, eager to be the first to establish a foothold in the market. None were successful and when the boom went bust four years later, Thomas came back to Colony Creek. In his absence, two businessmen tried their hand at running the brewery. The first was Peter Poulin, the owner of a Main Street liquor store called the "Big Bottle." With partner M. E. Roy they changed the name to the Winnipeg Brewing & Malting Company. Poulin also owned the Manitoba Soda & Water Works and had been bottling beer for the Winnipeg Brewery. For reasons unknown he left the partnership in 1883. Roy, along with the aptly named Samuel Porter as brewmaster, carried on until 1885, when the establishment finally fell back into the hands of Celestin Thomas. Once again the veteran brewer was forced to search for a suitable candidate to buy his brewery. The next two men came with impressive credentials.

John Cosgrave hailed from an established brewing family in Toronto. Along with his brother Lawrence they built their father's struggling business into the successful Cosgrave Brewery of Toronto. As for William Blackwood, his family had business ties in St. Thomas, Ontario and Montreal. The plan was to lease the brewery from Thomas under the name Cosgrave & Company. Blackwood was already operating a soda water business and brewery on Colony Creek just south the Portage Avenue. After only three months he dropped out of the Cosgrave partnership to concentrate on the Blackwood Bros. growing business concerns.

Cosgrave immediately set out to make improvements to the plant, tearing down the original structures and adding new ones fitted with the latest in brewing equipment. Celestin Thomas stayed on as brewer. An article in a June 1886 publication held high aspirations for the new establishment.

Roy & Poulin, Proprietors.
THE WINNIPEG
Brewing & Malting Co.
ALES, PORTER AND LAGER.
WINNIPEG.

NOTICE.
—COSGRAVE & CO.—
Beg to announce that they will commence to deliver
Lager Beer, Ale and Porter!
On Saturday Morning, June 5th, and that they feel confident that the quality of the articles which they are prepared to offer will merit a fair share of patronage.
HIGHEST PRICE PAID FOR BOTTLES.
Grains and Spent Hops Sold at Reasonable Rates.

Cosgrave and Co. 1886

"There is every probability that brewing will become a prominent industry in the city. The water to be had seems well suited for brewing and it is now conceded that in Manitoba there are better facilities for raising first class barley than anywhere on the continent. One brewery has been an unqualified success, and there can be no doubt but Mr. Cosgrave and the second institution will prove that the number and capacity can be increased just in proportion to the increase of the population of the City and surrounding area."

THOMAS & RAYWOOD.
HAVE COMMENCED BUSINESS AND are ready to furnish ale & Porter to any amount of customers. Satisfaction garaunteed. Orders to be left at the Manitoba House or the Broadway Brewery Winnipeg. Sept. 9th · 2

Far Left: Winnipeg Brewing & Malting Co. 1881 – 1885

Left: Thomas & Raywood (Broadway Brewery) 1874 – 1876

Unable to live up to the newspapers glowing prediction, within 13 months Mr. Cosgrave's brewery was broke. The Commercial responded by writing that he began the business with a "flourish of trumpets" but little cash. Cosgrave owed the bank $8850. The expansion was more than he could afford (or willing to gamble) and so the bank stepped in to protect its interest. On July 19, 1887, the stock and plant was sold at auction to Duncan MacArthur, a private banker. The banker now owned a fine brewery with great potential, but Duncan MacArthur held no aspiration of becoming a brewer. It was now up to John McDonagh & Patrick Shea to turn the fortunes of this brewery around. As we will later see, good fortune would play a large part in Patrick Shea's life for many years to come.

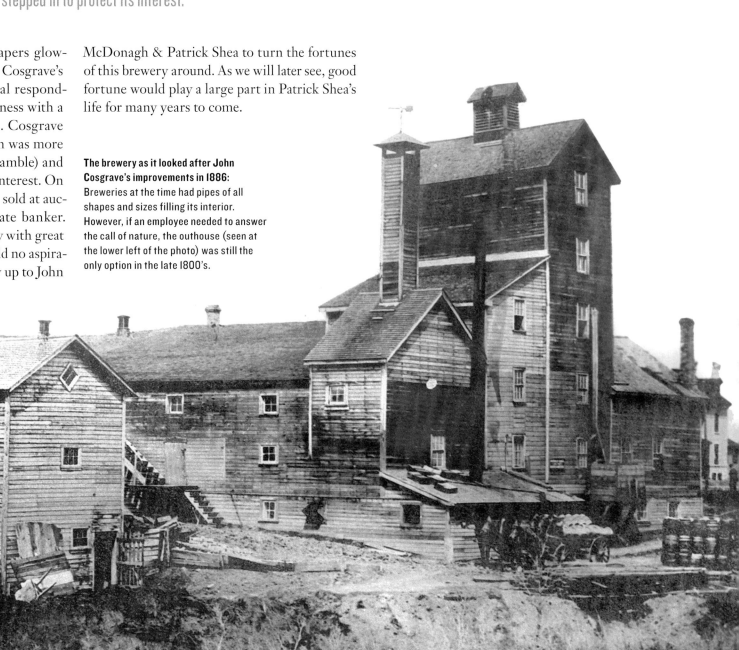

The brewery as it looked after John Cosgrave's improvements in 1886: Breweries at the time had pipes of all shapes and sizes filling its interior. However, if an employee needed to answer the call of nature, the outhouse (seen at the lower left of the photo) was still the only option in the late 1800's.

MULVEY & SONS, IMPERIAL BREWERY (MULVEY'S BREWERY),
MULVEY BREWING AND MALTING CO. 1883–1885
TODD, HEAP AND COMPANY – THE EMPIRE BREWING & MALTING CO. 1887–1891

As one of Winnipeg's pioneering businessmen, E.L Drewry's contribution to the city and province were exceptional. A businessman and politician, his name was synonymous with success. But one thing he doesn't have is a street named after him. Or even a school. Stewart Mulvey does. Just like E.L Drewry, Stewart Mulvey owned a brewery too. But the key difference between these two men is; Drewry was a brewer first and politician second. In Mulvey's case it was quite the opposite.

Irish-born and as ambitious as they come, Stewart Mulvey was encouraged to come to Canada by educator Dr. Egerton Ryerson in 1856. After spending 14 years as a teacher in Ontario he arrived in Winnipeg with Colonel Wolseley's 1870 expedition to put down the first Red River Rebellion. When the troops disbanded in 1871, Mulvey stayed in Manitoba and became exceedingly active in the community. He founded a newspaper, The Liberal, and in 1873 was appointed Collector of Internal Revenue. As a school trustee, he helped draft the provinces first educational act.

Why Mulvey, a teacher and public servant, decided to enter into the brewing business is not known. His role as Collector of Internal Revenue gave him a certain degree of insight into the local business scene and where the financial gain was. He was an incredible busy man and may have been looking to set up a business for his two sons. In 1881

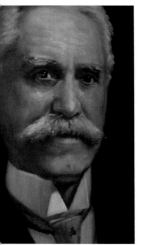

Stewart Mulvey

he bought 2 acres of land along the west side of the Red River just off of Pembina Street—later to become Osborne Street. In 1883 construction began on a three-story brewery and malt house. Costing $25,000 (a huge sum at the time) the brewery was fitted with modern equipment and was up and running by the fall of 1883. That same year he was elected to city council. Mulvey and E.L. Drewry, who was also an Alderman at the time, would bring samples of their beers to council for others to taste. Having so much in common the two brewery owners enjoyed a friendly rivalry.

Mulvey School - Broadway and Maryland

Mulvey had taken on his two sons, Stewart Jr. and Walter as partners, but the call of duty was too much for the fervent Orangeman. He left the business to his two sons while he went off to fight against the 1885 Riel Rebellion. The brewery ceased operation in 1886.

In 1896, Mulvey was elected to the Manitoba Legislature for the constituency of Morris as a Liberal-Conservative. He served as Grand Master of the Orange Order and was also a director of the Winnipeg General Hospital. Mulvey

Street and Mulvey School are named in his honour, but his brewery has long been forgotten.

If there is a common thread that's runs through the early history of brewing in Manitoba, it is this. Like an ongoing flood, as one brewery fails another entreprenuer rushes in to fill the void. After Mulvey and Son's ended their foray in the beer business the brewery sat vacant until 1887 when two more men reached for a piece of the pie. Charles F. Todd and Richard Heap were former owners of the South End Brewery. Todd, a chemist by trade, once worked for Gambles Brewery in Newmarket, Ontario. He soon bailed out of the partnership and new investors were found. They managed to raise $40,000 in capital, proving that regardless of the previous failure, investors still believed that beer was a viable commodity. More improvements were made and a spur line was built next to the brewery. Travellers were dispatched to cover the territory from Winnipeg to the west coast. The Empire

HEAP'S
SOUTH END BREWERY
Corner Kennedy and Graham Streets.
ENGLISH HOPPED ALE
In Wood and Bottles. Equal to the best "Burton" Brands.
EXTRA DOUBLE STOUT
Warranted Equal to Guiness' Dublin Stout, and Superior to any Brewed in this Country.

Put up in Eight Gallon Kegs and in bottles for family use.   TELEPHONE NO. 454

Brewing and Malting Company was incorporated in May of 1888. They boasted of having the finest beer, ales and porter ever produced in Canada, a lofty statement considering there were hundreds of breweries opening and closing during the 1880's. Whether that statement was true or not didn't matter. The company fell into financial trouble and went into receivership in 1891.

E.L. Drewry knew a good deal when he saw it, and snapped up the brewery from its liquidators for $14,000, a fraction of what Stewart Mulvey and the other investors had spent. He kept it operational for a while, but gradually moved the equipment over to his Redwood plant. During this time he changed the name of his

EMPIRE
Brewing & Malting Co.
WEINER LAGER, ICE COOL
ALES, XXX PORTER.
Orders for Families Receive Immediate Attention.
TELEPHONE 537.
Brewery at Fort Rouge
City Office 389 Main St.

Richard Heap acquired the Calcutt Bottling House from Henry Calcutt in 1885. The South End Brewery operated for two years until Heap and C. F. Todd bought Mulvey's Brewery in 1887. The name was changed to the Empire Brewing and Malting Co.

brewery to the Redwood & Empire Breweries and hired Richard Heap as his brewer. Heap never became the rich beer baron he may have set out to be; but never the less ended up working for Drewry for 32 years.

This wasn't the end of the line for the breweries at the south end of Osborne Street. In fact it was still just the beginning. Two more breweries would make their home at this location and brew beer right up until 1969. It wouldn't happen just yet because the next brewery to move in had its beginning not here, but at the other end of the street—Colony Street to be exact.

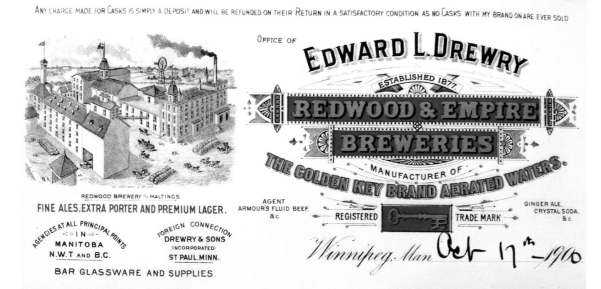

ANY CHARGE MADE FOR CASKS IS SIMPLY A DEPOSIT AND WILL BE REFUNDED ON THEIR RETURN IN A SATISFACTORY CONDITION AS NO CASKS WITH MY BRAND ON ARE EVER SOLD

OFFICE OF

EDWARD L. DREWRY
ESTABLISHED 1877
REDWOOD & EMPIRE
BREWERIES
MANUFACTURER OF
THE GOLDEN KEY BRAND AERATED WATERS.

REDWOOD BREWERY ~ MALTINGS
FINE ALES, EXTRA PORTER AND PREMIUM LAGER.

AGENCIES AT ALL PRINCIPAL POINTS
—IN—
MANITOBA
N.W.T. AND B.C.

FOREIGN CONNECTION
DREWRY & SONS
(INCORPORATED)
ST. PAUL. MINN.

BAR GLASSWARE AND SUPPLIES.

AGENT
ARMOUR'S FLUID BEEF
&c.

REGISTERED   TRADE MARK

GINGER ALE,
CRYSTAL SODA,
&c.

Winnipeg, Man Oct 17th 1910

PRAIRIE

LAGER

TRADE MARK
REGISTERED.

TRADE MARK
REGISTERED.

THE MANITOBA BREWING AND MALTING CO. LIMITED. WINNIPEG, CANADA.

BULMAN BROS. LITH. WP'G.

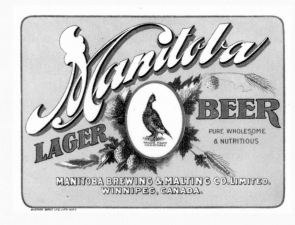

Manitoba

LAGER · BEER

PURE WHOLESOME
& NUTRITIOUS

TRADE MARK
REGISTERED

MANITOBA BREWING & MALTING CO. LIMITED.
WINNIPEG, CANADA.

BULMAN BROS. LTD. LITH. WP'G

BLACKWOOD BROTHERS 1882–1902,
BLACKWOOD'S LTD 1902–1919,
MANITOBA BREWING & MALTING CO. 1904–1914

The Hudson's Bay Store stands as a majestic reminder of the vibrancy downtown Winnipeg once enjoyed. It lies at the foot of Memorial Boulevard and as you drive by the store your eyes are drawn down the street to the Legislative Building in the distance. But once long ago, none of this was here. Way back in the 1880's Colony Creek occupied that space with Colony Street running alongside. This is where the Blackwood Brothers built their soda water business in 1882. The building stood at 315 Colony Street just south of Portage Avenue. They were known for packaged provisions, condiments, and soft drinks. It was a multifaceted business manufacturing a myriad of products including: mineral water, flavour extracts, syrups, apple cider, mustard, pickles and packaged tea. In 1884, they began to brew beer.

The Blackwoods' owned a successful soda water business in Montreal before coming out west. Initially there were three brothers: William and Thomas Blackwood, along with a third brother, D. M. Blackwood, who left for St. Paul in late 1882, but later returned to the fold in 1902. The brothers did very well for themselves and by 1896 they built a grand mansion to celebrate their success. This wasn't any ordinary mansion. The twenty-two-room home at 311 Colony Street may

Looking down Memorial Blvd with the Blackwood family mansion at right: The Winnipeg Art Gallery now stands in its place.

not have been the grandest house in Winnipeg, but it had one very cool convenience anyone would love to have—a tunnel to their workplace.

In Lillian Gibbons' book Stories Houses Tell she describes the tunnels as ghost-like "catacombs" that conjure up thoughts of Edgar Allen Poe and The Cask of Amontillado. The tunnels ran under Colony Creek and were built to connect the house with the brewery on the other side. She visited the house in 1936 before it was demolished a year later. Gibbons went on to describe the tunnel's entrance as having big iron doors, crusted with rust. The tunnel itself was shaped in an arch, made of brick and curved as far as the eye could see. After the Blackwood's moved out, the home was turned into a rooming house and in 1911 the Hudson's Bay Company

In Lillian Gibbons' book Stories Houses Tell she describes the tunnels as ghost-like "catacombs" that conjure up thoughts of Edgar Allen Poe and The Cask of Amontillado.

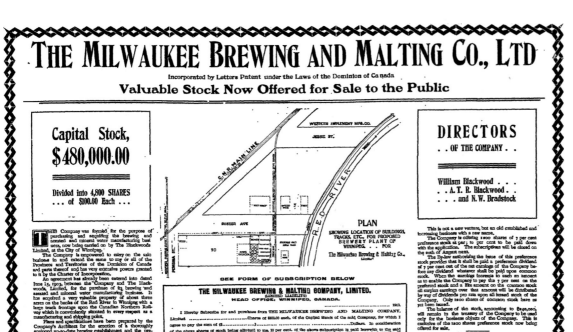

THE MILWAUKEE BREWING AND MALTING CO., LTD
Incorporated by Letters Patent under the Laws of the Dominion of Canada
Valuable Stock Now Offered for Sale to the Public

Capital Stock, $480,000.00

Divided into 4,800 SHARES ... of $100.00 Each ...

PLAN

SHOWING LOCATION OF BUILDINGS, TRACKS, ETC. FOR PROPOSED BREWERY PLANT OF WINNIPEG . . . FOR

The Milwaukee Brewing & Malting Co., Limited

DIRECTORS
. . OF THE COMPANY . .

William Blackwood . . .
. . A. T. R. Blackwood . .
. . . and N. W. Bradstock

SEE FORM OF SUBSCRIPTION BELOW

THE MILWAUKEE BREWING & MALTING COMPANY, LIMITED.
(LIMITED LIABILITY)
HEAD OFFICE, WINNIPEG, CANADA.

Prospectus for the Milwaukee Brewing and Malting Co.

PHONE 487

The Beer Season is Here
Have you tried PRAIRIE LAGER?
PRAIRIE LAGER is made in Winnipeg
PRAIRIE LAGER is Pure and Wholesome

─ SOLD BY ALL HOTELS AND DEALERS ─

Manitoba Brewing and Malting Co. Ltd., Winnipeg

bought it. In 1931 they renovated it to become the home of the Company's Beaver Club. Today the site is occupied by the Winnipeg Art Gallery.

As the Blackwood brothers prospered, the business eventually outgrew the Colony Street location. In 1902 the company changed its name to Blackwood's Ltd. and an ambitious plan emerged. A new company was formed with the peculiar name of "The Milwaukee Brewing and Malting Company". It was peculiar because it didn't have anything to do with Milwaukee, or the beer that made it famous. It was only a sales ploy to attract investors. The company planned to raise $480,000 worth of stock and build a new brewery on the same site where others had tried and failed. The company bought the old Empire Brewery on Osborne Street and had all the buildings torn down. When the Fort Rouge plant was completed in November 1904,

The Manitoba Brewing & Malting Company brewhouse ca. 1905

the name game continued. Now it became The Manitoba Brewing & Malting Company, but was often referred to as the "Prairie Chicken Brewery". The firm had adopted the Greater Prairie Chicken as their trademark to go along with their flagship brand—Prairie Lager.

The Blackwood's continued to operate the soft drink plant on Colony Street since the new firm only took the brewing operation. That changed when fire destroyed part of the plant on May 2, 1910. Seventy men were employed at the plant and the damage was $85,000. The operations were eventually moved to a new building next to the brewery on Mulvey Street.

The fire was the beginning of the end for the brewery. Even with the wide range of products the company produced, it was hit hard by Prohibition. Financially over-extended, it shut down in 1919. William Blackwood moved to California in 1922

Ask for BLACKWOOD'S
HOP BEER
A Temperance Beverage
GUARANTEED NON-INTOXICATING.
BLACKWOOD'S LTD., WINNIPEG

Above: Fire destroyed the Colony Street plant in 1910

Far Left: "Hop Beer" was Blackwood's version of the Temperance Beers that began to appear around 1909.

Left: Maltbru conformed to the Manitoba Temperance laws, c. 1917

Here are just a few of Blackwood's product line. For nearly forty years the company produced teas, soft drinks and even condiments. Of course, they also made beer. The Bond brand of stouts was named for their brewmaster, Louis Bond.

Prohibition era label

Blackwoods Beverages William Avenue location in the early 1950's.

and died 13 years later. After being in business for almost 40 years the Blackwood name disappeared until 1935. Ironically, it was an outsider that resurrected the name and for the next 60 years it was a Winnipeg institution.

Max Gray came to Canada from Russia when he was 19 years old. By 1923 he had joined the Whistle Bottling Co. as a sales manager at their new plant on Jarvis Avenue. During the depression the company fell on hard times. Grey reorganized the operation and bought controlling interest. Since Whistle owned Blackwood's product line the family name was resurrected. The new company's success was not built on any of the old Blackwood soft drink formulas, but on a new one. In 1935 Blackwood Beverages began bottling 7-Up, a drink invented by Charles Grigg in 1929.

Max Grey died in 1944 and his son Gerald became president in the mid 1950's. Gerald took the company to new heights when he built a large modern plant on Ellice Avenue. He continued to expand when they began bottling Orange Crush in 1965 and Pepsi-Cola in 1978. The company

The new company's success was not built on any of the old Blackwood soft drink formulas, but on a new one.

was finally sold to Pepsi in the 1990's; so ending the Blackwood's name. Since then Gerald Grey has become one Winnipeg's most generous philanthropists. One of his last acts of charity before passing away in October of 2010 was a donation of a million dollars to the restoration of Central Park in downtown Winnipeg.

There is one more story to tell of the brewery at Mulvey and Osborne Street. A new family took over to guarantee that beer flowed out of this location for another 45 years. Scott Bryant, the great-great grandson of founder Henri Pelissier tells the story of his family's brewery.

Ellice Avenue Plant before expansion.

PELISSIER'S

The Pelissier Brewery rose from its humble beginnings in the late 1890s out of Henri Pelissier's fledgling venture, The Pelissier and Gobeil Soda Water Manufacturers. It evolved into an important player in the burgeoning brewing business that was growing in Winnipeg in the early 1900s. The company underwent several name changes in the early years, from Pelissier and Sons to the Beaver Brewing and Bottling; the Home Brewery Co. to Pelissier's Limited (where it saw its greatest expansion and success), and finally to Pelissier's Brewery.

What started as a small family-run business would see relocation and expansion, transfer from father to son, takeovers and mergers with outside interests, and the gradual decline and eventual phase-out of the company name entirely.

But it's best to start at the beginning.

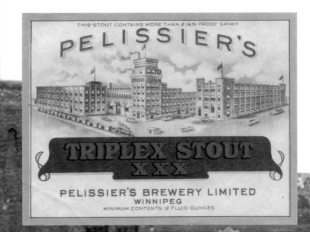

EARLY BEGINNINGS

Pelissier Brewery founder Louis Henri Godefroi Pelissier was born November 10, 1858 in the small farming community of St. Michel d'Yamaska, Quebec. Upon the death of his father, Joseph, in 1864, Henri's mother Adeline packed up her five children and moved to Fall River, Massachusetts. This was a natural move for the recently widowed Adeline as many French Canadians were moving to the New England states in response to the huge demand for unskilled labour in the rapidly growing textile industry. The majority of these jobs were centred in the towns of Woonsocket, Rhode Island, and Fall River. An added incentive for Adeline was that her mother and sister had already relocated to the Fall River area.

Henri Pelissier grew up in Fall River, where he met his future wife, Philomene Vandal. The two were married in Bristol, Rhode Island in 1877. The Pelissiers celebrated the birth of their first child, Henri Jr. in 1878. A couple of years earlier, Henri Sr.'s older brother Joseph had moved to Winnipeg; so in 1880, Henri, Philomene, and Henri Jr. followed suit and headed west.

The two brothers began their working careers in Winnipeg in the early 1880s as clerks at various hotels in the city. After a couple of years, Joseph and Henri purchased the St. Boniface Livery Stables on Dumoulin Street. In 1888, Henri and Joseph moved their stables to 110 Garry Street and changed the name to the Pelissier Brothers Stables.

It was at this time that the Pelissier brothers went their separate ways. Older brother Joseph moved to Saint-Jean-Baptiste, Manitoba, and became the proprietor of the town's most

Founder Henri Pelissier

successful hotel. Younger brother Henri also purchased a hotel, the Bellevue Hotel (later called the Bank Hotel), which was located at 186 McDermot in the Exchange District. It was most likely here that Henri first learned the art of brewing and used the new skill to supply his hotel guests with beer and ale. This was the earliest beginnings of what later became the Pelissier Brewery.

In 1902, Henri Sr. partnered with his son-in-law George Gobeil in a new venture – they purchased a soda water manufacturer from the O'Kelly Brothers and renamed the business Pelissier and Gobeil Soda Water Manufacturers, located at 184 James Street. Henri learned about the availability of this business from his son Cleophas (Pete) Pelissier, who worked for a time as a driver for the O'Kelly Brothers. By 1904, Pelissier, who had then split with his son-in-law, relocated the newly named Pelissier and Sons to the larger facilities that he had started building

Pelissier & Gobeil Soda Water Manufactures, 184 James Street ca. 1902

Henri Pelissier and Son's

Furby street plant ca. 1919

in 1903 on a plot of land located at the corner of Furby Street and Notre Dame Avenue.

The new Furby Street facility was outfitted with machinery purchased from a plant in Minnesota. It was from this location that Pelissier and Sons really began to become a growing concern in the brewing industry. In fact, in addition to their own brands, the Pelissiers began bottling beer for other breweries. For a time, they acted as bottlers for Labatt (with the kegs shipped in from its plant in London, Ontario), as well as for the Kuntz Brewery in Berlin (now Kitchener), Ontario. In 1905, they acted as agents for the Don Brewery of Toronto, Ontario.

The company continued to flourish, and in 1915 reorganized under a new name, Beaver Brewing and Bottling. The value of the transfer was an impressive $281,000, and Henri Sr. continued on as president with his sons, Pete, Philippe, Alphonse, Joseph, and Henri Jr. also involved.

The little company was not without its share of controversy, however. Beaver Brewing and Bottling was fined several times for various Prohibition infractions, including a 1917 fine of $200 for selling liquor without a license. An article in the Manitoba Free Press reported a scheme where a druggist ordered beer from the Beaver Brewing Company for "medicinal purposes." The prescription was kept and the order was repeated for the "patient" when he desired it. The patient then supplied his friends with

beer. This scheme worked very well until some Temperance Act enforcers caught wind of it. It appears that, eventually, the Beaver Brewing and Bottling Company pressed their luck a little too far. In May 1919 the company lost its license after being fined for the fifth time in the past year. But it seems the loss of its license was only a minor stumbling block as the company again reorganized and reopened under a new name—The Home Brewery.

Home Brewery founder Henri Sr. and his wife Philomene had 10 children – six boys and four girls. All of the children worked at the brewery in one capacity or another. But it was second oldest son, Pete, who emerged and took control of the company after his father's death.

THE NEW BOSS

Pete Pelissier was born in Winnipeg on August 19, 1881. He had spent his early years working for different breweries in the city, including Drewry's, learning as much as he could about the business of brewing. This would all come in handy when he took over control of Pelissier's.

While 1922 marked the beginning of a prosperous era for the Pelissier Brewery, it was a terrible year for the Pelissier family personally. In March, at the young age of 37, Henri son Phillipe, passed away, followed in May by the death of company founder, Henri Sr., at the age of 63. Among the honourary pallbearers at Henri's funeral were the former mayor of St. Boniface, J.A. Bleu. The elder Pelissier was remembered in his obituary as one of the leading parishioners of Sacré-Coeur, and he was interred at St. Mary's Cemetery on Osborne Street.

What had already been a sad year for the family was compounded by the death of Pete's oldest son, Henry, in a tragic fire at the St. Boniface College dormitory in November. Young Henry, age 14, fled the burning building but re-entered to search for his younger brothers; Louis (12 – my grandfather), and Ernie (9). Sadly, he was unaware that his brothers had already escaped the fire. Henry, a Jesuit brother, and eight other students died in the blaze and were later

TEN LIVES LOST, SCORE INJURED, IN COLLEGE FIRE

St. Boniface Institution In Ruins With Valuable Library And Seismograph Destroyed

List Of Dead Includes Rev. Bro. Stormont And 9 Students Of Ages From 9 To 16

Right: Cleophas "Pete" Pelissier hoisting a sample of the many different beers his company produced in the 1920's.

buried in a mass grave in front of St. Boniface Cathedral. The tragedy made headlines around North America, and The New York Times of December 1, 1922, noted that a strange man had been seen several times in the vicinity of the college on the day of the fire. This unknown man, however, was not identified, and the cause of the blaze was never determined.

Henri Sr.'s death signalled a change in control of the company. His will described his son Pete as a co-partner in the business and, as such, granted him controlling interest in the Home Brewery. Under Pete's command, the little family operation would thrive.

Pete recognized that the brewery's success in the mid 1920s was pushing the production limits of the Furby Street location. This necessitated a move to a larger facility, so Pelissier decided to purchase the former Blackwood's property down by the river. The new location cost the company $70,000 and with $100,000 worth of upgrading, the facility could now produce ale and beer on a large scale.

The family business saw its ups and downs over the next few years, but the 1920s were

The new location cost the company $70,000 and with $100,000 worth of upgrading, the facility could now produce ale and beer on a large scale.

generally quite prosperous for the small company. The growth of the business culminated in 1927. At that point, the company reorganized again and made another public offering on the Winnipeg Stock Exchange, with its capitalization reaching nearly $1.4 million. This was an astonishing 28 times its value in 1922 when Pete Pelissier took control of the company after the death of his father. Casting aside the Home brewery moniker in 1924, the business entered a new phase in 1927, when it was formally incorporated as Pelissier's Limited—a name that would last until 1939.

With the new name of Pelissier's Limited, the brewery launched a product line that included soft drinks like Club Ginger Ale.

Right: Pelissier's Banquet Ale was introduced in the early 1930's.

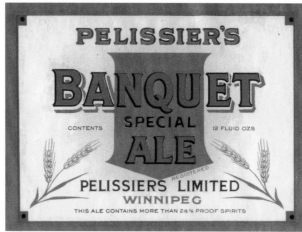

Country Club

SPECIAL

A special brew of particular flavor and quality, that is becoming more popular every day. Made from the finest of malt and imported hops — brewed and aged with expert care. Country Club Special is a marvel of quality and flavor—an instant favorite wherever served.

Golden Glow Ale

is made from high-grade malt, Bohemian hops and specially distilled water. Expert brewing and proper ageing produce a fine quality ale of delightful flavor.

Country Club Special and Golden Glow Ale are brewed under ideal conditions in a modern spotless brewery. Aged in glass lined vats to maintain absolute purity, and bottled in sterilized bottles.

Pelissier's Limited
WINNIPEG

Community Spirit

On a personal level, the Pelissiers were in a somewhat-unique position among Francophone Winnipeggers. The Catholic Church essentially viewed Manitoba francophones as rural people, but the promotional nature of the brewing business of Pelissiers spilled over into the personal lives of Pete and his wife, Rose Anna. They were known to entertain mostly English-speaking business associates with vaudeville, theatre, and opera performers most notably, at the many parties they hosted in their home at 180 Ethelbert Street. The Pelissiers deftly moved between the two cultures by making sure that they also acted as benefactors to the Sacre-Coeur parish and by encouraging involvement in the cadet movement.

Of Pete and Rose Anna's two surviving sons, Louis and Ernie, my grandfather Louis spoke often about his involvement in the family business. Louis Pelissier, like his father before him, was involved in the brewing business from an early age. He told me stories about driving a beer delivery truck around the city at the age of 12. He said that his father was so well known and liked that anytime the police pulled him over, they would immediately release him, saying, "Oh, you're Pete's son. Carry on."

Louis's exploits behind the wheel actually led to meeting his future wife, Kay Kreger (my grandmother) who also lived on Furby Street. When asked, years later, how they met, Kay exclaimed, "We met one day when I was crossing the street and he just about ran me over with his damn delivery truck!"

Another favourite story was one my grandfather told me about delivering beer on a sweltering summer day in the early 1920s. Louis was about 13 or 14, and after a long day making deliveries, he arrived back at the Furby Street plant tired and thirsty. He looked around at all the beer and decided that a nice cold brew would do the trick. He told me, "I grabbed a cold bottle right off the assembly line and downed the whole thing in one long gulp. The next thing I knew, I was lying flat on the floor looking up at my father who was standing over me laughing and laughing."

Above: The Pelissier name reached all the way to Wisconsin with this American Prohibition era (1920-1933) "Kingsbury Pale" near beer. Produced using a recipe from Pelissier's, it was made by Manitowoc Products. In 1933 its corporate name was changed to Kingsbury Breweries Company. Of interest is the swastika under the name. The symbol was widely used in western culture before its association with Nazi Germany.

Left: This unidentified couple are a vision of contrasts. The women with her 1920's flapper look and the gentlemen, sporting work clothes and keg apron.

The Evolution of Club Beer

Introduced in 1927, Country Club Special became Pelissier's flagship brand and remained that way until the late 1960's. In 1969 the plant at Mulvey and Osborne closed and Pelissiers merged with Kiewels in St. Boniface. The Labatt's controlled brewery re-launched the brand as "Club Beer" but that name actually goes back to the early 1930's. For about four years in a row Pelissier's released a seasonal Christmas brew called Club Beer and today, along with Standard Lager, it is the last remaining vestige of our brewing past.

Country Club Stark was ahead of its time. Inspired by his wife's distaste for beer, brewmaster John Prost created a recipe he hoped would attract non-beer lovers. Red in colour and with a sweet taste it was more suited for today's craft brew market. Unfortunately in the late 1950's Manitoba wasn't ready for this type of beer and it lived a short life.

Can You Tell The Difference? In the days before the big national breweries sold their beers across the country, smaller breweries like Pelissier's used stock labels offered by printers such as Winnipeg's Bulman Bros. Pelissier's Country Club Special was almost identical to the Country Club label from the M.K. Goetz Brewing Company of St. Joseph, Missouri. The markets for these two breweries were so far apart that copyright infringements were never an issue. On the other hand, the folks at Anheuser Busch, a national brewery, frequently had to protect their famous Budweiser label.

THE LATER YEARS

Despite the prosperity of 1927, that year sparked the beginning of the end of family control as Pete Pelissier saw his involvement with the company lessen and eventually come to an end. Pelissier sold his controlling interest in Pelissier's Limited for a whopping $750,000. He remained the company president for one more year. He then stepped aside in favour of T.C. Anderson and left the company entirely to pursue other interests.

In 1928, Pelissier took the considerable fortune he made from the sale of Pelissier's and started a new company, Superior Finance Corp, which he later called Empire Construction and Investment Company. The company financed the construction of several apartment buildings, but this venture did not turn out well. Unfortunately, the launch of his new business coincided with the start of the Depression, and Pete lost most of his fortune in the stock market crash the following year. Pete was known for his generous nature and it was said that, in spite of the Depression, he refused to lay off any of his workers. He even went as far as to give out loans to friends in need. Pete hung in there as best he could, but, with the money gone, and no other options, he returned to what he knew best – working at Pelissier's as a director. He remained at this position for a year until his death in 1934.

The year 1930 saw the remaining shares held by Pelissier family members bought out by the company, and the family involvement in the brewery came largely to an end. The years 1929 and 1930 were profitable, but the early years of the depression were a loss. The only Pelissier family member still connected to the business, in any capacity, was Pete's brother Joe, who continued on as brewmaster until his death in 1939.

T.C. Anderson took control of the company for a period of time. He was elected president of the Winnipeg Stock Exchange in 1933, but was forced to resign 1936 after charges of conspiracy and theft were laid against him by the attorney general's office. Meanwhile, Anderson had placed Pelissier's Limited in the hands of liquidators.

In 1935, Pelissier's Limited was sold to a consortium of Drewry's and Shea's breweries in a 60/40 split. Shea's eventually bought Drewry's shares. Later, Labatt took control of the Pelissier brand after buying out Shea's in 1953, and carried on the Pelissier name with its own sales staff. Although the last remaining Pelissier brand, Club Beer (originally Country Club), still lives on, it is now brewed in Edmonton. Labatt continues to hold the trademark on many of the brewery's brand names to this day.

The operation of the Pelissier Brewery plant at Mulvey and Osborne in Winnipeg continued until 1969, when the facility was closed and the production of Pelissier's lone brand was moved to the Kiewel plant in St. Boniface. The three buildings that made up the Pelissier complex on Mulvey Avenue were occupied by several different businesses over the past 35 years, until the brewhouse was demolished in 1994.

A beautiful Pelissier calender for 1932.

Unfortunately, the launch of his new business coincided with the start of the Depression, and Pete lost most of his fortune in the stock market crash the following year.

Shea's
INTERNATIONAL CHAMPIONS

JOHNNIE   UNITY   CAPTAIN
ALADDIN   HARRY   MAJOR

OWNED BY PATRICK SHEA, WINNIPEG, CANADA

CHAPTER 5

THE HOUSE OF SHEA

HIGH CLASS AND CLYDESDALES

By the mid 1880's, E.L. Drewry was by far the dominant brewer in town. While other upstart breweries wrestled their way to profit, it proved to be a tough challenge to match Drewry's professionalism. Even an old hand like Whiskey Thomas struggled to compete. But all that changed when an Irishman named Patrick Shea entered the game.

Born in County Kerry, Ireland in 1854, Patrick Shea left home at the tender age of 16. Arriving in New York in 1870 the young lad soon landed a job with a company building railroad bridges across America. In 1882, when the CPR began building in the West, Shea headed north to Manitoba and found work overseeing the water supply for the construction of the railway from Oak Lake westward. Working for the CPR proved to be the perfect stepping stone for Shea's growing ambition. In two years time he quit the railway and began a partnership with fellow Irishman, John McDonagh. Aware of the thriving business the railway was bringing to Winnipeg, they purchased the Waverley Hotel on Main Street right next to the CPR Station. Considered one of the good hotels of the time, it wasn't immune to living up to Winnipeg's rough reputation. In 1883 a salesman from Chicago was found murdered in his room—the sad result of

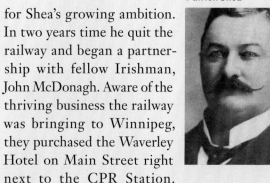

Patrick Shea

Waverley Hotel ca. 1892: John McDonagh and Patrick Shea's hotel stood beside the second of three CPR depots that have been built over the years. Opening in 1906, the Royal Alexandra Hotel occupied this site for 65 years. (Drawing of a photograph from C.E. Steele)

The brewery in the late 1890's before the plant expanded in 1903.

Acquiring the land for $5000 and the brewery for 80 cents on the dollar, in two months time he found a buyer and secured himself a handsome profit.

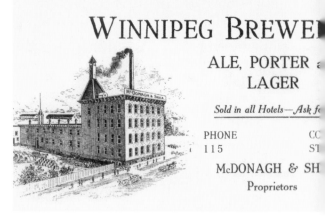

WINNIPEG BREWE[RY]

ALE, PORTER [and]
LAGER

Sold in all Hotels—Ask f[or]

PHONE   CC
115   ST

McDONAGH & SH[EA]
Proprietors

an apparent robbery. With the burden of owning a busy hotel and saloon, perhaps the two young men realized the real money lay in making beer, instead of selling it. With the failure of Cosgrave & Company they found the perfect opportunity.

When banker Duncan MacArthur took title of the Winnipeg Brewery, his only interest was to make a quick buck. Acquiring the land for $5000 and the brewery for 80 cents on the dollar, in two months time he found a buyer and secured himself a handsome profit. McDonagh and Shea scraped together their assets, sold the hotel and in November of 1887 bought the brewery for the princely sum of $16,000. For Patrick Shea and his partner it was an enormous gamble. But he had confidence in Winnipeg's future and its potential growth. Unfortunately, John McDonagh would not live long enough to witness the immense success his company was to enjoy. Leaving Shea to run the brewery, McDonagh was content to work as a 'traveller' (salesman), until

his untimely death in 1894 at the age 38. He left his share of the business to his partner's young son, Frank. In his honour, the company name remained unchanged for 32 years.

In line with the common practice of the day, McDonagh & Shea hired a brewer from Milwaukee with the skills and expertise to make the best beer they could. Starting with only seven men, including themselves, the company began to prosper. Throwing all of their profits back into the business the brewery grew as the city did and by the turn of the century was ready for a building expansion that took it to new levels of success. Regardless of competition from local, eastern Canadian and a few U.S. breweries, McDonagh & Shea managed to secure sales outside of Winnipeg, including Saskatchewan and northern Ontario. The brewer's strength was in their relationships with the hotels they dealt with. Every hotel keeper in the province was known by his first name. Brand loyalty was created by using discount incentives or even going so far as holding the hotel mortgage. By 1916, when Prohibition took hold in Manitoba, McDonagh & Shea's was considered to be one of the largest breweries on the Canadian prairies.

As with all of Manitoba's breweries, Prohibition forced Shea to rely on any means possible to keep his business going. With the soft drinks market already saturated, he instead relied on sales outside the province. To take advantage of this and to bring his name to prominence outside the established market, Patrick Shea created a promotional legacy still recognized today.

The brewery used dray wagons to haul their product and, by 1920, their horses could be seen pulling the company's temperance beers around town. Of all the different dray wagons that roamed the city before the advent of the automobile, it was the big brewery wagons children of the day most fondly remembered. With the jingle of their harness, these burly animals lumbered along the streets, the wagons stacked high with barrels of beer. This was the image Patrick Shea would use to promote his company.

McDonagh & Shea's first motorized truck, a 1916 Willy's Knight: Pictured is George Maitland and driver Henry Worster.

Shea's Billboard, Fort William, Ont.

Right: Shea's Champion Clydesdales made a name for themselves across the country and even into the United States where they caught the eye of August Busch Jr., scion to the famous Anheuser Busch empire.

Far Right: Part of the breweries stable of Clydesdale show horses in front of Manitoba's Legistature Building, from left to right; Alladin, Harry, Unity, Warrior, Johnny, Wiley, Major, Captain, Sandy, Brunstane and Renown.

Above: Lithograph of an Arthur Hider painting: Hider, (1870–1952) was a Canadian artist with a penchant for painting horses. His extensive portfolio includes advertising art for Dawes Black Horse Ale & Porters. When Patrick Shea commissioned to have his Clydesdales immortalized, Hider was the natural choice. Today Arthur Hider's work is in the collection of the Canadian Archives, the Canadian War Museum, the Jockey Club of Ontario as well as numerous private collections.

In the spring of 1921, Shea purchased his first team of Clydesdale geldings from Arcola, Saskatchewan. Named Donald and Sandy, these two Canadian-bred show horses made their first appearance on the Western Show Circuit in 1922 and immediately brought positive results. Building upon this success, the first six-horse team began showing in 1923. With a custom-built wagon prominently displaying the Shea's logo on the side, these teams went on to make a name for the brewery, winning prize after prize everywhere they entered. From 1922 to 1933 Shea's dominated the circuit at fairs and exhibitions across the country and at shows in Minneapolis and Chicago. It was in Chicago that the brewery horses caught the eye of August Busch Jr.

The year was 1932 and with the repeal of American Prohibition in sight, the board of directors at Anheuser-Busch approved a motion to spend $15,000 for a six-horse team of Clydesdales to promote their beer when the taps began to flow. The company wanted to claim their show horses as Grand Champions, but unfortunately they weren't. Shea's owned that claim and so August (Gussie) approached Patrick Shea about acquiring his team. After a long series of negotiations, Busch finally gave Shea an offer he couldn't refuse (some reports say it was $31,000, well over the approved amount) and eight of the Shea horses along with harnesses and wagon were sold to Anheuser-Busch. Included in the deal was trainer and handler Andrew Haxton. Along with Shea's ability to buy the best horses, it was Haxton's acute knowledge and skill that made the horses the success they were. Haxton had great passion for the four legged animals and when he immigrated to Canada from Kinross, Scotland, he brought his own horse with him!

The Budweiser Clydesdales were first introduced to the public in St. Louis on April 7, 1933 to celebrate the repeal of Prohibition. Down the street from the brewery stables on Pestalozzi Street, Gussie presented the hitch as a surprise gift to his father Augustus Sr. who was coaxed outside the brewery after being told his son had just purchased a new automobile. Instead of a car, Busch was greeted with a team of horses pulling a

From 1922 to 1933 Shea's dominated the circuit at fairs and exhibitions across the country and at shows in Minneapolis and Chicago.

red, white and gold beer wagon. Accounts of the day have the team thundering down the street carrying the first case of post-Prohibition beer from the brewery.

Andrew Haxton went on to win more prizes for his new employer and today Anheuser-Busch has six "hitches" or teams of horses. Five travel around the United States and one team remains at the company head-quarters in St. Louis. Descendants of Shea's original Clydesdales still serve the company in its ubiquitous ad campaigns around the world.

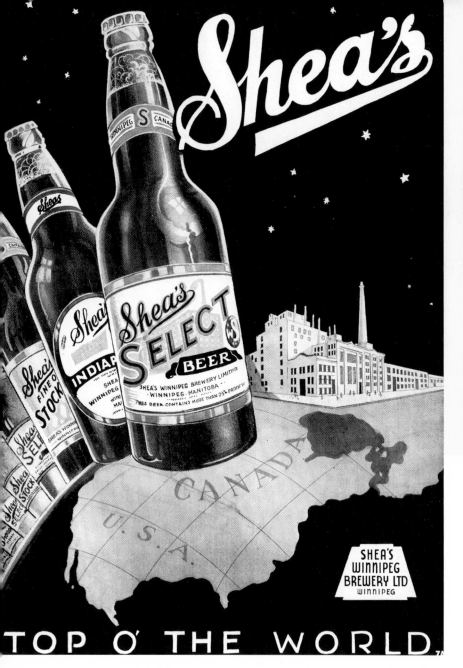

TOP O' THE WORLD.

Patrick Shea, (middle between Charles Byrnes and nine year old son Paul)
with brewery employees, 1905.

Labels from the 1920's

Born in 1896, Paul Ignatius Shea had been attending school in New York City since the age of 14. In his senior year at Fordham University he was stricken ill with appendicitis and died of complications in April of 1917. In 1932, Paul Shea Hall was built as an addition to St. Paul's College campus on Ellice and Vaughan (seen at the right of the main building). With funds donated by Patrick and Margaret Shea, the building was dedicated to the memory of their young son. The College eventually outgrew the Ellice Avenue location and moved to the U of M in 1958. The building was demolished in 1964.

Having survived to the end of Prohibition in 1923, the brewery was back on track and in 1926 a name change was in order. For nearly 40 years the brewery went under the Winnipeg Brewery/ McDonagh & Shea banner, but on October 9, 1926 a new company was incorporated and would be known as Shea's Winnipeg Brewery Limited. The Shea family retained complete control of the newly incorporated company.

By this time, just as E.L. Drewry had become, Patrick Shea was a wealthy and well-respected citizen of Winnipeg. The two men shared many qualities. Both had a soft spot for their employees and in fact the owner was often referred to as "Papa Shea" by many of his faithful workers. Public-spirited, he never hesitated to support a worthy cause that benefited the community and his acts of kindness and generosity were countless. Both were shrewd businessmen, but they had their differences too. During Prohibition Shea had no qualms about

Both had a soft spot for their employees and in fact the owner was often referred to as "Papa Shea" by many of his faithful workers.

ordering whiskey in twenty and forty-case lots from Sam Bronfman. On the contrary, Drewry was quite proud of the fact that he survived Prohibition by playing by the rules.

In his younger days Patrick Shea lived up to the image of the quintessential brewer. Stout like the beer he produced and sporting a handle-bar mustache, he was a gregarious man who easily fit into the lifestyle of a millionaire. But life had not always been a bed of roses. Three of his five children died in infancy. Son Paul died at the age of twenty-one and a year before that their maid committed suicide by shooting herself in the Shea family home across the street from the brewery. That left son Frank to follow in his father's footsteps. In 1926 he was named Vice-President and General Manager.

As a wealthy man, Patrick Shea enjoyed all the trappings of his success. Pictured is Shea's driver Ed Penston in front of a 1916 Packard Twin-Six Touring Car.

THOROUGHBRED

Shea's

IN A QUALITY RACE
IS WINNER

SHEA'S WINNIPEG BREWERY LTD.

The Shea family at Polo Park Race Track.

Frank Shea

Big and handsome, Frank Shea was as popular and well-liked as his father. A natural athlete, the sportsman became a generous promoter of local amateur athletics. He was the financial backer for the St. John's Rugby Club. They later merged with the Winnipeg Rugby Football Club and we now know them as the Winnipeg Blue Bombers. Having inherited bachelor John McDonagh's share of the company back in 1894, he had the means to live the life of luxury and easily embraced the role of the wealthy man-about-town. In 1928, he built a palatial home on Park Boulevard for $50,000, but it was horse racing where much of his money was spent. His Green Brier Stables met with considerable success in California and Mexico as well as Polo Park. Along with this international success came some rather negative press back home.

In 1927, when a Royal Commission on Customs and Excise did some probing, it found the racing stable had been charged to the brewery malt account and had been done so without the knowledge of Patrick Shea. A total of $33,650 had been charged to the profits of the business and no income tax had been paid. As soon as this fact became public the tax bill was promptly settled. Customs Counsel N.W. Rowell recommended the brewery have its license cancelled, but in the end that proved to be too severe. The breweries had become cash cows for the government and rarely were licenses suspended. Frank managed to dodge a major bullet and soon after began scaling back his horse racing in the United States. Green Brier Stables trainer Bert Michell left in 1927 and became famous the next year when he won the Kentucky Derby with American Horse of the Year "Reigh Count". Frank continued to race and was a presence at both Polo Park and Whittier Park.

John T. Boyd became President and General Manager of Shea's Winnipeg Brewery after the death of Patrick and Frank Shea in 1933.

His funeral was the one of the largest the city had ever seen up to that point and as a tribute beer parlours across the city were closed until 1:00 p.m.

As Depression gripped the nation, the year 1933 proved to be a very dark one for the brewery. On July 8, Patrick Shea died at his home after a lengthy illness. His funeral was the one of the largest the city had ever seen up to that point and as a tribute beer parlours across the city were closed until 1:00 p.m. Now it was up to Frank to succeed his father, but he too was suffering from poor health. Only three months after his father's death, Frank passed away at John's Hopkins Hospital in Baltimore, Maryland. Suffering from cirrhosis of the liver, he was just 44 years old.

A key to Patrick Shea's success was his ability to surround himself with competent men and John T. Boyd fit that to a tee. Boyd entered the firm as an office boy in 1904 and rose to the position of Secretary Treasurer in 1926. In 1934, Boyd became president and general manager and steered the company through the Great Depression and World War ll. As one final comparison to the other great brewery across town, a non-family member guided the business through to the 1950's where a major shift in the industry was to take place.

Brewery Offices on Colony Street in 1947: Next door was the Winnipeg Amphitheatre seen at the right hand edge of the photo. Originally built in 1909 as a venue for horse shows, it was later converted to a hockey rink and for a time was the only artificial ice surface between Toronto and Vancouver. Often referred to as Shea's Amphitheatre, the brewery never owned the hockey rink, however it did supply steam power for the facility.

Cleaning interior of the brew kettle and polishing the pecolator; 1942.

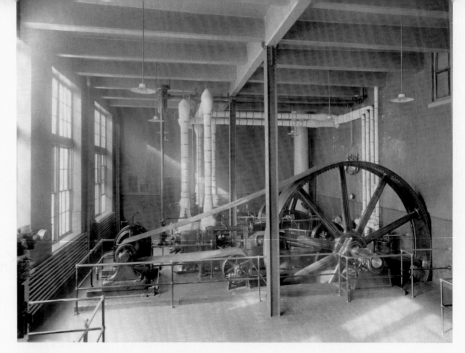

Compressor Room: The giant wheel of a 150 ton compressor used for refrigeration. There is no doubt refrigeration was one of the most important advancements in the brewing industry and by the 1890's most breweries were using the new technology.

John Streib tending to the giant wooden fermenting tanks: Constructed with staves of Cyprus, these tanks were installed in 1895 and used until 1943.

Racking (filling) barrels, 1947: Wooden kegs were used in Manitoba until 1956 when they were replaced by lighter metal kegs made of steel and aluminum.

Coronation Beer was introduced in 1937 to commemorate the crowning of King George VI.

Above: Bottle capping machine, 1942.

Right: Filling wooden beer crates by hand, 1942.

Brewmaster John Dries and assistant Brewmaster Carl Zimmerman in Shea's Hospitality Room, 1936

Select Beer

Serving Tray, 1925

Labatt's Manitoba brought back the Shea's name when it re-branded Select beer in 1982. The new recipe was based on a formula used in Patrick Shea's day. Bottles were capped with historical images from Manitoba's past. Unfortunately, sales dwindled when American beers became all the rage. It was eventually discontinued.

Select label, late 1940's

Shea's flagship brand was also their only beer to outlive the brewery name. Inherited by Labatt's in the 1950's, Select's popularity continued until Labatt's own national brands eventually overtook the market

CONTENTS 11 FLU OUNCES

Riedles

PORTER

A. W. RIEDLE, BREWER
WINNIPEG, MAN.

THIS BEER CONTAINS MORE
THAN 2½% PROOF SPIRITS

NET CO... LEO OUNCES.

Riedles

BEER

THIS BEER
CONTAINS
BEST QUALITY WHEAT

THE RIEDLE BREWERY LIMITED
WINNIPEG, MAN.

THIS BEER CONTAINS MORE THAN 2½% PROOF SPIRITS.

Riedle's

RICE
BEER

Riedle's

EXPORT

Riedles

OVERSEAS
BOTTLED BEER
CHAMPIONSHIP
BRITISH EMPIRE
LONDON
1937

PRESENTED BY
BOTTLING.
THE RIEDLE BREWERY
LTD.

Awarded
The Gold Championship Medal
Silver and Bronze Medals
London, England
1937

PHONE
57 241

Riedles
EXPORT
XXX

THE RIEDLE BREWERY LIMITED
WINNIPEG, MAN.

Riedles
EXP
B

THE RIEDLE BREWERY
WINNIPEG, MAN

Independently
Owned
and

A NEW CENTURY

SUCCESS AND FAILURES

Main Street looking south from the CPR subway, 1904: This stretch of Main was crowded with hotels, saloons and liquor stores. The Oriental Hotel was part of this group and its owner, A.W. Riedle later became a successful brewer in Elmwood.

The phrase "Chicago of the North" reminds us of a time when Winnipeg was thought to be on the verge of greatness. At the same time it brings a hint of disappointment for what might have been. All these years later, it hard to imagine the kind of optimism that was in the air at the dawn of the twentieth century. Manitoba was on the cusp of a new era where anything seemed possible. The agricultural engine was firing up as new immigrants flocked to the countryside. In the city, a building boom grew to proportions never seen before or since. Winnipeg was on its way to becoming the third largest city in Canada and for the business community, opportunities abound.

It's not surprising then, we find this period in the annals of local beer history as a very active time for brewery startups. But much like Winnipeg's first boom and bust in the early 1880's, there were winners and losers. For the businessmen that believed they could be another Patrick Shea or E.L. Drewry, the future wasn't going to be as bright as they had bargained. The opening of the Panama Canal in 1914 put a damper on Winnipeg's reputation as the gateway to the west. The outbreak of World War I in the summer of 1914 cut off trade from Europe as well as immigration. Recession gripped the nation and the rapid growth Winnipeg enjoyed in the first decade slowed to be more moderate and steady. Of course, the threat of Prohibition was in the air. From the new group of breweries that began after 1900, only Henri Pelissier and Arnold Riedle survived after 1916. For the other startups—they failed before the Prohibitionist ever had a chance to close them down.

THE BRITISH BEER BREWERIES

In a six-year period between 1904 and 1910 there were no fewer than 8 new breweries started in Winnipeg. Everyone from lawyers, merchants and even retired farmers were investing thousands of dollars to turn cold beer into cold cash. In 1904, one such group formed a company with a bold plan to brew English style ales and stouts with the appropriate name of the British Beer Breweries. Ginger beers, soda water and extracts were also in the works. They opened in January of 1905 at 142 Nena Street on the northwest corner of William Avenue. This corner is now occupied by the Health Science Centre and Nena is now known as Sherbrook Street. The building proved to be too small and so the brewery was moved north to larger premises at Logan and Nena.

Unlike other contemporary breweries of the time, management brought in an English brewing expert instead of the customary German brewer. This alone wouldn't be enough to set them apart from the rest of the pack. They needed a new idea, a different way to brew beer and with something called Hobson's Concentrate, they had it. A publicity campaign began by claiming this new concoction was made in London, England from the very best English malt and hops using a new and improved process. From this concentrate, they asserted, "a much purer and more wholesome ale, stout, and lager beer could be obtained and is

> Unlike other contemporary breweries of the time, management brought in an English brewing expert instead of the customary German brewer.

superior to what was possible under the old process. The accolades continued; "the concentrate is shipped in sealed cans and received in perfect shape as when first made, whereas the large quantity of malt used in this county and which is imported from Germany deteriorates with shipping, making it impossible to procure a good wholesome beer." This last statement was pure advertising hyperbole. Most local breweries were malting their own barley or at the very least buying it from Canadian sources.

The concentrate was being used in other breweries in Nova Scotia, British Columbia and elsewhere around the world. British Beer Breweries held the sole rights to Hobson's Concentrate for the Prairie provinces for 40 years which was rather optimistic, to say the least. By 1905, the company had begun manufacturing a Bitter Ale, Burton Ale and Double Stout in their temporary premises on Logan and Nena. Their target customer was Winnipeg's large English population, guaranteeing them the same flavour to which they were accustomed, and at regular prices.

The British Beer Breweries plant was on the corner of Logan & Nena Street. Nena later became part of Sherbrook Street.

The X Label

In today's market it's rare to find a brand of beer with an X label; the most popular would be Mexico's Dos Equis, which literally translates as "two x's". The double X on that beer was originally used to commemorate the new century and was introduced in 1897. Usually, a double X or more meant the beer was extra strong in taste or alcohol content, but there might be other reasons too. Here are a couple of suggested origins for the use of the "X" mark on labels.

When beer was originally brewed in the monasteries, it was customary to place the Sign of the Cross upon each cask. However, when the particular monk responsible for brewing made an exceptionally good cask of ale he put an additional "X" upon it for the purpose identification. Hence the XXX was extra, extra special ... and so on.

The "X" was simply the mark placed on the cask by the Excise Officer to show that he had examined and passed this cask for payment of duty.

It is believed that (b) is more likely to be the correct explanation, but undoubtedly (a) is the more "picturesque"!

Stouts and ales are usually more robust and richer tasting than lagers and many local brands advertised this fact with an X label.

By 1906 plans were in place to build a more suitable brewery at Portage and Langside but this never materialized. Although the company had a large capitalization of $50,000, it wasn't enough. George Drewry, brother of E.L Drewry, came on board as an owner but even his experience couldn't save the company. After only two years of operation, the brewery shut down in October of 1907 and the contents were auctioned off. Why they failed isn't known. Perhaps it was the quality of the brew or most likely, a failure to crack the market. Whatever the cause it didn't seem to deter the next group that thought they could do better.

In 1908, H.J. Miller, as manager and M.R. Miller, as brewer took over the premises and changed the name to the English Beer Breweries Co. Ltd. No other information or brewery artifacts exist and so it seems that, like its predecessor, it closed in short order.

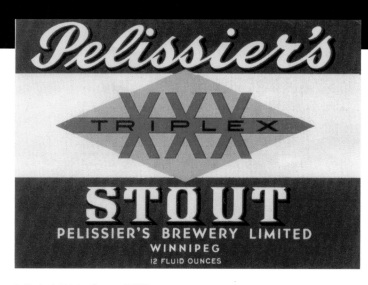

Pelissier's Triplex Stout - 1950's

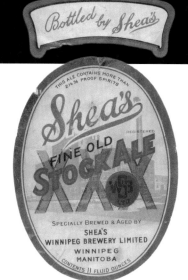

Shea's Stock Ale - late 1920's

Riedle's Ale - early 1930's

STELLA AVENUE:
THE LITTLE BREWERY THAT COULDN'T

In the heart of Winnipeg's north end is a street name Stella. City pioneer E.L. Barber named the street after Stella Hayden, a long lost sweetheart he reluctantly left behind when he moved north from the United States. Along a short strip of this street between Salter and Aikins sit a variety of homes, some boarded up, a few brought back to life. Once, over a hundred years ago, there was a small brewery among these homes. With a variety of owners it tried in vain to make a name for itself under the shadow of the bigger breweries in town and today all that remains are a few tokens to remind us of its brief existence.

LYONE BROS. 1905–1907
IMPERIAL BREWERY 1907–1908

The saga of four breweries at one location begins with the Lyone brothers. Martin and Albert Lyone operated a pickle factory on the south side of Stella Street between Aikens and Salter in 1904. They built their brewery the next year.

The brewery earned a fair share of publicity when it ran roughshod with the law. It seems that the brothers had a habit of selling beer on the brewery premises, which at the time was against the law. Charges were laid, but that didn't stop them from selling beer on Sundays, also against the law. For this they were fined $200 since it was their second offence after selling two kegs to inspectors. During the raid the inspectors found the accused "freely filling orders for a number of foreigners." In 1907, it became the Imperial Brewery but closed just a year later. Businessman George Nagy became the new owner in 1908.

THE CROWN BREWERY
1908–1910

The Crown Brewery has its roots connected to one of Winnipeg's foremost pioneer families. George Nagy happened to be married to the former Rachel Gomez Fonseca. Her father was Don Derigo Nojada Gomez da Silva Fonseca, but history remembers him as William Gomez da Fonseca. Born in Santa Croix in the West Indies he immigrated to New York before moving to north to Minnesota and finally to Winnipeg in 1860. He owned a dry goods store and eventual began buying property in Point Douglas where he married the daughter of Thomas Logan and niece of Alexander Logan, another of Winnipeg's pioneer families. His daughter and son in-law operated the Crown Brewery for two years before passing the business to her brother Benjamin Fonseca. Benjamin changed the name to the Blitz Brewery in 1910.

THE BLITZ BREWERY 1910–1911

Benjamin already had other business concerns. He owned several hotels in Winnipeg, including the Alberta, the Patricia and the Wolseley Hotel on Higgins Avenue. Higgins was known as Fonseca Street until 1906. Owning three saloons wasn't sufficient enough to guarantee a profit for his brewery and the Blitz Brewery closed a year later.

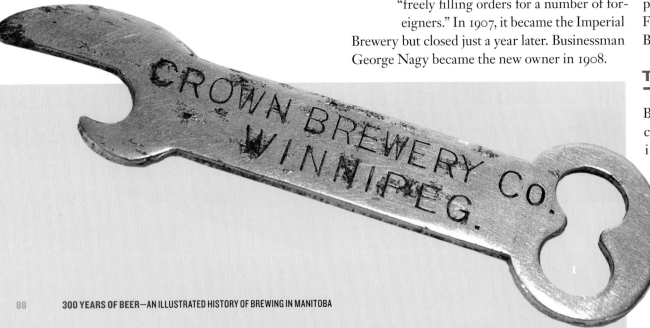

Imperial Brewery
MALSTERS and BREWERS

LYONE BROS
Proprietors.
LAGER BEER
PORTER & ALE

CROWN BREWERY Co. WINNIPEG.

Hidden Treasures

Most people consider old beer bottles junk, worth the 10 cent deposit the man at the beer vendor will give you. But what about an one-hundred year old bottle, how much is that worth? If you're a collector, it will depend on rarity, and this story is about a very rare bottle.

In 1986, an article in the Winnipeg Sun created a stir among local collectors. While renovating the old Warwick Apartments on Qu'Appelle Ave, construction workers discovered a few long neck beer bottles above the ceiling of one of the rooms. Built back in 1908, it was assumed the men building the apartments tucked them away after quaffing a few on their lunch break. Perhaps they thought they'd leave their own little time capsules. As it turned out, that exactly what happened!

Warwick Apartments

arwick Apartments, Winnipeg, Man.

When the late Jim Angus, a Winnipeg police officer at the time, read the article he decided to investigate. Jim was a member of the Keystone Breweriana Collectors Club and just happened to have his uniform on when he visited the construction site. At 6'6" with gun in holster, the cop was an imposing presence when he asked the foreman to see the alleged bottles. The foreman stated 24 bottles were found; some with full labels, others with the labels eaten away. He took four of the bottles and gave three away. Jim was horrified to discover the rest of the bottles had been thrown out. Fortunately, the foreman managed to produce one piece of evidence and it was a beauty; a Crown Brewery Lager bottle with the label still intact and in good shape, a very rare find considering most old bottles stored in building or barns have the labels eaten away by mice and insects. Most importantly, it was the only label or bottle ever seen from this brewery.

Jim bought the bottle that day and it still stands as a rare item. Like undiscovered ancient tombs of Egypt, who knows what other brewery treasures lay hidden behind the walls of Winnipeg's past?

Crown Bre
bottle, 190

THE BREWERIES OF ELMWOOD

Prone to flooding, Elmwood was one of the last areas east of the Red River to be settled. The first person to live in this heavily wooded area was Charles Midwinter who built a cabin in 1877. The area remained secluded for a few short years until Winnipeg built the Louise Bridge in 1881. Constructed as part of a deal to lure the CPR to re-route the mainline through Winnipeg instead of Selkirk, the Louise was Winnipeg's first bridge and shortly after it was built, a group of buildings grew up around it. Nairn Avenue was all but a two-block street of mud. Soon, homes were built and Elmwood eventually became a working class neighborhood filled with noisy enterprises, several rail lines and other busy industries. The first application to join Winnipeg was on November 2, 1905 and in 1906 Elmwood became Ward 7 in the City of Winnipeg.

THE ELMWOOD BREWERY/ BENSON BROS. 1904–1905

In 1904, P. A. Wiborg along with brothers Oliver and Benjamin Benson built a small brewery near the foot of the Louise Bridge on Nairn Avenue next to the post office. Often referred to as the Elmwood Brewery, its official name was the Benson Brothers Brewery. Benjamin Benson had garnered his brewing experience working for McDonagh & Shea in the early days of that brewery and was no doubt influenced by its success. Wiborg had been trained in Sweden and worked in Great Britain before arriving in Winnipeg and taking on the duties of brewmaster.

In 1905 A. W. Riedle joined the brothers as brewery manager. Arnold Riedle was still in his teens when he got his first job as a shoeshine boy at a local hotel. The young man eagerly worked his way up to eventually become owner of the Oriental Hotel on Main Street. This strong work ethic contributed to the next phase in the breweries growth.

Named after the plant's brewmaster, Wiborg's Table Beer was a low alcohol brew suitable for the whole family. Typically table beers are about 1% alcohol content and are served with meals

LOOK HERE!

Wiborg's Table Beer

a wholesome and delicious non-toxicant malt drink, is for the first time being brewed in the great Northwest of Canada, and is now for sale at

Benson Bros. Brewery

LOUISE BIRDGE P. O.
Tel 2987.   Box 24.

BENSON BROS.
LOUISE BRIDGE

ALE STOUT
AND TABLE BEER

We are no won the market to supply you with the finest line of pure malted goods, unsurpassed in quality; manufactured by strictly up-to-date method. Ask your dealer.

Phone 2987.

P.O. Box 41, Louise Bridge.

THE EDELWEISS BREWERY 1905–1923

When Ben decided to retire, the brothers sold their brewery to Riedle in July of 1905. Rechristened in 1906 as the Edelweiss Brewery, construction on a new brewery began with a larger, brick building about a block north of the Louise Bridge at 49 Stadacona Street. The architect was a specialist from Chicago and the goal was to make the operation modern in every way.

Possessing the same qualities as Patrick Shea and E.L. Drewry, Arnold Riedle became a good corporate citizen and while he preferred anonymity, his employees were aware he regularly sent food hampers to the needy and bags of coal often showed up for others during the harsh Winnipeg winters. He was especially good to his employees, supplying hotel facilities for weddings and on one occasion Riedle paid three employees to help a fourth put a basement in his house.

For all his good intentions, there was one thing Riedle couldn't defend himself against. In the atmosphere of the First World War and the prevalent anti-German sentiment, Riedle's German background sparked an event that nearly turned tragic for his company.

It happened on Sunday, January 26, 1919 at a Communist-inspired rally being held in Old Market Square and attended by many European immigrants. Recently returned WW I veterans and youths, holding resentment because they could not find jobs, began disrupting the meeting.

The melee quickly spread with a mob vandalizing German and other "alien" social clubs, businesses and anything thought to be foreign.

The melee quickly spread with a mob vandalizing German and other "alien" social clubs, businesses and anything thought to be foreign. One group hi-jacked a passing street car and took it to Elmwood where they commenced a destructive rampage against the Edelweiss Brewery. Countless bottles, interior fittings and many windows were broken. Finally, the owner of a nearby restaurant and general store arrived at the scene saying he was a war veteran. He told the rioters about the many good deeds that Riedle had done for the community, one of which was loaning money to a group to build a hall for meetings. This group was the forerunner of the Canadian Legion. These remarks finally settled the crowd down and they dispersed leaving behind a badly damaged brewery.

By 1919, when his brewery was ransacked, Riedle and his fellow brewers were at their lowest production

EDELWEISS
BREWERY

Lager, Ale
and Stout

A. W. RIEDLE
PROPRIETOR

Phone 2987   Winnipeg

level. The strong temperance forces were enjoying greater success and called for an extension of the control on inter-provincial liquor trade. Many smaller breweries in Canada were on the verge of collapse if it were not for one saving grace. The United States finally succumbed to Prohibition on January 16, 1920. Winnipeg is only 65 miles (100 km) from the North Dakota/Minnesota border and it was fairly easy to run beer across the many small crossings and border farms.

With the repeal of Prohibition in Manitoba in 1923, the company became the Riedle Brewery Limited.

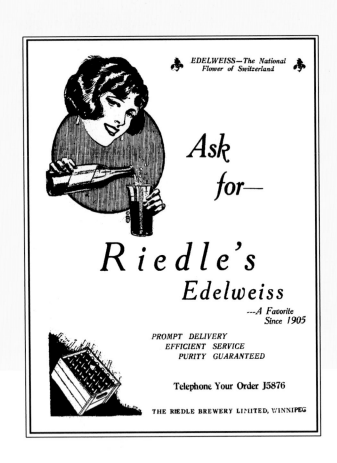

Above: Edelweiss ad, 1923.

Right: John Hauser at the Hineson Keeler
Filler machine , 1938.

Top Right: Riedle dray wagon in front of the
brewery cash & carry store, Stadacona
Street, early 1940's.

THE RIEDLE BREWERY LIMITED 1923–1950

As his bank account grew, Riedle bought farms at Petersfield, Elm Creek and Whitemouth and was a popular figure at local fairs. Owning seven rural hotels as well as five in Winnipeg, he began to share his growing success with other members of his family. He and his wife Natalie were childless but a nephew of Natalie's, Albert Dietz was invited to live in their house and work at the brewery. His new job was in sales and public relations. Arnold brought over his nephew, Ted Kling from Germany and he also moved into the house. Later, he returned to Germany to attend a brewing school and while there he picked up two recipes that raised the company's profile another notch.

Before his company moved into its second phase of success, Riedle died on July 11, 1937 at the age 64. When the company was reorganized an unusual situation was created. Natalie Riedle was named president of the company, the first time in Manitoba that a woman became head of brewery. More ironically, it put her in a scenario where a woman owned a beer company and 12 hotels in a time when her gender was prohibited from drinking or even working in a beer parlour.

After A.W. Riedles death Ted Kling became brewmaster and vice-president, while John Popp, Natalie's brother and company attorney, becoming general manager.

The two recipes that Ted Kling brought back from Germany were tested and samples entered in London's 1937 British Empire Bottled Beer Competition. They won both the Gold and Silver Medals and in 1939 they took a Gold medal again.

With this good fortune they launched a campaign with numerous newspaper ads, trays, glasses and openers to help boost the brewery's new found fame. The promotions worked and sales soared. The increase was so great that an immediate expansion was started which doubled the size of their brewery. A new fermentation and storage building was erected. A new brewhouse, boiler room, general offices and employee facilities were also built. These changes took until 1948 to complete, due mainly to wartime materials restrictions.

Ted Kling had the idea that locally grown hops should be used. Employees were taken to a Middlechurch farm to pick the hops. At least two

> More ironically, it put her in a scenario where a woman owned a beer company and 12 hotels in a time when her gender was prohibited from drinking or even working in a beer parlour.

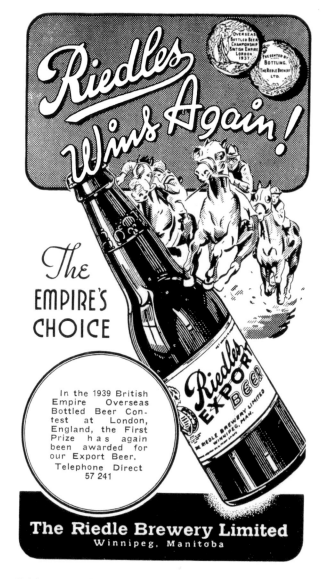

In the 1939 British Empire Overseas Bottled Beer Contest at London, England, the First Prize has again been awarded for our Export Beer. Telephone Direct 57 241

The Riedle Brewery Limited
Winnipeg, Manitoba

Celebrating another brewing award, 1939.

When you take home a case of RIEDLE'S "GREEN LABEL," you'll discover how truly good beer can be!

Phone 50 118 DIRECT

The RIEDLE BREWERY Limited

WINNIPEG MAN.

This advertisement is not inserted by the Government Liquor Control Commission. The Commission is not responsible for statements made as to quality of products advertised.

Above: Winnipeg Tribune ad, Christmas, 1941.

Both Riedle's Ye Olde Town Beer and Black Top Beer were brewed with Manitoba grown hops until they were deemed unsuitable. Ye Olde Town Beer was specially made for Winnipeg's 75th birthday in 1949.

brews were made—Black Top and Ye Olde Town Beer—but this project eventually failed as the local hops proved to be unsuitable.

Kling, whose recipes started the sales boom, soon became complacent. He had his own plane and would fly off to ski. His summer home was 100 miles away. As a result he spent less and less time at the brewery. The outcome was what all brewers fear the most—a bad batch. Not just one, but several. Sales fell.

In January 1950, Natalie Riedle, who owned 51% of the shares, called a meeting with Ted Kling and John Popp. She announced her shares in the brewery had been sold to George M. Black. Mrs. Riedle spent her later years managing Jack's Hotel on Main Street; a far cry from the social-ite lifestyle the wives of Winnipeg's other beer barons had enjoyed in the past.

Riedles gave away a variety of promotional items that included, of all things, a broom hanger.

What the Heck is Bock Beer?

o doubt, of all the different kinds of beers, bock has the most misinformation and conjecture. The most likely expla-
ation of the name is it was one of the principal products of the city of Einbeck, in Germany, and the "bock" part of it
ame from the reference to the city. The brewers from Munich later adapted the style to fit their new lager method of
rewing. They pronounced "Einbeck" as "ien Bock", a reflection of their Bavarian accent. This pronunciation sounds
milar to the German word for "Billy Goat" and this is why we see the bearded fellow on Bock beer labels.

Bock beer is usually prepared in the spring around Easter. If someone tries to tell you that Bock beer is made
om the end of the season residue from the vats, don't believe it! This is simply a carrying on of the German custom
of brewing beers in either October or March, (prior to refrigeration), when temperatures were favour-able. The brew is a special one, heavy in flavour, usually darker in colour and richer in taste than regular lager beers.

Winnipeg has had its fair share of Bock beers over the years, but just try finding one in your local beer vendor these days!

The American Temperance Brewery and the Canadian Temperance Brewery were two companies established before prohibition became a reality in 1916. Both breweries were short lived.

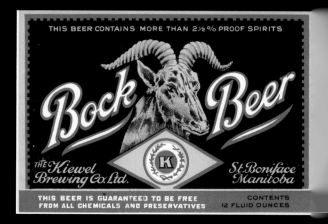

THE BREWERY THAT NEVER WAS:
THE STANLEY MINERAL SPRINGS AND BREWING CO, LTD

How do you take a thriving business with great potential and just make it disappear? In the case of one particular company, it was a wildly ambitious plan to build a brewery at a time when the "Banish the Bar" campaign was at full stride. Throw in a pinch of political intrigue involving the premier of the province and top it off with the First World War. With those ingredients we bring you the folly of the Stanley Mineral Springs & Brewing Company.

On the banks of the Kaministiquia River twenty miles west of Thunder Bay, Ontario lies the little hamlet of Stanley. One of its main attributes was an underground spring percolating from an immense natural filter bed of sand. It was a perfect source of water for the manufacturing of table waters and ginger ale. The Stanley Mineral Springs Company had taken advantage of this spring and by 1911 it was a well-established business with markets stretching from Ontario to the west coast. In fact, they were so successful that at full capacity they could only fill half their orders. This soon attracted the attention of a few businessmen from Winnipeg. In 1912, the group announced they had acquired the flourishing little company and would enlarge the plant. But they had a much more grandiose plan than just plain expansion.

In a prospectus that later become problematic; it was announced that the company would build a brewery with a capitalization of one million dollars. To raise such a large amount of money, the prospectus made a variety of claims that soon caused a political firestorm fanned by the Manitoba Free Press and dodged by Manitoba Premier Sir Rodmond Roblin for several years.

The plan was to build a brewery in St. Boniface with a capacity of 100,000 barrels a year as well as a separate bottling plant for soft drinks. Company directors included a handful of the city's business elite. Wholesale merchant and Union Bank director John Galt; Hugh Sutherland, director of the Winnipeg Electric Railway and D. E. Sprague, president of Sprague Lumber were just a few of many successful businessmen on the Board. The company estimated about 70 percent of new immigrants came from beer drinking countries, making it an opportune time to build a new brewery. But it was two more statements that set off a storm of controversy.

> The Stanley Mineral Springs Company had taken advantage of this spring and by 1911 it was a well-established business with markets stretching from Ontario to the west coast.

Men Who Know "Stanley"

STANLEY
Extra Dry
GINGER ALE

Know how sparkling, Invigorating and enjoyable a non-alcoholic Drink can be. When Clear brain and steady Nerves demand abstinence from other beverages, drink "STANLEY" —it refreshes and stimulates without any "let-down" Afterwards.

Unvarying insistence upon the highest excellence in the Ingredients and preparation keeps "STANLEY" true to its Reputation, as "one of the few non-alcoholic drinks that Are really enjoyable."

"STANLEY" Ginger Ale blends perfectly with spirits. "STANLEY" Mineral Water has the same natural blending excellence.

Phone for a case. Main 8638

YES, SIR !
IT'S
STANLEY
Extra Dry Ginger Ale And Mineral Water

PHONE FOR A CASE—
MAIN 8638

A hundred point home
Product
Bottled at the Springs

The Stanley Mineral Springs Company was a successful Ontario business until a few prominent Winnipeg business men got a hold of it. Here are two ads for their popular Ginger Ale from 1913.

The first was a candid admission to the existence of "tied houses" when it was mentioned that the directors controlled 18 liquor licenses in Winnipeg. The concept of brewery ownership of hotels was a contentious issue during these times as many felt it was an inappropriate control of liquor sales. Already putting their foot in their mouth, a letter accompanying the prospectus stated such men as Sir William Mackenzie, Sir Donald Mann, and the premier of Manitoba, Sir Rodmond Roblin were interested in the welfare of the company, sufficiently guaranteeing the success of the enterprise.

The Manitoba Free Press, being the Liberal publication that it was, took no time pointing out in an editorial that the premier of Manitoba, a Conservative and anti-Prohibitionist, was involved in building a new brewing enterprise. While they allowed he should be able to invest his money in any venture that would bring him dividends, they also felt this was a conflict of interest and at the very least poor politics. The premier immediately denied he was a shareholder or had any involvement whatsoever in "some brewing company." He even went so far as calling it slanderous, but the paper refused to back down.

> It wasn't bad publicity that finally killed the brewery but the uncertainty of the times.

Another sticky issue the Free Press brought to light was that one of the company directors was Daniel Sprague, the same D. E. Sprague who happened to be a license commissionaire for district 4 in the City of Winnipeg. The MFP suggested that this must be an impropriety that should be obvious to everyone.

Through all the controversy and the growing strength of the temperance movement, the Stanley Mineral Springs & Brewing Company kept busy building its plant in St. Boniface at 714 Tache at Rue Messager. The man responsible for the design of the building was the eminent railway architect, Ralph B. Pratt, who later designed many other local landmarks including the Winnipeg Civic Auditorium on Vaughan Street. Basic construction was completed in early June of 1913, but that's as far as it got. In the end no manufacturing was ever done.

It wasn't bad publicity that finally killed the brewery but the uncertainty of the times. With men marching off to war and the country in a recession, further plans for the company were at first put on hold until after the war. Not knowing how long that would be and with creditors knocking at their door, the venture fell into the hands of liquidators on December 22, 1914. Stanley's Ginger Ale was still sold until August of 1915.

Although the brewery never made a drop of beer, alcohol was still a part of its future when the building was bought by the Canadian Industrial Alcohol Company in 1924.

Premier Roblin ran into a bigger scandal involving the construction of the Legislative Building and he was forced to resign in 1915,

Sir Rodmond Roblin: Manitoba's Premier was forced to defend himself when his name was associated with a new brewery being built in St. Boniface. At the time Roblin's Conservative Party had been resisting the temperance movement's pressure to hold a popular vote on the proposal to "Banish the Bar."

resulting in a new provincial election. The Liberal government of T.C. Norris was swept into power and with them, a new resolve to finally make Prohibition a reality.

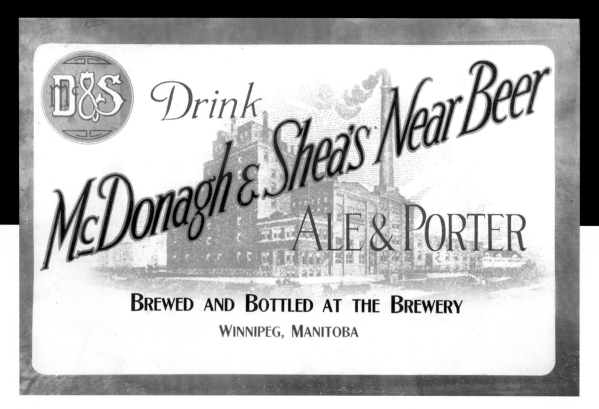

Fate may have played a part in the discovery of this prohibition ad for McDonagh & Shea's Near Beer. Found on the underside of an old picture bought at a garage sale, the new owner was John Penston. John's father, Ed Penston, was Patrick Shea's driver before moving up the corporate ladder to become sales manager.

CHAPTER 7

PROHIBITION
THE TEMPERANCE BEER BLUES

Canadian prohibition was not as long lasting as America's "Noble Experiment." In Manitoba, prohibition was from 1916 to 1923. The United States suffered for another ten years after that and so Canada became a popular destination for the American "booze tourist."

When the word Prohibition comes to mind, many people's thoughts turn to images of bootleggers, speakeasies and Al Capone. Mostly cultivated by popular movies and TV shows, these pervasive images are of American Prohibition. Few people realize Canada had its own version of the "Noble Experiment." Our story played out quite differently than in America and its ultimate outcome determined how alcohol would be bought and consumed in this country. Manitoba's role in all this was at the forefront. In western Canada, Winnipeg was the inspirational centre for the temperance movement. And it was the financial help from Manitoba breweries that enabled the Moderation League to sway the public to vote for repeal, and government control. Although these events came to a head in the early part of the twentieth century, the temperance movement in Canada began much earlier.

By the mid 1800's, alcohol had become so ingrained in the fabric of Canadian life that it's no surprise there was a backlash. From the taverns of Ontario to the fur trading outposts of the West, men overindulged. The negative impact to society was obvious and slowly groups were formed to combat the demon drink. It wasn't beer that was being blamed for the social ills of the day, at least not in the beginning. The early temperance societies had hard liquor in their sights, while beer and wine were considered the lesser of evils. Gradually the movement took a harder stance aimed toward total abstinence.

After years of political pressure, the Dunkin Act of 1864 was passed (that's not a typo). This legislation only applied to Ontario and Quebec and allowed each county or municipality the right, by vote, to prohibit the retail sale of liquor. The idea of this "local option" was carried over when the Canadian Temperance Act, otherwise known as the Scott Act, was passed in 1878. It wasn't quite the victory the "drys" had hoped for. Although Fredericton, New Brunswick voted dry in 1879, the implementation of local option wasn't widespread until the turn of the century. Out west things were just starting to heat up. If ever there was a place that could draw the attention of the Prohibitionist, it was Winnipeg in the early years of the 1880's.

Main Street's reputation for decadence is infamous. Journalist James Gray wrote a wonderful description of those heady times; smoke filled saloons on every corner, beer for a nickel a glass and whiskey, "two-bits a slug." Grifters, knockabouts, and tough characters abound. At night; a Wild West town full of men stumbling about the muddy streets. Today that may seem exaggerated, but consider the facts. In the boom times of 1882, the number of hotels peaked at eighty-six, many of them with saloons attached. And if you didn't feel like standing up to the bar, there were twenty-four wine and liquor stores, fifteen of them on Main Street alone. The best option of all; the sixty-four grocery stores that sold whiskey by the bottle—at half the price it would cost for a night on the town. If you felt like it, there was no law saying you couldn't plunk yourself down on a sack of flour and pass the bottle around. The numbers are quite staggering, even when you consider the population grew from 9,000 to 14,000 in one year. This out-of-control boom town was also inhabited by God-fearing teetotalling Christians. A collision was about to occur.

In response to all this debauchery, the Protestant clergy formed the Manitoba

Cecil Hotel Saloon, Rivers, Manitoba circa 1915.

Temperance Alliance in 1883. Soon others followed, including the non-sectarian Women's Christian Temperance Union. The movement took years to build steam, but finally in 1892, the provincial government was persuaded to hold a plebiscite to settle the issue on where the public stood on the liquor question. The results were more than two to one in favour of banishing alcohol from the province. Nevertheless, the government was slow to act. Unsure of whether the province had the authority under the British North American Act to enforce Prohibition, the Greenway government passed the political hot potato on to the federal government for a ruling. When that ruling came back, it was so vague and indefinite the Manitoba government had to employ a lawyer to give a legal opinion. But his opinion also lacked clarity. The issue was left in limbo until an 1896, when Canada's highest court ruled that the provinces held jurisdiction over the retailing of alcohol, while the federal government would control the production and inter-provincial export (this decision was a godsend to the breweries when Prohibition finally took hold). Two years later the Laurier Government came under pressure from the dry movement and a national plebiscite was held in 1898.

Right across the country each province voted for Prohibition—except Quebec. One has to remember that this was before women were allowed to vote. Given this fact, it's quite remarkable how Laurier responded to the results. He rejected it. Fearful of a backlash from his home province, Laurier justified his decision by blaming poor voter turnout. It was a setback for Temperance leaders nationally, but with Manitoba facing a general election, Prohibition once again became a major issue.

THE LAST THREE DAYS

MONDAY, TUESDAY
WEDNESDAY

REFINED ALE

EXTRA STOUT

DO you realize just what this city is going to be like after June 1, with the bars closed and the soldiers out at Camp Hughs? You are going to notice it very plainly then. You will wonder what makes it so quite in town.

Then you are going to be glad you ordered in a supply of beer against those quite days and months.

We know you will order some beer, but will it be enough?

There is added expense and inconvenience after next Wednesday.

Order your Drewry's American Style Rice Beer, Redwood Lager, Extra Stout or Refined Ale NOW. It will keep indefinitely in bottles.

E. L. DREWRY LTD.
WINNIPEG, - - MAN.

"Get Your Beer Before It's Gone" Newspaper ad warning of the impending doom in the days leading up to June 1, 1916.

After jumping on the dry bandwagon, the Conservative Party led by Hugh John Macdonald (son of John A. who was no stranger to the odd drink) trounced the Liberals and soon after their victory passed a Prohibition bill. Named the "Macdonald Act", the law was set to become legal on June 1, 1901. Finally, for Manitoba's Temperance leaders, the battle had been won. Or so it seemed. Before the law came into effect, Macdonald stepped down as premier to run in the upcoming federal election and Rodmond Roblin slipped in to take his place. Unlike Macdonald, Roblin was no staunch Prohibitionist. With a pro-business stance and the reluctance to lose a major source of tax the liquor trade provided, Roblin immediately put the Macdonald Act before the courts. When that failed, he then decided that a new plebiscite was in order. Outraged, the Temperance leaders boycotted the vote. Without their campaigning and support, the call for Prohibition was rejected. But tales of cheating abound. In St. Boniface there were more votes cast as there were eligible voters. In spite of the uproar, the vote held firm and again it become an uphill battle to banish the bar.

"Banish the Bar." Now that sounds like a slogan if there ever was one! Manitoba's Temperance leaders thought so, and a new catch phrase was born. As the province moved into the Twentieth Century the population exploded with new immigrants. This phenomenon only heightened the social plight already gripping Winnipeg. Together, with the fight for women's suffrage, a new atmosphere for social change was in the air. Premier Roblin was vehemently opposed to the suffrage movement, as much as he was to Prohibition. The scales were already tipping when the country went to war in 1914. When Roblin was forced to resign as a result of the Legislative Building scandal, the biggest obstacle was finally removed. The new Liberal government of T.C. Norris called for a plebiscite to resurrect the Macdonald Act in March, 1916. The result was a resounding "yes". On June 1, 1916 the Manitoba Temperance Act came into effect. After thirty-three frustrating years the battle was finally won.

> Together, with the fight for women's suffrage, a new atmosphere for social change was in the air.

So what were the Beer Barons to do? And how would the hotels survive without their lucrative saloons? Before the hammer came down the breweries put up a fight, albeit a rather tepid one. In order to sway public opinion, full page ads were placed in the news papers. Made to look like articles, the ads contained headlines on the virtues of the beer business and how positive it was for the local economy. The bartenders' union brought in famous American labour lawyer Clarence Darrow to speak against Prohibition on the grounds it violated civil liberties. These attempts were all too late to make a difference.

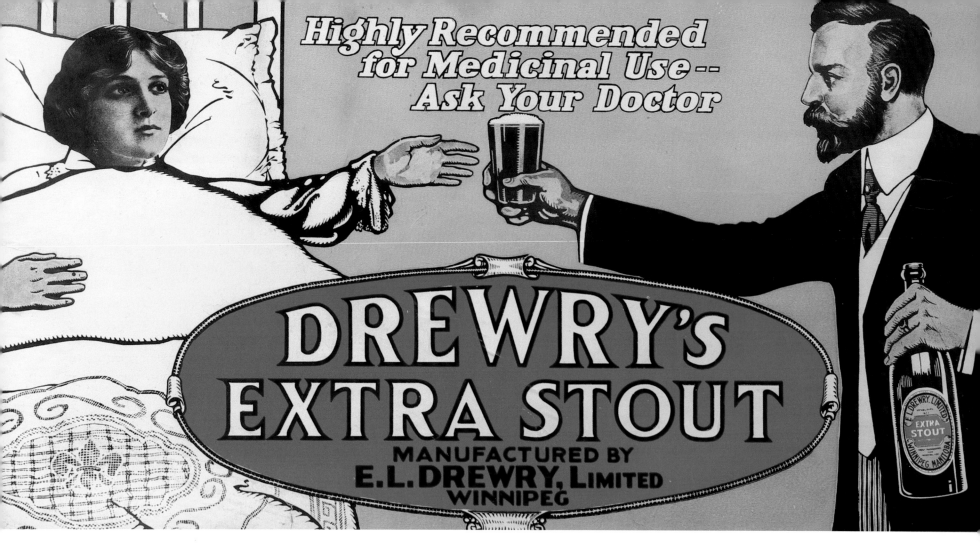

Highly Recommended
for Medicinal Use --
Ask Your Doctor

DREWRY'S EXTRA STOUT

MANUFACTURED BY
E.L. DREWRY, LIMITED
WINNIPEG

Full strength beer was still available during prohibition—as long as you had an understanding Doctor. E.L. Drewry and other Manitoba breweries took advantage of this loophole. This streetcar placard from the era suggests it was as easy as a visit to your physician.

Fortunately for the likes of E.L Drewry and Patrick Shea, the tap handles weren't completely shut off.

As James Gray wrote, "What Good Were Laws without Loopholes?" The number one loophole for Manitoba's seven breweries (and for that matter everyone in the liquor trade) was the distinction between federal and provincial jurisdiction when it came to liquor. The feds controlled the manufacture and import of alcohol and so, constitutionally, the province couldn't shut them down. Before the federal government's outright ban on alcohol in 1918 which lasted until November of 1919, full strength beer could still be made and shipped outside the province.

Loophole number two was "Temperance Beer". In Manitoba and Saskatchewan, beer containing two percent or less was not considered a beverage alcohol and was permitted in hotels as well as shipped inter-provincially, even after 1918. It wasn't hard to disguise one from the other. With a good imagination, there was all kind of ways to sneak a barrel or two of strong beer into a shipment. Sometimes they didn't even bother with the weak stuff and carloads of strong beer were confiscated. Loophole number three; full strength alcohol could be purchased with a prescription for medicinal purposes, creating a stampede to the doctor with pleas to "cure my rheumatism" as TV's Granny Clampett would later say.

Unfortunately for the hotels, surviving in this fashion wasn't feasible. In some cases, when caught serving the strong stuff, it took the help of the breweries to pay their fines. To settle the debt, scores of hotels fell into their hands after Prohibition. The idea of breweries owning "tied houses" was controversial and was only settled in the late 1950's when they were forced to sell their holdings (in 1955 two thirds of the provinces 286 beer outlets were owned by the breweries.)

In 1920, the province voted to ban the importation of alcohol and the wide-open cross border trade was again shut down. These were lean years for Manitoba's breweries but remarkably most survived. In spite of the huge hit the beer companies took, they began throwing their financial weight toward the newly formed Moderation League. The public had become weary of the whole situation and it was obvious Prohibition was impossible to enforce. Bootlegging persisted and Manitobans felt like a criminal every time they took a drink. Returning from overseas, war veterans began joining the Moderation League and their call for repeal. Their platform was simple; let the government control and profit from the sale of liquor and as a result the bootleggers would be out of business. It turned out to be a convincing argument.

In June of 1923, Manitoban's voted in favour of repeal. Less than a month later the public was asked to vote on a second question. The Moderation League had been pushing for the sale of beer and wine in hotels, but with the memory of the saloon still fresh in their minds, the public vetoed the proposal. For the breweries, it was a bitter pill to swallow. A victory to be sure, but nevertheless, the new Government Liquor Commission and its rules would be harder to live with than anyone ever expected.

In 1920, the province voted to ban the importation of alcohol and the wide-open cross border trade was again shut down.

If you were a drinker in Manitoba during the mid 1920's, here is how life was under the new liquor laws. Liquor could only be bought with a permit and ordered from the government liquor outlet which closed at 6:00 p.m. Your order would be delivered by the GLCC to your home as it was illegal to drink in any other place other than the address on the permit. Each permit holder was allowed a 24 case of beer a day but only up to 10 cases per month (very generous actually—that's eight bottles a beer a day). There were liquor stores or agencies scattered around the province, but they were pretty scarce compared to the party times before 1916.

With these tight restrictions in place, most drinkers went back to their old Prohibition ways. The breweries tried to beat the system too. Since

The label says "Temperance Lager" and it probably was, but when it came to beer in barrels, it was a different story. Breweries were sometimes guilty of shipping carloads of temperance beer along with a few specially marked barrels of strong beer to prevent detection from government liquor inspectors.

they couldn't deliver beer directly to the customer, the customer went directly to them. Before long there were calls to bring back hotel drinking. The "Beer by the Glass" campaign strived to convince the public that beer and wine in hotels would finally drive the bootleggers out of business for good. Of course the breweries were behind this push. In order to protect their investments they became the driving force in creating the Manitoba Hotel Association.

Another plebiscite was called in 1927 and the vote was unanimous; the breweries finally succeeded in getting their beer back in the bars. Only this time they wouldn't be called saloons. The term "beer parlour" was created and under the tight watch of the government monopoly, drinking in Manitoba would never be the same.

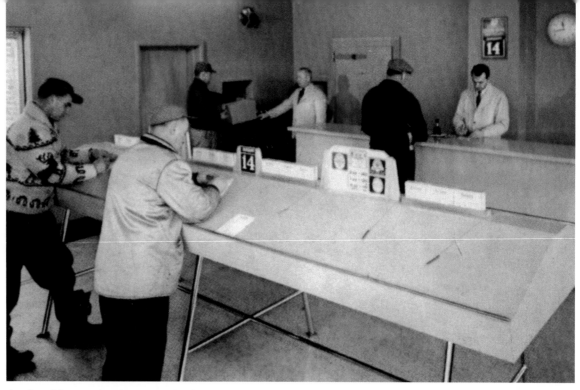

Another of the sweeping changes to take place was the restrictions on where to buy liquor. Initially, the Government Liquor outlet was the only point of purchase but this changed after hotels were allowed to serve beer in 1928. Soon hotel vendor and brewery outlets were established. Here is the interior of the Carling's retail store in 1958. No casually perusing the goods here! Instead a customer filled out a form and waited for his order to be retrieved from the back of the store.

Form No. 143-28A

The Government Liquor Control Commission

OFFICIAL SEAL

WARNING

This package shall not be kept or opened elsewhere than in the premises designated in purchaser's permit as his residence or as the place where such package may lawfully be delivered.

If a person is convicted for a first offence against the above provision he may be punished by a heavy fine or by imprisonment or by both fine and imprisonment—Sec. 151.

One of the regulation to come into affect after the government took control of liquor sales was the requirement of a liquor permit. Permit holders could only drink in the premise stipulated on the holder permit. Left is the official seal that was taped over the lid of every cardboard beer case purchased by the public. The permit system lasted until 1956.

For Men Only—Manitoba's Beer Parlour

In 1975, a curious ad began to appear in the newspapers and the headline said it all; "Beer parlours were places to drink...period." These ads—sponsored by the Manitoba Liquor Commission—were celebrating how far the province's liquor laws had come in the last 20 years. By the mid 1970's, the beer parlour was in the latter stages of being phased out and replaced by the beverage room—a more people friendly environment where both sexes could enjoy a drink, listen to music and have fun. Quite the opposite of what the government set out to do when they invented the beer parlour fifty years before.

It was only five years after Prohibition when the public voted to bring back drinking establishments—but this time it would be different. The wild days of the saloon were over and these new bars would be strictly controlled. The idea was to make the hotel beer parlour staid and restrained. Only beer was served and no food could be ordered; if you got hungry, hopefully, you would go home. There was no entertainment—music, dancing, singing and card playing (gambling) were forbidden. Unlike the saloon, standing while holding a drink was not allowed; it was harder to pick a fight while sitting.

Of course, what set the beer parlour apart the most from today's establishments was the exclusion of women. Although there was a provision in the liquor act for separate beer parlours for women, most hotels were not prepared to spend the money for such a small clientele. In post Edwardian society, men, beer, and women were still viewed as an unhealthy mix. As the 1975 newspaper ad went on to say, "Beer parlours were dismal places designed just for drinking, and too often, places to drink to the extent of drunkenness".

Gradually liquor laws were relaxed. In the 1950's a Royal Commission led by former Premier John Bracken was established to look at the liquor laws. Known as the Bracken Report, the exhaustive investigation led to the updated liquor act of 1956. Mixed drinking in restaurants and the establishment of cocktail lounges and beverage rooms finally brought the liquor act into the twentieth century. In 1961, women were allowed to work and serve alcohol in beverage rooms, and the beer parlour was starting to look like a relic of days gone by.

Regardless of all the changes, it wasn't until the 1980's that the last of the male only watering holes began to close. In 1982, Manitoba's Human Rights Commission ruled that men-only pubs would have to serve women by the end of March, 1986. In 1985, the Woodbine Hotel opened its doors to women leaving the Roblin Hotel as the last male-only bar west of Quebec. Because of this, the MHRC didn't push the issue and the Roblin remained a bastion for men only drinking until 1990, when owner Tommy Roy decided to close the doors for good.

Women were finally allowed to work in beverage rooms in 1961. This created an uproar from the Bartenders Union who feared their jobs would be lost to lower paid female workers. Because of a provincial ban on liquor advertising, the beer bottles in this photo had the labels retouched to hide the brand's name.

The Kiewel Brewing Company's aggressive ad campaign proved to be very effective and it wasn't long before White Seal beer became a popular brand in the province.

THE NEXT GENERATION

1925-1953

Charles E. Kiewel

The 1920's proved to be a defining decade for the brewing industry in Manitoba. Surviving Prohibition, the next challenge was the "beer by the glass" campaign. The fight to land their product back into hotels lasted five years and during this period, breweries learned to live within the confines of new liquor laws. It was also a time for a changing of the guard. By 1924, pioneer brewer E.L. Drewry had retired. On the other side of town, Frank Shea was poised to take over his father's brewery. At the same time, American Prohibition was in full swing and all over the United States brewers were forced to find other outlets for their skills.

In the case of Minnesotan Charles Kiewel, he decided Prohibition wasn't going to stop him and his family from doing what they did best—brewing beer. He needed to think outside the box, or rather outside the country. Winnipeg's size made it the ideal location for starting over and so Charles looked north to carry on the family's tradition. Minnesota's loss became Manitoba's gain and in the process Kiewel's became a St. Boniface institution for the next 50 years.

Charles Kiewel's father immigrated to the United States from Prussia, a portion of the German Empire, in 1856. He was part of the huge influx of German immigrants that brought their beer drinking culture with them and settled into the American Midwest. States like Wisconsin, Minnesota and Missouri became hotbeds for the manufacturing of beer and produced now famous names like Miller, Pabst, Hamm's and of course Anheuser-Busch. The Kiewel name is not among these famous national brands but throughout the Midwest they became very well known for a beer named White Seal—a brand Manitoban's embraced as their own.

The KIEWEL BREWING CO.Ltd., St. Boniface, anounce their opening of the first brew from the $200,000 new brewing plant recently completed in St. Boniface and now in full operation.

"WHITE SEAL," the new beer, will appeal at once to discriminating tastes. It is made from specially selected malt and finest inported hops to compare favorably in quality with the most noted brands of traditional fame.

We want you to taste "White Seal." Try it! Realize for yourself from the first glass, the zest and sparkle of this mellow, pure and perfect beer.

Order a Case by Telephone for Delivery Direct to Your Home—
Our Trucks Go Everywhere.
Deliveries After Monday.

Phone N1888 for Delivery to Permit-Holders' Residence

KIEWEL BREWING CO. LIMITED,

St. Boniface, Man.

Kiewel's St. Boniface brewery opened in June, 1925.

JACOB KIEWEL BREWING CO. – LITTLE FALLS, MN

The Kiewel family began brewing beer when Charles' father Jacob bought into a brewery near Fergus Falls, Minnesota in 1883. Jacob's time in Fergus Falls was anything but easy. A couple of disastrous fires to the brewery in 1884 and 1892 bookended more bad luck when he served a short jail time for selling a keg of beer on a Sunday. The brewery roof blew off in 1889 and when the city voted to suspend all saloon licenses in 1893 that was the last straw for Jacob. He gave up on Fergus Falls and landed in Little Falls, Minnesota where he started his next brewery. A substantial investment and a lot of hard work finally brought him enough success to purchase a second brewery in 1899 at Crookston, Minnesota.

KIEWEL BREWING CO. – CROOKSTON

Jacob Kiewel and his wife Rosa had ten children, six becoming active in the brewery. Eldest son Charles took over management of the Crookston brewery and a new beer called White Seal was developed to serve as a companion to the White Rose brand produced at the Little Falls plant.

Fire managed to haunt the family again as the Crookston plant suffered two blazes in 1905 and 1910, but they didn't give up, and the business

continued to grow. In 1913, the Jacob Kiewel Brewing Co. was the fifth largest manufacturing firm in the Little Falls area. When America surrendered to Prohibition in 1920, the Kiewel family rolled with the punches. Changing the name to Kiewel Associated Products, the company diversified into candy and the Little Falls brewery was used as an ice cream plant and creamery.

KIEWEL BREWING CO. LTD. – ST. BONIFACE, MANITOBA

With American Prohibition in full force and Manitoba's ending in 1923, Charles Kiewel moved north and commenced building a $200,000 brewery at 191 Dumoulin Street in St. Boniface. This had previously been the location for an open-air market where farmers came to sell their produce and to gather the latest news. Bits of equipment came from the Minnesota brewery and in fact the brew kettle had the name Jacob Kiewel engraved on it.

The new plant opened in June of 1925 and St. Boniface finally had its own brewery. All through its history the plant would cull its workforce from within the community. Francophone and Belgians alike would always be found manning the equipment somewhere in the brewery.

Kiewel immediately launched a bold business plan. He flooded newspapers with ads extolling the virtues of White Seal Beer. It was a huge campaign that even outstripped what Drewry's was doing at the time. White Seal became the

In 1913, the Jacob Kiewel Brewing Co. was the fifth largest manufacturing firm in the Little Falls area.

first beer in Manitoba to be bottled in clear glass after Prohibition and it wasn't long before the other local breweries followed suit. His aggressive approach paid off. A major expansion took place in October of 1925 when two additional floors were added over the stock house. A second bottling line was installed, capable of filling 120 bottles per minute (modern breweries can fill bottles at the lightning speed of 1100 BPM).

In the euphoria of post Prohibition, local breweries could not foresee how difficult it would be to adhere to the new rules imposed on them by the GLCC. One has to wonder if Kiewel knew what he was getting into, for it wasn't long before the company's name was being dragged through the courts on charges of the illegal sale of liquor.

- -

White Seal became the first beer in Manitoba to be bottled in clear glass after Prohibition and it wasn't long before the other local breweries followed suit.

With their permit, customers could buy beer from the government liquor outlet or have it delivered to their home. The brewery was required to balance the number of sales per week, against the issued permits. In 1927, the brewery and three employees were charged with a scheme to resell beer that had been shipped out of the brewery. The men made sure every brother and sister; aunt or uncle had a convenient permit number that could be used. They were caught when police were informed 72 cases had been delivered to a residence with a plan to eventually redirect 500 cases of beer to a U.S. destination. The charges against the brewery were dropped when it was found the employees had acted alone.

This case wasn't the only infractions to the Temperance Act the company had endured, but it may have been enough to sway Charles Kiewel to sell his brewery. The Brewing Corporation of Canada had just purchased the Empire Brewing Co. of Brandon on July 1, 1928 and was looking to add to its stable of companies. Kiewel sold the brewery on October 28, 1928. These were the first two breweries in the west to fall into the grasp of the growing number of eastern holding companies. They wouldn't be the last.

Of course this isn't the end of the story for Kiewels. Two years later the company landed in the hands of tycoon E.P. Taylor. In 1930 Taylor was in the midst of a buying frenzy. Before swallowing up Carling Breweries of London, Ontario, he bought the Brewing Corporation of Canada. Taylor's modus operandi was to close the less profitable breweries; concentrate the production of the more popular brands into one brewery and make sure the equipment was dismantled so that the building couldn't be used by another brewery. Unfortunately, this was the fate of the Empire in Brandon in 1931. In 1936, Shea's Winnipeg Brewery and the Drewrys Limited wrestled Kiewel's away from Taylor's holding company in a 60/40 split bringing the brewery back into local hands.

Bootlegging Beer

Since bootlegging was such a clandestine affair, it's difficult to know how widespread it really was. We do know hard liquor was the product of choice. Packing more bang for the buck than beer, folklore tends to be inhabited by stories of rum runners and whiskey stills. The business of bootlegging beer isn't as well known and what little evidence remains can be found in newspaper clippings of the day.

The bewildering laws of Canadian Prohibition allowed breweries to continue to make beer and export it to other provinces and to the United States. On the other hand, the Americans banned the importation of booze into their country and so, if you were a brewery or an individual and wanted to "expand" your market, the product had to be smuggled across the international border. Finally in 1930, after years of pressure by the Americans, exporting liquor into the U.S. was made illegal—leaving the stakes too high for cross border sales.

But the Americans weren't the only fodder for the illegal booze trade. As it was law in the 1920's—and remains so to this day—all beer must be bought through the liquor commission. Since this was a relatively new idea after Prohibition, breweries were often charged with violations of the Manitoba's Temperance Act. More often than not, it was the brewery workers themselves that got their employer in trouble. In 1926 alone, breweries were fined a total of $4,500 for violations of the Temperance Act. Beer became more available in 1928, when the hotel beer parlour opened for business and the practice of bootlegging beer slowly began to fade.

Kiewel's Buffalo Beer ad, 1926.

The Brief Life of Kiewel's Buffalo Beer

In October of 1926, the Kiewel Brewing Company introduced a new style of beer to the Manitoba market. Launched as a winter alternative to the lighter tasting White Seal, "Buffalo Beer" was advertised as a "Wonderful, Rich, Fully-Matured, Dark Beer" and different than anything else from a Canadian brewery. While the beer inside the bottle may have been unique, the label wasn't—at least that's what the Calgary Brewing Company thought. Their logo used a buffalo too, and so, after only two months on the market, a new name had to be found. A $100 cash prize was offered for a new name and the winner was . . . Grain Belt! They went from one trademark infringement to another; at least it seemed that way.

Grain Belt, a popular Midwestern beer, was introduced in 1893 by the Minneapolis Brewing Company. Even the label Kiewel's chose was similar to the American brand. They only catch here; America was in the throes of Prohibition and Grain Belt Beer wasn't being produced. Was the name chosen for its familiarity to the U.S. market? Were they counting on thirsty Americans crossing the line to find temporary relief? Or perhaps Kiewel had secured the Canadian rights for the simple reason that it was a great name. All these years have passed and we still don't know the full story, but interestingly enough, later in his career Charles Kiewel became president of the Minneapolis Brewing Co.

Grain Belt Beer, Kiewel's Brewing Co. Ltd.

Grain Belt Beer, Minneapolis Brewing Co.

Two labels from 1927.

The St. Boniface plant continued to brew beer under its own banner even after Labatt's took control of Shea's Winnipeg Brewery in the 1950's. In 1969 Pelissier's merged with Kiewel's and finally, after 50 years of brewing, the plant closed in 1976. Employees moved over to the new Labatt's facilities on Notre Dame Avenue.

Charles Kiewel returned to the United States after American Prohibition ended and became president of the Minneapolis Brewing Company. The Little Falls brewery returned to production in 1933 and began brewing the old Crookston label, White Seal. The venerable brand lived on in the States with different versions including a Strong beer and a Super White Seal. After leasing the brewery to the Minnesota Brewing Co. in 1959, the old brewery was shut down two years later.

In 1969 Pelissier's merged with Kiewel's and finally, after 50 years of brewing, the plant closed in 1976.

Kiewel's Dumoulin Street brewery, 1961: In 1979, while removing a beer vat, sparks from a torch caused a $40,000 fire. Fortunately, it didn't destroy the former brewery. Along with the Blackwood's annex on Mulvey and Osborne, this building is the last reminder we have of Winnipeg's brewing past.

A Genuine "Quality" Product

White Seal BEER

Brewed and bottled without any chemical process.

Delivered direct to permit-holders on phone order to the brewery.

Phone 81 178 or 81 179

KIEWEL BREWING CO., LTD.

ST. BONIFACE

White Seal was based on the Crookston, MN product of the same name. In the 1930's and 40's the label with the diamond inset was produced in Flint, Michigan, Minnesota and the State of Missouri. After the Canadian Corporation of Canada bought out Kiewel's St. Boniface plant in 1928, its Dominion Brewery in Toronto also produced a version of White Seal with a label almost identical to Kiewel's.

Above: Labatt's gave White Seal a different look for the late 1970's.

Top Left: A White Seal label from the early 1970's.

LOST AND FOUND

Collectors are never satisfied! It doesn't matter if its stamps or automobiles, hobbyists are always looking for that next big find. Brewerianists—a fancy term for people that collect items related to beer—are constantly on the lookout for rare bottles, advertisements or anything else with a brewery name on it. The Great White North Brewerianists is a Manitoba-based club devoted to the cause. A few club members have been collecting for over thirty-five years. With all this experience behind them you would think they have seen it all, but remarkably there are still treasures to find. Kiewel's Buffalo Beer label is one such gem that was once lost and now found.

Until 2012, the only known remnants of Buffalo Beer were various magazine and newspaper ads of the day. While making a request for permission to publish a Grain Belt label from an American collector, the authors related the Buffalo Beer story and commented on what a rare label it would be if one existed. Much to everyone's surprise, the collector stated he owned a Buffalo Beer label and it was for sale. Not only that—he had two other Kiewel labels collectors were unaware of. These labels originally came from a collection in Crookston, Minnesota, once home to the Kiewel family brewery.

The Kiewel labels have been repatriated and are now back where they belong. And the quest continues. There are a few breweries from the late nineteenth century that have no surviving artifacts—until we find one, that is.

> Brewerianists—a fancy term for people that collect items related to beer—are constantly on the lookout for rare bottles, advertisements or anything else with a brewery name on it.

After 86 years these labels have returned to Canada. Originally in the hands of an American collector they were previously unknown to local beer historians.

The Extra Stout Lager label may be a mistake in printing as the term contradicts itself. Stout beers are ales and thus are brewed with different yeasts than lagers.

The illustration includes handwritten names: Rolly Marion, Bill Hill, George Mitchell, John Kock, Madelaine, Josie Porier, Hy Beatty

best wishes for a happy holiday season

THE KIEWEL BREWING C

1965

Above: A Kiewel Christmas card from 1965.

Left: Starting his career with McDonagh & Shea in 1901, Charles F. Byrnes was General Manager of Kiewels from 1936 until his death in 1946. The cigar chomping manager was a keen sportsman and a well known figure in the local curling scene. The C. Byrnes Trophy competition was a popular event in the 1940's. In the background might be the worlds ugliest lamp—but highly collectible, if it still exists.

MACPHERSON BREWERY LIMITED

By 1925, the Pelissier family had outgrown their premises on Furby Street. They shifted their business to the old Blackwood's plant on Osborne Street and Winnipeg businessman Harold C. Macpherson moved in to fill the void.

The first beers left the plant on April 16, 1926. Apparently, the first cheque Harold Macpherson ever received was framed and hung in his office. A newsman at the time was so optimistic, he suggested the cheque would be in the Macpherson Museum in 2026. The writer went on to say, "when entering the plant, one is instinctively constrained to remove your hat, because of the cleanliness and good order." A unique feature of the brewery was a courtyard reminiscent of an old Norman farmhouse. Macpherson spent thousands of dollars improving the plant and equipment which included a new brewhouse. With

Harold C. Macpherson

assistance from Bert Ryland as sales manager, sales began to pick up.

By 1928, the public voted for the sale of beer by the glass. With the opening of hotel beer

Christmas Greetings

Macpherson's

OLD SQUIRE ALE

Brewed by one of England's Best Brewers

Realize for yourself the zest and sparkle of this mellow, pure and perfect ale . . .

PHONE

24 841

Macpherson Brewing Limited

H. C. MACPHERSON,
PRESIDENT

Furby at Notre Dame   Winnipeg, Man.

parlors, it seemed Macpherson's was in a perfect position to take advantage of the new market. But as swift as Harold Macpherson was in building up his company, he was just as quick to let it go. In 1928, he abruptly sold the company to brewmaster Anton Braun. We will never know the real reason he sold his brewery after such a short period of time, but perhaps the government crackdown on illegal sales was a strong point of contention. In April of 1928, his company pleaded guilty to charges of the illegal sale of liquor and the weeklong suspension of his license was lifted. Even in the beer business, a week of lost sales can be devastating to a young company under huge debt. But this was just a fork in the road for the prominent business man who

had worked his way up from Langside Street to a home in Tuxedo. In 1933, he packed his bags and moved his young family to New York, leaving the future of the brewery in the hands of family from Saskatchewan who were no strangers to the beer business.

In addition to these three brands, Macpherson also made a Wheat Stout and a Bock Beer.

In April of 1928, his company pleaded guilty to charges of the illegal sale of liquor and the weeklong suspension of his license was lifted.

FORT GARRY BREWERY LTD.

The most remarkable facet of the original Fort Garry Brewery is not the beer it produced—although it must have been very good. Its ability to survive under difficult times was the true measure of its success. When the Hoeschen family took controlling interest in the Macpherson Brewery in April of 1930, it was the dawn of the Depression, hardly an ideal time to start a new business. As a small independent brewery, Fort Garry took on the challenges of the Great Depression and the Second World War all on its own. They were the new kids on the block and not only did they survive, they prospered.

Fort Garry began as a family enterprise; the president, Ben (B.W.) Hoeschen, was well-heeled when it came to the beer business. His father John, was a businessman from Minnesota who in 1902 began investing in Saskatchewan real estate. Impressed with the potential of the prairie province, he set up a consortium of Minnesota businessmen and raised $100,000 to build a brewery in Saskatoon, (it ended up costing twice that amount). Along with Fred Wentzler, a brewer from St. Cloud, Minnesota, the Hoeschen-Wentzler Brewing Company was formed in 1906. John never took an active part in managing the brewery. He chose to remain living in Melrose, Minnesota while his son Ben became secretary-treasurer. Brewmaster Fred Wentzler took on the task of managing the company and brewing the beer, but by 1915, he sold out and the firm was solely in the hands of the Hoeschen family. The company then became the Saskatoon Brewing Co—just in time for Prohibition.

Ben, a lawyer by profession, used his expertise and some of the obvious loopholes in the law, to keep his business afloat when the province went dry. Some of those loop holes were so big you could drive a beer truck through them and most breweries eagerly did just that. In spite of the many lucky gaps in the law, the Saskatoon Brewing Company was the only brewery in Saskatchewan to survive Prohibition.

Fort Garry's first labels and ad, 1930.

In 1930, the controlling shares of Macpherson's were acquired from brewmaster Anton Braun and the name was changed to the Fort Garry Brewery Ltd. Just like his father, Ben chose his sons to run the brewery. John C. and his brother Norm didn't disappoint their father and rose to the challenge. By May of 1930, Anton Braun was brewing two new brands of beer.

Frontier Beer and Frontier Stout were mainstay products from their introduction in 1930. The brand gained recognition in England, when it won the award as the best in its class in competition with other Commonwealth breweries. Frontier became so popular, it was still being brewed by Molson 50 years later.

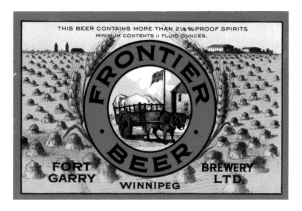

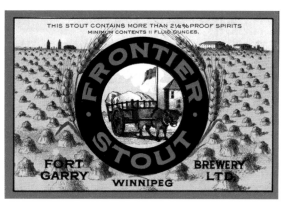

Fort Garry was the only brewery in Canada to use the American Style "Steinie" bottle. Above is an ad from 1939.

As the company grew in sales and in size, many building expansions took place. But the one thing that didn't grow much was their product line. Only one more brand was added; Fort Garry Pilsner. Instead of confusing their customers with many different brews, they launched a marketing ploy that set them apart from all the other breweries in town.

In 1935, after a trip to the United States, J.M. Davidson from the Manitoba Development Board brought back a strange beer bottle that would soon become popular in the U.S. Described as a squat little affair, it held 12 ounces and was obviously very different than the sleek long necks of the day. None of the breweries were very much interested in this odd looking bottle except for one. In 1938, Fort Garry broke from the pack and began using what became known as the "Steinie". Since FGB wasn't a member of Brewery Products

(a recently established beer distributor owned by Drewry's and Shea's) they could use any kind of bottle they wanted. The Steinie became a part of the Fort Garry image until 1950, when it was replaced with the standard long neck bottle. The popularity of the style declined and the brewery decided that being different was too expensive.

In 1940, Ben disposed of his shares to his four children, John, Norm and their two sisters. The war years were a difficult time for the brewery as it went into expansion and then had their sales limited when the government imposed beer rationing. As the war ended and business picked up, a new threat began to emerge in the late 1950's. All across the country breweries were being bought out by big eastern companies like Labatt's and Canadian Breweries Ltd. In Winnipeg, the Furby Street brewery was the last holdout.

Fort Garry's Furby Street Plant in the late 1950's

Top Left: Tony Kehrer scanning washed bottles for debris; one the most mundane of tasks to be found in a brewery.

Top Right: Charlie Sabo at the labelling machine.

Above: Feeding the soaker and washer, Bill Chorney (Left) and Fred McMullen.

ONE DOZEN PHONE 2484

FGB

Frontier BEER

FRONTIER BEER FORT GARRY BREWERY *Limited* WINNIPEG

119

PELISSIER'S LIMITED

MULVEY & OSBORNE ST.

WINNIPEG
CANADA

PHONES 41 111
42 304

FOR
FAST
DELIVERY
SERVICE
TO
YOUR
HOME

PHONE

41 111

42 304

42 305

42 306

The home of the famous "Country Club"

Pelissier's delivery fleet included a motorcycle and sidecar for "fast" home delivery, c. 1929.

THE DELIVERY MAN

Thanks to Anheuser-Busch, the high stepping Budweiser Clydesdales have become a symbol of brewing tradition. It takes us back to a simpler time when city streets were crowded with horses drawn carriages and delivery wagons. With teams of big sturdy Clydesdales pulling barrel laden wagons amongst all this activity, the beer delivery man was king of the road. At least that's the image that might come to mind all these years later. As romantic as that may seem, it's not quite accurate. Unlike the specially bred show horses from the commercials, real working Clydesdales were subjected to heavy daily labour. In fact Clydesdales were not always used and rarely were there more than two horses in a team. In reality, delivering beer was hard back breaking work.

Imagine if you will, the drayman (as they were known) arriving at the brewery stable in the early hours of the morning to collect his team and begin the task of loading his wagon with the heavy barrels full of beer. Depending on the size, each barrel could weigh over 300 lbs and so draymen were usually big burly men and tough as nails. Once on the road, the driver and his helper, (sometimes referred to as a trouncer, an old English term, named so because he had to trounce or manhandle the kegs when unloading),

> Depending on the size, each barrel could weigh over 300 lbs and so draymen were usually big burly men and tough as nails.

navigated their team of horses through traffic until they got to their destination—the busy Main Street hotel strip. Many of the old hotels stored their barrels in the basement and so delivery was done through a hole in the sidewalk. When the day was done it was back to the brewery to unload the wagons stacked full of empty kegs and bulky wooden beer cases. Although the men were paid at the top end of the brewery scale, they worked six days a week in heavy rain or 30 below weather. For man or beast, life before the automobile age was a far cry from those idyllic beer commercials.

Jules Supeene at the reins of a McDonagh & Shea wagon, c. early 1920's: Shea's kept 12 teams of delivery horses as well as their stable of champion Clydesdales. Supeene's career spanned 46 years, ending with Labatt's in 1966.

BREWERY PRODUCTS

As the age of the automobile gradually took hold, horses were retired to pasture. Motorized transport was definitely cheaper for the breweries than looking after a stable of horses and employing the men to care for them, but it was still a very labour intensive job. In 1936, Manitoba's two top breweries, Drewry's and Shea's made a move to simplify their delivery system. Brewery Product Limited was formed to warehouse, deliver and handle bottle exchanges. The beer distributor also handled products from Kiewel's and Pelissier's, since both were now owned by the big two local breweries. Reidles and Fort Garry continued to deliver their own beer.

In later years BP branched out to handle eastern brands such as Dow and Molson's but as the local brewery scene began to change and grow in the 1950's, the company's four-storey James Avenue building became inadequate for the job. With the loss of Shea's and Drewry's to the big eastern breweries, control of the company now fell into the hands of Labatt's Breweries and Carlings (Canadian Breweries Limited). Labatt's was soon to have their own bottle shop and warehouse on Notre Dame Avenue and since both breweries decided to take over home deliveries, BP was rendered obsolete. At the end of 1960, after 25 years, Brewery Products was closed. Many of the 134 employees found themselves back working for the original breweries from where they started.

Even after breweries changed over to motorized trucks for delivery, it hardly made life easier for employees. The following is an excerpt from a 1982 edition of "Blue Prints", the Labatt's Manitoba employee newsletter.

In 1928, Shea's Winnipeg Brewery bought a couple of REO Speedwagon 3 ton trucks. Henry Worster and Alex Kahler were assigned to drive these vehicles on the daily Winnipeg to Brandon run. Their day started at five am. By six a.m. they had the big Reo loaded with anywhere up to eight tons of keg and bottled beer, and they headed for Brandon, 150 miles of gravel road. They were frequently plagued with blow-outs, but on good days were back at the brewery by nine o'clock that night. Then they had to unload the truck, grease and gas up for the next day's run, which would start at five a.m. This was a six day per week schedule, and Henry remembers that in one nine month stretch, he ran up a total of 63,000 miles. He drove that 1928 Reo for 240,000 miles. He also recalls that he worked from 1916 for 17 years, 6 days a week, without a holiday or vacation. These were the "good old days?"

Top: Brewery Products fleet and warehouse, 132 James Avenue, 1938.

Above: **Big and Small:** This cute little delivery wagon was used for home delivery.

Bottom right: Brewery Products truck delivering to the Green Brier Inn, late 1940's.

THE WAR YEARS

The Second World War presented a number of challenges for Manitoba's breweries, not unlike many other industries across the country. Raw materials such as grain were rationed and that meant malt—one of beers key ingredients—was in short supply. When glass for bottles became scarce, ads encouraging the return of empty bottles were placed in newspapers. Cardboard boxes began to replace the heavy wooden cases. The practice of reusing beer cartons as "seconds" or "re-trippers" was widely adopted. As young men were sent overseas, women began working in breweries for the first time.

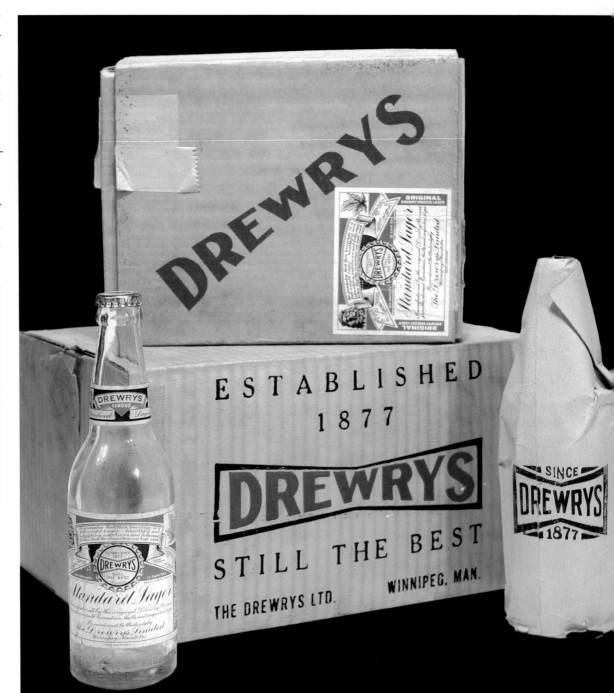

In Manitoba cardboard beer cases were used as early as 1925. The bottles were packed on their sides and a paper shroud was used for protection. The top case is a unique "3 pack" of the era.

During the war years rationing was a necessary part of life. Since fuel was needed for the war effort, Brewery Products briefly went back to using dray wagons for delivery. But gas wasn't the only commodity to be rationed. In 1943, liquor rationing went into effect creating a run on beer sales. Breweries often ran dry when their production quotas for the month were exhausted.

Beginning in 1942, liquor advertising was banned and this particular regulation lasted well beyond the war. It wasn't until 1967 that legislators finally allowed Manitoba breweries to advertise their products.

Beer parlour and delivery hours were cut and beer rationing was instituted. Brewery sales were limited to 90 percent of the beer consumed in the previous year. Restrictions were lifted in 1944 and by the time the war ended beer sales were back on track. By 1950, sales were three times what they were during the Depression.

- -

Restrictions were lifted in 1944 and by the time the war ended beer sales were back on track.

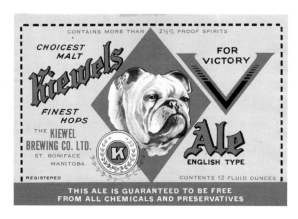

Kiewel's Bulldog "Victory" Ale

In 1942, liquor advertising was banned and so breweries could only pay for public service announcements.

EASTERN INVASION

THE END OF AN ERA

The 1950's was a watershed period in Canadian history. World War II had transformed the nation and the country's economy exploded. As wages increased and more disposable income became available, consumers were now able to afford the finer things in life most families couldn't enjoy during the depression. New automobiles, a first home and modern appliances were now within reach of the common man. With this new lifestyle, the average Joe could sit at home and enjoy a cold beer, fresh from his new refrigerator.

Home consumption of beer soared and sales in general had risen steadily since the war. Huge profits were at stake and Canada's brewing industry needed a make-over. Based on the expansion of the eastern giants, this was the time when the country's brewing structure changed from individual local brewers into national brewing empires.

Long before the 1950's, brewery expansion and empire building were already taking place.

Starting in the 1930's, Drewrys had morphed into a chain of breweries in western Canada. The huge Sick's brewing empire stretched across the west and even into the States. In Quebec, National Breweries was formed as far back as 1909. It was only when Toronto business man E.P. Taylor began buying up and consolidating breweries in the 1930's that a clear trend was starting to form. By 1939, Taylor controlled 60 percent of the Ontario market, but there was one brewery he couldn't buy.

As Taylor continued on expanding into the 1940's, Labatt's began to rise from their roots as a family-owned business when they became a public company in 1945. Founded in 1847 by John Kinder Labatt, the London, Ontario brewery slowly moved beyond the local market by exporting their product across the country by rail. With an excellent management team and a family controlled board they were able to ward off any kind of a takeover from Taylor and in fact he would refer to their company as "filthy rich." Fending off the advances of E.P Taylor wouldn't be enough if the company was to remain competitive. They needed to beat Taylor at his own game by expanding their brewery and branching out.

In 1939, Labatt's purchased land next to their brewery in London for a planned expansion, but

John and Hugh Labatt, grandsons of founder John Labatt, launched Labatt's 50 Ale in 1950 to commemorate fifty years of partnership. A year later, Labatt's Pilsner was debuted.

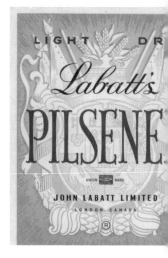

wartime restrictions placed on brewers regarding production, raw materials and sales delayed those plans. After the war those restrictions were lifted. Along with expanding their London plant they made their first step towards branching out. In 1945, John Labatt Limited was formed to raise capital for their acquisition of the old Copland Brewery. Toronto was Ontario's largest market and Copland's was the last brewery in Toronto not yet absorbed by E.P. Taylor. The old plant, with its decrepit equipment, would give Labatt's the needed emergency capacity to stave off Taylor's total dominance of the Toronto beer market. As far as Taylor was concerned, this was just fine. While Labatt's was busy expanding and upgrading their two breweries, Taylor was contemplating his move into Quebec.

National Breweries was in trouble. Its four plants in Montreal and Quebec City needed transformation as their products were old and losing appeal. In 1947, its chairman, Norman Dawes, sought out Hugh Mackenzie, the man leading Labatt's and offered him the presidency. Mackenzie felt his loyalties and future were with Labatt's and the great things he saw coming to them. Between 1947 and 1951, National's share of the lucrative Quebec and Ontario market plummeted leaving them with the unrelenting cost of over capacity, too many plants and too many brands. To get an injection of cash, Dawes next move was to offer Labatt's the Frontenac Brewery. Labatt's management team, led by John Cronyn, made their own appraisal, assuming beforehand that Taylor would out bid them. Their offer was a generous $3,400,000 for the plant built in 1925. While he very much preferred selling to Labatt's, Dawes felt obligated to his investors to make E.P. Taylor aware of the offer. Taylor countered with 110 percent of any legitimate offer and so the deal was made. By 1952, Taylor took full control of National and the company was renamed the Dow Brewery Ltd.

Realizing in the previous year that this was the most likely outcome, Cronyn had informed the board that if Labatt's was to remain competitive they would have to build a brewery in Quebec and do it without delay. In 1952 the board authorized the purchase of 26 acres in the Montreal suburb of Ville LaSalle for $204,000.

Unprecedented risk for Labatt's meant the previously very conservative company which Taylor had called "filthy rich" had seen a continual outpouring of large sums of money since 1946 for brewery acquisition, upgrading and expansion and now faced a towering bill with the potential to risk destabilizing their carefully nurtured world. The fifties had brought huge changes – Labatt 50 Ale was introduced, then Pilsener, now expansion and possible overwhelming debt. What could possibly top this?

LABATT'S COMES TO MANITOBA

In Manitoba, Shea's Winnipeg Brewery was a local institution with brewing tradition that went all the way back to 1887. Although a percentage of voting stock was in public hands, Shea's had remained family owned, even after the death of Patrick Shea and his son Frank in 1933. More than 50 percent of the shares were divided evenly between Shea's management and the widows of both Patrick and Frank. When Frank's widow Ethel died in 1952, she left the largest legacy ever bequeathed to a hospital in Manitoba at that time. The value of $2,500,000 in shares was divided equally between the Misericordia and Winnipeg General Hospitals. This generous gift proved to be very profitable to both groups until the spring of 1953. At the time the two hospital boards indicated that they would be interested in selling their shares in order to finance some large building projects they were about to undertake. Shea's management realized the sale of the hospitals' shares would leave them vulnerable to an unfriendly takeover by someone like E.P. Taylor—who had already "Taylorized" Drewrys with his acquisition of Western Breweries Limited. Neither Shea's management, nor the Manitoba government was happy at the thought of this big brewery in Taylor's hands and thus giving him a monopoly for Manitoba's beer market. Shea's decided they had to find a friendly buyer and do it quickly.

The call came from Manitoba in the spring of 1953. Labatt's Hugh Mackenzie was informed that Shea's Winnipeg Brewery was for sale.

Labatt's board of directors immediately set up a team to determine the feasibility of making the purchase and what that might entail. Interestingly, that decision was made at the same meeting that authorized the construction of the Montreal brewery.

Based on earnings, and appraisals of stock, structures, equipment and market share, Labatt's figured a fair price for Shea's was $9,000,000. The proposal was enticing for Labatt's but the timing was not good. How could they possible raise this amount and still maintain the current debt for their huge Montreal project which was already in motion. If they passed on the Shea's opportunity, would they be locked out of the West in the future?

Wise financial heads amongst management, and the Labatt family connection to London's establishment came through with sound support when it was needed. Raising cash by releasing Labatt Treasury shares, which had been held back

With John Boyd looking on, company matriarch Mrs. Margaret Shea hands out service awards at the 60th anniversary banquet in 1947. Mrs. Shea and her daughter in-law Ethel enjoyed great wealth from the success of their late husband's brewery. When Ethel Shea died in 1952, she left $2.5 million worth of company shares to the Misericordia and Winnipeg General Hospitals.

in 1945 and issuing an additional 500,000 shares proved to be a huge business undertaking and was completed in a remarkably short time. By November of 1953, the offer was accepted.

E.P Taylor was surely surprised at Labatt's ability to carry out these two gigantic undertakings within the same year. He must have realized at that moment that Labatt's was not just a little London brewery but now was a formidable challenger to his bid for dominance in Canada's beer market.

Brewmaster Carl Zimmerman (left) and Jack Labatt (middle) looking over plans for the new brewery

One of the few negative aspects of the Shea's plant was the property could not be expanded. This meant that Labatt's would eventually have to build a new modern brewery in Winnipeg. They used the value of the Shea's property to raise funds for current projects by selling the land to Great West Life for $2,500,000 and then leasing it back for ten years.

When Labatts bought the Shea's plant in 1953, it also gave them the majority shares in the two smaller Winnipeg breweries—Pelissiers and Kiewels, which Shea's had picked up when they bought them back from E.P. Taylor in the 1930's. Labatt's needed the extra capacity and continued operations at all three plants until a new brewery could be built within the next ten years.

The Shea's Winnipeg Brewery name was finally put to rest in 1958 when the company was renamed Labatt's Manitoba Brewery Limited. That same year Labatt's announced that it had purchased land for its new Winnipeg brewery at the site of the old Carpiquet barracks. The new brewery was to be built gradually (as money was available) in sections. The first section completed was the warehouse and bottling plant.

For many years beer was transferred by tanker truck from the brewery on Osborne Street to the Notre Dame Avenue bottling plant. The big gold trucks proved to be an effective way to advertise the Labatt's name.

It wasn't until 1970 that Premier Ed Schreyer turned the sod for the new brewhouse, the fifth and final section of the plant. When the new brewery was finally completed in 1973, it cost Labatt's $13,000,000, an increase of $5,000,000 over the 1954 estimate. The brewhouse was geared for a capacity of 390,000 barrels a year and its opening signalled the end of Labatt's lease on the Shea's site. The plant was shut down followed three years later by Kiewel - Pelissier's in St. Boniface.

Grown men cried at the sight of the old Shea's plant engulfed in flames. Beer had been brewed at this location for 100 years. The 1975 fire destroyed the building that had already been slated for future demolition.

CARLING BREWERIES MANITOBA LIMITED

While E.P. Taylor may have been concerned over the bold moves Labatt's were making, he wasn't about to let them have western Canada all to themselves. In fact, in the late 1940's his Canadian Breweries Ltd. was already buying up shares in two western Canadian brewers: Western Breweries Limited (the parent company to the Drewry empire) and Brewers & and Distillers of Vancouver. In 1950 these two holding companies amalgamated to become Western Canada Breweries Limited (WCBL). By 1953, Taylor took full control of WCBL and along with it, Winnipeg's largest brewery—Drewrys.

Now controlled by the two eastern brewing titans, it wasn't long before the long standing local names of Shea's and Drewrys would disappear. In April of 1957, the Drewrys plant officially became The Carling Breweries (Manitoba) Limited. To prepare for the manufacturing of Carling brands, a state of the art fermentation building was erected at the Redwood and Main plant at a cost of $1,000,000.

THE BEST BREWS IN THE WORLD COME FROM CARLING'S

A gleaming new addition to the old Drewry's plant featured open fermenting vats. Carling brands included Red Cap Ale and Carling Pilsener as well as Drewry's Standard Lager— soon to be rechristened with the Carling name.

Why did Canadian Breweries Ltd. change their name to Carling? Although the name itself goes all the way back to 1843, when Thomas Carling established his brewery in London, Ontario, by the 1950's, under the ownership E.P. Taylor, Carling had become synonymous with Black Label Lager and Red Cap Ale. At the time Carling's Black Label was Canadian Breweries flagship brand and was enjoying international success after Taylor began licensing its production in the U.S. and Great Britain. It was a natural fit to go with the Carling name when CBL finally became a national brewery.

132

GRANT'S BREWERY AND THE O'KEEFE BREWING COMPANY (MANITOBA) LIMITED

It wasn't enough for the ambitious Taylor to own just one brewery in Manitoba. By the time Canadian Breweries took full control of WCBL and Drewry's in 1953, he was already in possession of another brewery in town.

When Natalie Riedle, Ted Kling and John Popp sold the Riedles Brewing Company to George M. Black in 1950, there were grounds for suspicion that it was another ploy by E.P. Taylor to add to his empire and eliminate a competitor. Black claimed that after heading the large Drewry operations for Manitoba and Saskatchewan, he still had an interest in brewing and wanted a small brewery to work with. The skeptics proved to be right and as was expected, a year later Black sold the brewery to the company his son George Jr. who was now president of—Canadian Breweries Limited.

With the sale of Riedles in 1950, the Elmwood plant's name was changed to Grant's Brewery Limited. Jack Grant became general

manager and William Hauser, who had been Ted Kling's assistant, was promoted to brewmaster.

Grant's Brewery continued to do fair business in spite of no advertising or promotion attempts. This may have been due to customer loyalty as the brewery still had its own retail store and hotels that catered to the local clientele.

The Grant's name enjoyed a short run before E.P. Taylor began plans to introduce another eastern beer into the Manitoba market. O'Keefe's was a long establish name in the brewing business. Beginning in 1862, Eugene O'Keefe's Toronto brewery flourished as the city's population expanded. In 1934, O'Keefe's fell into the clutches of Taylor's Brewing Corporation of Canada and when the 1950's arrived, O'Keefe breweries were popping up in places like Ottawa and Saskatoon. Before it was Manitoba's turn, a major renovation and expansion began in the winter of 1956-57. With the completion of construction the name was changed to O'Keefe's on April 1, 1957.

The acceptance of the O'Keefe brands in Manitoba surpassed all expectation and it was necessary to immediately start construction on additional fermentation and storage facilities. E.P. Taylor was transforming the industry and like a feeding frenzy local breweries across the country were being "Taylorized." In Winnipeg, there was one independent left and North America's oldest brewery was about to head west.

Grant's Brewery was in business for only seven years before the Elmwood plant's name was changed to O'Keefe Brewing Co. (Man) Ltd.

This Old Vienna bottle is from 1958. In 2011, a bottle like this was found in a case of empties at Brewers Distributors Winnipeg warehouse.

Fifty-three years later someone finally got their ten cent deposit back—even though, to a collector, the bottle is worth much more than that.

Right off the hop, no pun intended, Manitoban's took to the O'Keefe line of products. It wasn't until August 6, 1970, when the brewery finally introduced Extra Old Stock to the Manitoba market. To celebrate the launch, the brewery carted a dray wagon through the streets to various hotels. Seen above is sales manager Julian Klymkiw presenting the Oxford Hotel with their first case of Old Stock. A long established Ontario brand, Old Stock became popular, in part, because of the higher alcohol content (originally over 10%.) Now known as Carling Black Label Extra Old Stock, the alcohol content is down to 5.65%.

Old Vienna's was O'Keefe's best seller. So much so that in 1965, they changed the name of the brewery to the O'Keefe Old Vienna Brewing Co (Manitoba) Ltd. Sales were so great the brewery outgrew the old Elmwood plant. Canadian Breweries decided to move production over to Carling's Redwood location and the plant was shut down on August 31, 1969. In 1973, Canadian Breweries official name was changed to Carling O'Keefe Ltd.

MOLSON'S FORT GARRY BREWERY LTD

It's a bit surprising that Canada's second oldest company, after the Hudson's Bay of course, took as long as it did to react to the rapid transformation sweeping across the Canadian brewing landscape. Since 1786, Molson's has been brewing beer on the banks of the St. Lawrence River in Montreal and much like Labatt's, its growth was steered by a strong management team with deep-rooted family ties. Beer wasn't the only business the family was familiar with. As his brewery grew, founder John Molson began to diversify into other areas such as transportation, which included steamships and Canada's first railway. John the Elder, as he was later referred to, passed on his business to his two sons John and William. They were also successful and went on to establish their own bank. The Molson Bank later merged with the Bank of Montreal in 1925. Generations of the Molson family became pillars of Montreal society through their many successful businesses and philanthropy.

Molson's had always enjoyed a healthy share of the Montreal beer market and by the end of the Second World War sales were climbing. With an eye to the future, company president Bert Molson decided that after 159 years it was time to make Molson's a public company. The Montreal plant took on a six-year $10,000,000 expansion, without borrowing a single cent. The company's healthy balance sheet served them well, at least until E.P. Taylor entered the scene.

Taylor's takeover of National Breweries came as a surprise to Molson's, but it shouldn't have. Norman Dawes previously offered to sell Molson's control of National in 1944, but Bert Molson had declined, leaving the door open for Taylor to maneuver a hostile takeover. With Labatt's announcing the building of a brewery in Montreal, the writing was on the wall. Molson's would have to respond to the growing competition and do what the others had done, become a national brewery. Their first move was on E.P. Taylor's home turf—Toronto.

Newly appointed president Hartland Molson opened Molson's Fleet Street Brewery in Toronto in August of 1955, a mere fifteen months after construction began. It was quite the accomplishment, especially since part of the property had been owned by none other than Canadian Breweries, (the purchase had been made through a second party; a trick "Uncle" Ben Ginter would later perform in Manitoba.) To celebrate the entry into the Ontario market Molson's introduced its first lager, Crown and Anchor.

> The Montreal plant took on a six-year $10,000,000 expansion, without borrowing a single cent.

Molson's Furby & Notre Dame Brewery and Retail Store.

It's sparkling light...

It's dry...

...and bright!

It's CROWN & ANCHOR lager beer

The gay Crown & Anchor label signals a promise of pleasure this lager beer fulfills. It's light and bright for cheery refreshment — the DRY beer you'll call MY beer!

a product of MOLSON'S Brewers since 1786

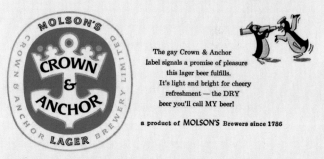

Molson's Crown & Anchor Lager was renamed Molson Canadian in 1959.

There's something new on the old Frontier...**Us!**

Off with the new...on with the old!

When you bought Frontier Beer last month, you may remember we warned you a label change was coming. This is it.

Why? Because our old label was just too **new**. Too modern for a fine, old-fashioned Manitoba brew like ours. Frontier is still the kind of beer your grandfather might have enjoyed. We figure it ought to have his kind of label. Take a look at one of these bottles and you'll see what we mean. (On second thought, better have a Frontier first and **then** look at the label. That may brace you for the sight of six Indians, three crows, a biplane, two rabbits and a stagecoach marching bravely across your beer bottle.)

More important, though, a sip or two will also reassure you that we haven't messed around with the beer inside. It's the same as always. Slow-brewed and naturally aged for good old Frontier flavour. We'll never change that.

MOLSON'S FORT GARRY BREWERY LTD.

To become a true national brewery Molson's had to have a presence in the West. After talks with the Calgary Brewing and Malting Co. failed to bring an agreement, Molson's set their sights on another successful Alberta brewery. With the unfortunate name of Sick's, owner Emil Sick managed to build up his brewing empire that included five breweries in western Canada, and two in the United States. Sick proved to be a tough negotiator, but in the end Molson's acquired the group of breweries in 1958 for an

astonishing sum of twenty-seven million dollars. Unfortunately for Molson's none of the Sick's breweries were located in Manitoba.

After thirty years of operation, by the late 1950's Norm and John Hoeschen's brewery on Furby Street and Notre Dame Avenue became a sitting duck, ripe for a takeover. Apprehension about the future of small breweries led Norman Hoeschen, manager and treasurer to enter into talks of a merger with a larger brewer, he told the Ontario Supreme Court on November 6, 1959. The court was conducting the trial of Canadian Breweries, Ltd. on a combines charge. He didn't reveal which company he was negotiating with, but told the court it was not CBL, or any of its subsidiaries. He also told the court the brewery had 7 percent of the Manitoba market and less than ½ percent of the total Canadian market. He added that the costs of selling and promotion had increased and felt it would be in his best interests to join a larger firm.

On Feb. 15, 1960, Hartland Molson announced that FGB had merged with Molson's. Norm Hoeschen stayed on as Managing Director. Molson's control was through their Calgary subsidiary, Sicks' Breweries Ltd. Hoeschen said he welcomed the merger as strengthening the financial and marketing position of the brewery. In June of 1961, the name was incorporated as Molson's Fort Garry Brewery Ltd. The first local bottle of Molson Canadian Lager Beer came off the line on June 23 and along with Molson Ale added to the market.

Left: In 1968, Molson's gave the long standing Frontier brand a new label design that was reminiscent of Sick's Old Style Pilsner label which dates back to 1926. Molson's still uses a version of this design for their current Old Style Pilsner brand.

Right: Molson's Canadian was first brewed in Manitoba in June of 1961. The bottle sported a new foil type label that had become popular in the late 1950's.

The same fate befell Ben Hoeschen's Saskatoon Brewing Co. in 1960 when it was purchased by John Labatt Limited. John Hoeschen died on November 28, 1962 age 55. His father Ben died in 1966 in Saskatoon at the age of 83.

And so the stage was set for the next 35 years. To maintain customer loyalty the breweries continued to brew a few of the original local brands and the industry remained an important cog in the local economy. As the swinging sixties began more changes were in the air. One major change was a new bottle shape that made Canadian beer distinctive from the rest of the world. The other was a brand that changed its name because Manitoban's said so.

INTRODUCING THE STUBBY

The official name was the Compact Bottle, and when it was introduced to the Canadian market in 1962, it was one of the most difficult packaging changeovers in business history. Three glass manufacturers were employed to make over 268 million bottles. But that was only half the task. Just as many bottles had to be taken out of circulation and either sold or crushed. It was a well coordinated effort and done in an amazingly short period of time.

It all started in late 1950's when the consolidation of the Canadian brewing industry was nearly complete. The Dominion Brewers Association felt the need for a standardized bottle that could be interchangeable between all breweries. The new bottle would replace the traditional long neck, which came in a variety of shapes and colours. The stubby would a have distinct amber tint to protect the beer from damage caused by the ultra violet light. Designed to be easily packaged and carried, the bottles were 25 percent lighter than

the long necks and that reduced shipping costs. Sturdier than the old bottles, the stubby could be reused more than twenty times and stacked higher than its predecessor.

It wasn't much to look at, but gradually the little bottle captured the hearts of Canadian beer drinkers. For twenty years it was an icon for the industry and is now considered to be as Canadian as maple syrup.

This odd looking contraption was made for the Manitoba Brewers Association and was used to convince customers that the new compact bottle held the same amount of beer as the old long neck. The bottles could be flipped upside down and like magic, the beer from the larger looking bottle would flow into what appeared to be the smaller bottle. Manitoba changed over to the compact bottle in 1963.

Sturdier than the old bottles, the stubby could be reused more than twenty times and stacked higher than its predecessor.

Big Blue—Labatt's Pilsener

Prior to the 1950's the Canadian beer market was split in its preference. Eastern Canadians were largely ale drinkers. In the west, perhaps because of the large American influence (both E.L. Drewry and Fritz Sick brewed beer in the United States before arriving in Canada) lager was king. Although Labatt's had dabbled with lager prior to Prohibition, it remained an ale brewery for most of its existence. That began to change in the 1950's with the increasing popularity of lager. In 1950, Labatt's began the task of developing a lager that would live up to the quality of its sister brand, Labatt's IPA. Under the direction of Czechoslovak Roman Vecosvky, the brewmaster of the famed Pilsen Brewery, Labatt's produced a brew they felt matched the old-world qualities of a true pilsener beer, (pilsener is a type of pale lager). In May of 1951, they introduced Labatt's Pilsener.

To promote its Bavarian heritage, a colourful little mascot dressed in lederhosen and wearing a green Alpine hat was developed. "Mr. Pilsener" as he was named, appeared on the neckbands, beer cases, and in print ads for Labatt's. This first marketing campaign ran nationally for many years before it was finally overshadowed by a curious series of events born in the beer parlours of Manitoba.

When Labatt's took control of Shea's in 1953, the parent company had a very hands-off approach to their Winnipeg operation. This most likely was because the Board of Directors were focusing on construction of their new Montreal plant. That changed in 1956 when they began brewing their new pilsener in Manitoba and Blue was ready to jump into the spotlight.

On a hot August night in 1957, Shea's sales rep Peter Langelle, was "treating" in the Waverley Hotel on McDermot Avenue when a guy called out to the waiter, "Hey give us another round of Blue." The waiter seemed to know what the man meant because he returned with refills of Labatt's Pilsener. Pete leaned forward, "Blue?" he asked. The customers were filling their glasses, "Sure, blue label, Blue—Great Beer!" This was a direct response to Labatt's main competitor in town and the beer they produced—Carling Black Label. Of course the slogan that came with it, "Hey Mabel, Black Label" was by then a well-known catch phrase. At the next morning's sales meeting Pete mentioned the "Blue" nickname he'd heard the night before. Other reps said they'd heard it too. Don Macbeth suggested they keep

Cactus Jack Wells enjoying a cold one with Blue Bomber GM and CFL Hall of Famer, Earl Lunsford: Wells did public relations for Labatt's and always referred to the football club as the Big Blue.

Left: Labatt's Pilsener label from the mid 1950's.

an eye on that. Beer drinkers have a great way of giving nicknames to their favourite beers such as "Club" for Pelissier's Country Club; perhaps Labatt could turn "Blue" to their advantage. Fortunately for the brewery, they had help from a local broadcaster with a great nickname of his own.

WHEN YOU'RE SMILING CALL FOR 'LABATT'S BLUE'

THE TRUE-BLUE FRIENDLY BEER!

By the late 1950's Labatt's was able to arrange sponsorships of the first televised CFL games. This was a great coup in Winnipeg where the football team was beloved by all and the biggest game in town. "Cactus" Jack Wells was the voice of the Western Conference for the CFL and also did public relations for Labatt's Manitoba Brewery. Although direct advertising on television, radio and in the print media within the province of Manitoba was illegal, Wells did his best to associate the Winnipeg Blue Bombers, the "Big Blue" with the blue label on Labatt's Pilsener.

At first, head office wasn't happy with this alternative to the little Bavarian, but sales figures won them over. Manitoba sold more Pilsener than anywhere else. From then on as Labatt's spread across the West, Pilsener's new nickname went with it.

In 1958, Labatt's Pilsener added to its prestige by winning the first prize, Prix d'Excellence, at the World Beer Competition in Brussels, Belgium. Labatt's responded by showing the award on special neckbands for Labatt's Pilsener, but in Manitoba, Labatt's Ed McManus made a milestone decision. They drew up a stylish advertisement, introducing a new Pilsner label adorned with the "Prix d'Excellence" medals and later, in sheer inspiration, added a strip at the bottom of the label that said, "Ask for a Blue." This was later changed to "Call for a Blue."

From that moment on Labatt's Blue began to move up the sales charts. First, Blue sailed across the West, at that time home to the bulk of Canada's lager drinkers. Then the Blue phenomenon began influencing Labatt's Pilsener sales in Ontario and Bleue appeared in Quebec.

By the late 1960's advertising laws were being relaxed and Labatt's saw Blue and Fifty Ale as key brands that could be advertised nationally on television and radio commercials. When Labatt's began their "When Your Smiling" campaign in 1968, Labatt's Pilsener had officially become Blue. A decade later Labatt's Blue became the best-selling Canadian beer in the world.

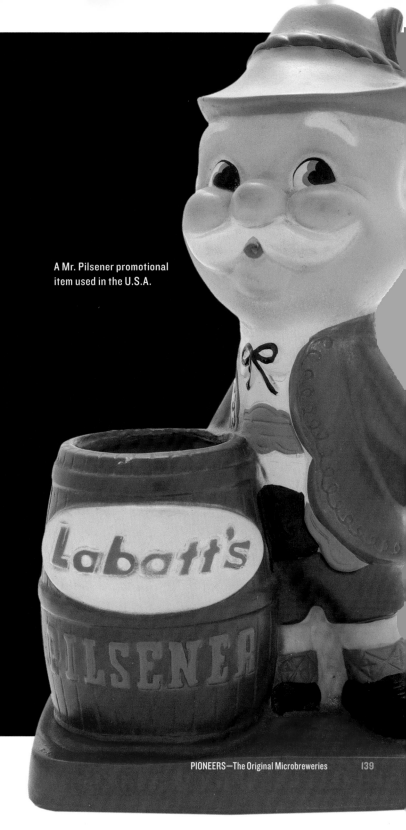

A Mr. Pilsener promotional item used in the U.S.A.

CHAPTER 10

UNCLE BEN

REBEL WITH A CAUSE

Industrialist Ben Ginter's maverick style clashed with breweries and government alike. Manitoban's got a taste of his beer and his style when he opened a brewery in Transcona in 1971.

He once called the beer business "the crudest, most discriminatory, dirtiest industry in Canada." A multimillionaire by the early 1960's, Ben Ginter bulldozed his way to success on his own terms. His fortunes were made building highways and up to that point, his stubbornness and sheer determination served him well. But when he reluctantly bought a brewery in 1962, he knew nothing of the industry or its challenges. He threw himself into the brewing game, primarily because the competition tried to keep him out. No one told Ben Ginter what to do and ultimately, this maverick attitude is what brought him down.

Born in Poland in 1923, Ben steadfastly claimed to be a Manitoba boy; born and bred. Spending his youth on a farm near Minitonas, Manitoba, Ginter learned the value of hard work when his father died. He was forced to quit school in the eighth grade and by the time he left home, he had become a strong-willed and ambitious young man. In 1948, he met Noel Smith, a heavy equipment dealer in Saskatoon and together they formed a construction company. Ginter

soon found himself building track foundations for the railway near the northern town of Prince George, B.C. and his career was launched. From construction to pulp and paper, mining and even a winery, the former cat skinner became one of British Columbia's most successful businessmen.

By far, Ginter's greatest success was the work he did for the B.C. government. He went on to construct over $300 million worth of roads for the province. If he had just kept building roads

we may never have heard of Uncle Ben. His decision to buy a derelict brewery was the beginning of one of the most controversial sagas in Canadian brewing history.

It all started innocently enough when Ginter bought the defunct Caribou Brewing Co. plant as a storage yard for his construction equipment. Soon the town convinced him to restore the brewery to its original use. After all, Prince George was full of beer drinkers and surely the growing market could support such a venture. He was reluctant at first, until a call came from a major brewery in Vancouver with a plea to buy his old brew kettle. Theirs was broken beyond repair they explained, but the savvy businessman became suspicious. When they offered him

Tartan Breweries was the first to introduce canned beer to the western provinces. When Ginter was forced to give up the Pilcan name after a lawsuit from Carlings, he introduced Uncle Ben's Malt Liquor with a picture of himself on the product. Ginter wasn't sporting a beard at the time of the photo shoot and so he donned a fake one shown here on the can. He later grew the real thing and the image of the burly and bearded beer tycoon became the company trademark.

$150,000 for the kettle, he was convinced they were trying to keep him out of the beer business. Ginter's competitive spirit got the best of him and with that, Tartan Industries was born.

As soon as his beer hit the market, Ginter's unorthodox marketing techniques brought him trouble. His first brand names were mis-spelled famous beers such as "Budd" and "Paap's" and it wasn't long before the big American beer companies put a stop to that practice. He was the first to introduce canned beer out west and this resulted in one of his most famous stunts.

When the big three (Molson's, Labatt's, Carling) finally brought out their own canned beers, they wanted to sell it at a premium. Ginter charged the same for cans as he did for bottles and didn't see any financial need for disparity. This partisan way of doing business just wasn't how things were done! The B.C. liquor board maintained price conformity from all the breweries in the province and so Ginter was forced to

raise his price or lose his license. Ben was adamant on keeping his price the same and so in an act of defiance he had his employee's tape a dime to every can of beer. Whether this was an inspired bid for publicity or just plain stubbornness, his actions didn't sit well with the government. Not only was Ginter forced to stop giving the "under the table" refund, he was shut out of the extra profit, since he hadn't requested the premium in the first place. That extra insult was eventually overturned, but it proved to be the beginning of a long series of battles with local governments and the competition.

After losing a hard-fought court case with Carling Breweries over the use of the word "Pil" in his Pilcan beer, he gave up and decided a new approach was needed. Ben Ginter finally became "Uncle Ben" when he introduced Uncle Ben's Malt Liquor in 1969. This new 10 percent brew not only sported a powerful wallop, it also gave a face to the brand. Every can was adorned with a

picture of the burly entrepreneur, beard and all. At six feet and 250 pounds, Uncle Ben became his own trademark. With this image and the tartan designs on his bottles and cases, Ginter decided to become a national force across the country. Regardless of his past troubles, he convinced himself he could take on the big three breweries. But because of inter-provincial trade barriers, he'd have to build plants in other provinces. Soon Ben Ginter would be barrelling his way into Manitoba.

When Ben Ginter opened his brewery in Prince George, BC, the names of his beers were rip-offs of big American brands, but with a slight change in spelling.

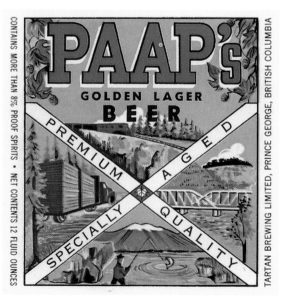

"WELCOME TO MANITOBA UNCLE BEN"

With unsuccessful attempts to establish breweries in Ontario and Newfoundland (Ontario reneged on a loan and Joey Smallwood demanded a cut of beer sales), Manitoba almost blew its chance too. In 1968, Winnipeg made Uncle Ben an honorary citizen when he announced plans to build a brewery in St. Andrews and then the city twice rejected his application for rezoning, (the City of Winnipeg was responsible for zoning at that time.) Then Selkirk and St. Boniface were in the running and the longer it took to find a location for his new brewery the more publicity he received. Finally, Transcona threw down the welcome mat when Ginter found a suitable building for his brewery. As always, there was a slight problem with the plan.

The former Catelli Foods plant on Regent Avenue was owned by Ogilvie Flour Mills and they in turn, were part of the Labatt's brewing empire. Ben knew his arch enemy would never let the property fall into his hands, so he handled it in pure Ginter fashion. He used the name of a trucking company he controlled and bought the building before Labatt's knew what hit them. He then reneged on paying the realtor their commission by claiming that the trucking company had terminated their services before the deal was made. Of course a lawsuit followed; an occurrence all too familiar to the industrialist. Whether it was railways, unions or breweries, Ginter was always in the middle of some sort of litigation. He gave the law profession so much business the students at the University of British Columbia law school made him an honorary lawyer.

Before his plant brewed its first beer, Ginter was making the establishment sit up and take notice. Just as he had in B.C., Ginter planned to market his beer at a lower price than everyone else, but first the MLCC would have to okay it. And then the Public Utilities Board had to give its stamp of approval; something Ginter hadn't counted on.

Tartan Breweries was up and running by the spring of 1971 and Big Ben was already in the papers publicly complaining about the whole bureaucratic process involved in getting his

prices approved. They were purposely making it difficult for him, he spouted. J. Frank Syms, chairman of the MLCC, was rather annoyed by Ginter's comments. He countered that the government wasn't setting up any barriers to his bid and the brewery hadn't yet submitted the proper financial information. In the past local breweries always applied for an increase and never had a single brewery ever asked for a reduction. Some felt Ginter's request was a publicity gimmick and he would later ask for an increase once his beer took off. In June of 1971, Tartan Breweries request was finally granted. It was a small victory because by November of the same year Ginter claimed his brewery was already in trouble.

Uncle Ben's took pride in brewing their beer with pure Manitoba spring water drawn from an underground source right on the brewery property. The bottles in this case of beer had the convenient Rip Cap, a new innovation at the time.

Don't let the beer shirts fool you—these boys were drinking Uncle Ben's Cola.

As one blogger recently put it; "Kids loved Uncle Ben's; every sip risked glances of disapproval, every sip a thumb of the nose."

Ben Ginter always thought big. The company boasted they could capture an astonishing 21 percent of the market in the first year and 60 percent four years later! But he hadn't counted on one thing. In Manitoba, most beer sales were handled by the hotels. Many of those hotels were once owned by breweries and the big three still held a certain amount of influence. In the late 1950's and early 1960's breweries began selling their interests in the hotels they'd owned since the end of Prohibition. A few of these hotels were sold to former brewery employees and at a very reasonable price—guaranteeing loyalty. Ginter hit the newspapers claiming the hotels were

shutting him out. The hotel association fought back and challenged Ginter about his allegations. Uncle Ben said sales in hotels and vendors were half of what he sold at the liquor commission and even Frank Syms agreed. One hotel employee wrote in the papers the reason for Uncle Ben's poor sales is the public didn't like it. The hotel ordered his beer and it just sat in the back of the vendor collecting dust. There may have been a ring of truth to this too. Ginter was extremely hard on his management. Former employees recall there was always a high turnover for brewmasters and thus the quality and consistency of the beer suffered.

In the middle of all this turmoil Ben found a bit of luck. As a result of a beer strike involving

Molson's and Labatt's in Vancouver, Uncle Ben's was allowed to ship in 60,000 cases of his brew from Manitoba. In 1972, his other new brewery in Red Deer, Alberta wasn't yet operational. With special permission, Ginter was able to ship beer from his Manitoba plant to pre-establish the Alberta market. And then of course there was another one of his ideas that hit the streets in 1972.

Uncle Ben's created a ruckus when he began selling soft drinks in beer bottles. In an exclusive deal with 7-Eleven, the brewery came under

Another of Ben Ginters famous marketing stunts was selling soft drinks in beer bottles, much to the chagrin of parents and teachers everywhere.

fire after high school teachers complained they couldn't tell if students were drinking beer or soft drinks on school grounds. Ginter said the claims were a lot of foolishness and the real complaints were probably lodged by the breweries.

It's safe to say the beer business will never see another character quite like the irascible "Uncle" Ben Ginter.

After weathering a strike in 1974 and the ongoing struggle to find a market, Ben Ginter was ready to throw in the towel. In 1973, he managed to convince the government to look into allowing beer sales in grocery stores but two years later nothing had come of the matter. In March of 1975, Ginter addressed the public in an article in the Winnipeg Free Press. He stated he would shut down the Manitoba operation in two months if he couldn't sell the brewery for five million dollars. He wanted the Manitoba government to take it over, so it wouldn't fall into the hands of the competition. He then said, with a bit of remorse, that when he decided to build a brewery in Manitoba he only wanted to do something good for the people and for his home province. He thanked the government and the public for their support.

In some ways it's hard not to feel sorry for the big man. He just tried too hard. There is no denying that his attempt to build a national brewery was too ambitious and that the roadblocks to success were not his alone. His foray into Manitoba was just a small part of that whole story. He may have been his own worst enemy, but in many cases he didn't get a fair shake either. Understandably, when his company was forced into receivership in January of 1976, he was incredulous. He maintained he hadn't been given a chance to pay back the loan and that it was a conspiracy led by the big breweries because the chairman of Labatt's was on the bank's board of directors, (an allegation that was never proven in court.)

His breweries in Manitoba, Alberta, and Prince George, B.C. were closed and then re-opened under the receivership of Dunwoody and Company. His brewery in Richmond remained incomplete and by 1978 everything was shut down.

Ginter's workaholic lifestyle, hard drinking and constant turmoil finally took its toll. On July 17, 1982 he died of a severe heart attack at the age of 59. He is buried in the family plot near his hometown of Minitonas. It's safe to say the beer business will never see another character quite like the irascible "Uncle" Ben Ginter.

KEEP SAYING «UNCLE»

Uncle Ben's beer and soft drinks are alive and well and available in all the usual places.

Many people were confused when Uncle Ben's Breweries (Manitoba) Ltd. went into recievership last January. The truth is, nothing changed except the administration. The brewery didn't shut down — it didn't even slow down. And will still deliver to your home.

We're still producing 4 different beers and a variety of Dad's and Uncle Ben's soft drinks.

So keep saying "Uncle." It's still the only way to make sure you're getting the best.

Uncle Ben's Breweries (Manitoba) Ltd.

Above: This ad was a last ditch plea to customers informing them that the company was still in business after going into receivership in early 1976.

Labatt's sales staff grew steadily after the brewery moved to Manitoba in 1953. At the time, Shea's owned over 40 hotels and kept as few as three salesman on board.

Before the rules for beer advertising were relaxed, it was the promotional skills of the local marketing department that every brewery relied on to build a loyal customer base.

CHAPTER 11

THE BIG THREE

GOING, GOING ... GONE

Someone once said about brewery work; "Hey, that's a great job; people will always drink beer, right?" It was the late 1970's when that conversation occurred and by all accounts, it seemed to make sense. But what this person didn't realize is; the brewing industry is always changing, always in flux. The forty years following the formation of the Big Three—as Molson's, Labatt's and Carling O'Keefe were called—had been a wild ride.

The all-important fight for market share was the driving force behind the so-called innovations that had been steadily offered to the beer drinking public. First it was canned beer, then light beer.

The biggest change of all happened when the breweries began licensing American brews, thus casting aside the little stubby and the pride we had in our own style of beer. New brewing techniques debuted when national marketing brought us the Extra-Dry-Cold-Filtered-Ice beers of the 1990's. By then local brands like

White Seal and Select had disappeared. One by one, Manitoba's long standing breweries would soon be gone too.

There were a fortunate few that started their careers when the Big Three moved in. They were the lucky ones that retired just before free trade brought the hammer down. Yes, it's true, people will always drink beer; where it comes from, is another story.

Canned Beer in Manitoba

It might be considered the first volley in what has been described as the battle for market share. In 1966, Ben Ginter's Tartan Breweries was the first to introduce canned beer in western Canada. Two years later, when the Big Three began marketing their own canned beer in British Columbia, Ginter had grabbed almost seven percent of the market. In 1968, Manitoba became the first prairie province to introduce domestic beer in cans, but had to settle with importing it from Ontario. Meanwhile Tartan Breweries, with a new brewery license in hand, brought their product in from BC.

Manitoban's had eleven brands to choose from. At $3.25 per dozen, 20 cents more than bottled beer, it proved to be a tough sell. It's hard to imagine now, but at one time canned beer was looked upon as an environmental scourge. With no return or refund policy in place the tin beer can became the poster child for environmental irresponsibility. It was also expensive to manufacture and in Manitoba sales were less than two percent. By 1973, Ontario stopped canning beer and finally in 1975, Manitoba discontinued the sale of canned beer.

In 1983, with the advent of the aluminum beer can, the breweries once again began importing cans to the Manitoba market. Carling O'Keefe invested $3 million dollars in a canning line at their Redwood and Main plant in 1985. With a refund system in place canned beer was here to stay, but the same can't be said for the canning line at Carling O'Keefe. In 1988, the line was shut down after it proved to be less than cost-effective.

As of 2012, canned beer holds more than 60 percent of the Manitoba market. With an increasing variety of package sizes to choose from and a number of brands selling at reduced prices, it doesn't look like bottled beer will ever dominate the shelves again.

Labatt's Hugh Hamilton enjoying a beer from the new 12 pack of canned beer that first became available in 1968: Beer in tin cans was not a success in Manitoba. It wasn't until the re-introduction of beer in the new aluminum can when the public slowly began to embrace the product.

This Old Vienna can from 1985 commemorates the first canning line in Manitoba brewing history. The only problem was— it wasn't true. Someone forgot that in the 1970's, Uncle Ben's Transcona plant had been canning beer with pure Manitoba spring water. Their canning line shut down in 1975.

FIRST EDITION

Just say

THIS SPECIAL COMMEMORATIVE CAN MARKS THE OFFICIAL OPENING OF THE FIRST CANNING LINE IN THE HISTORY OF THE MANITOBA BREWING INDUSTRY. NOVEMBER 1985
CARLING O'KEEFE BREWERIES
WINNIPEG, MANITOBA

THE BEER SALESMAN
THE MOST POPULAR MAN IN TOWN

As important as advertising is to the beer business today, in days gone by, it was the beer salesman who was worth his weight in gold. Before national ad campaigns ruled the airwaves, the sales representative was the important link between the brewery and the customer. Well travelled, these men were popular names in the community and for good reason. Buying beer parlour patrons a drink was an effective sales ploy; if word got out the brewery rep would be in town, the bar was

There are too many wonderful characters in the annals of Manitoba's brewing past to mention, so we give you just one—Labatt's Sales Rep, Pete Langelle. A big man with a big personality, Pete was the friendly good natured type that people are drawn to. It didn't hurt that he had a heroic past as a former Toronto Maple Leaf. Pete scored the winning goal in the seventh game of the 1942 Stanley Cup playoffs. His career spanned 30 years with both Shea's and Labatt's Breweries.

packed the next day. Although this sales technique was at odds with provincial liquor laws, it gradually faded away as more modern sales methods took its place.

Ian Coutts, in his book Brew North, describes beer salesmen as "glad-handed extroverts with cast-iron livers." But it took more than personality (and a strong constitution) to become a success. It was hard work too. Salesman might work every day during the summer months, travelling to rodeos, fairs and sporting events. Breweries understood the toll it could take on their staff and occasionally salesmen were able to bring their families along to events. There was a certain status to being a brewery representative and many old names are fondly remembered.

Selling beer is different today. Women are on board now and buying a round is a thing of the past. The same can be said of the brewery hospitality room. Every brewery had one and they served as ideal venues for promotional events and community functions. The "Blue Room" at Labatt's and Carling's "Carlsberg Hall" is just a groggy memory for the many people who were lucky enough to have visited them. And free beer in brewery lunchrooms is unthinkable in today's safety conscious environment. One has to ask; with all the old ways of doing business gone—is the job of selling beer fun anymore?

MOLSON'S
FORT GARRY BREWERY LTD.

721 FURBY STREET
WINNIPEG, MANITOBA

SP 4-4441

ED MAZUR

DAVE JOWETT
Marketing Representative

Notre Dame & Keewatin
Box 776 Winnipeg Man.
R3C 2N3
Tel: (204) 633-9286

OREST HORECHKO
SALES REPRESENTATIVE

CARLING O'KEEFE

CARLING O'KEEFE BREWERIES OF CANADA LIMITED
1149 MAIN STREET, WINNIPEG, MANITOBA R2W 3S5   •   TEL. (204) 586-8011

The "Blue Room" at Labatt's and Carling's "Carlsberg Hall" is just a groggy memory for the many people who were lucky enough to have visited them.

SPORTS AND SPONSORSHIP

Long before Park Avenue ad men hatched the "Tastes Great, Less Filling" debates of the 1970's, brewers had made the all important connection between men, sports and beer drinking. That they go together so well is a no-brainer of course, but before the days of mass marketing, it was the grass roots connection to amateur sport that brought in the customers.

In this province it was E.L Drewry, an avid sportsman himself, who began to see the merits of brewery sponsorship. As early as 1909, E.L. had become President of the Redwood Football Club. Organized by his factory employees, it wasn't the only club Drewry put his money behind. Lacrosse was another game dear to his heart and the brewery sponsored tournaments for the Western Canada Lacrosse Association. They also had their own

Far left: Redwood Football Club schedule, c. 1909.

Bottom left: Labatt's sponsored the Brier from 1978–2000. Carling O'Keefe also sponsored curling with the Carling O'Keefe Super Curling League in the 1970's.

Above: Shea's Winnipeg Brewery hockey team, 1926.

baseball venue called Drewry Park. As the years progressed, other breweries lent their names to a variety of clubs in hockey, curling, baseball and bowling leagues.

The practice of brewery sponsorship really took off in the 1950's when Labatt's began their association with the Winnipeg Blue Bombers. The brewery also supported the Manitoba

Amateur sport wasn't the only benefactor the breweries supported. Along with scholarships in education they also gave their assistance to the arts. Carling O'Keefe donated space above the company's garage to the Forum Art Institute in the 1970's.

Wildlife Federation with their popular "Sportsman's Friend" campaign in the 1960's. Amateur sport teams all over the province could count on a brewery to supply their team jersey and t-shirts. In turn, the team made an effort to drink the breweries beer after a game.

Today, local sponsorship is on a much smaller than those heady days of the 60's and 70's. With sales staff a fraction of what they were and budgets equally as small, the focus is now on the big picture. In 2012, Budweiser is the sponsor for the reincarnated Winnipeg Jets—the Labatt name is hardly mentioned.

Today, local sponsorship is on a much smaller scale that those heady days of the 60's and 70's.

Below: A "Sportsman's Friend" billboard on the side of Labatt's Colony Street brewery.

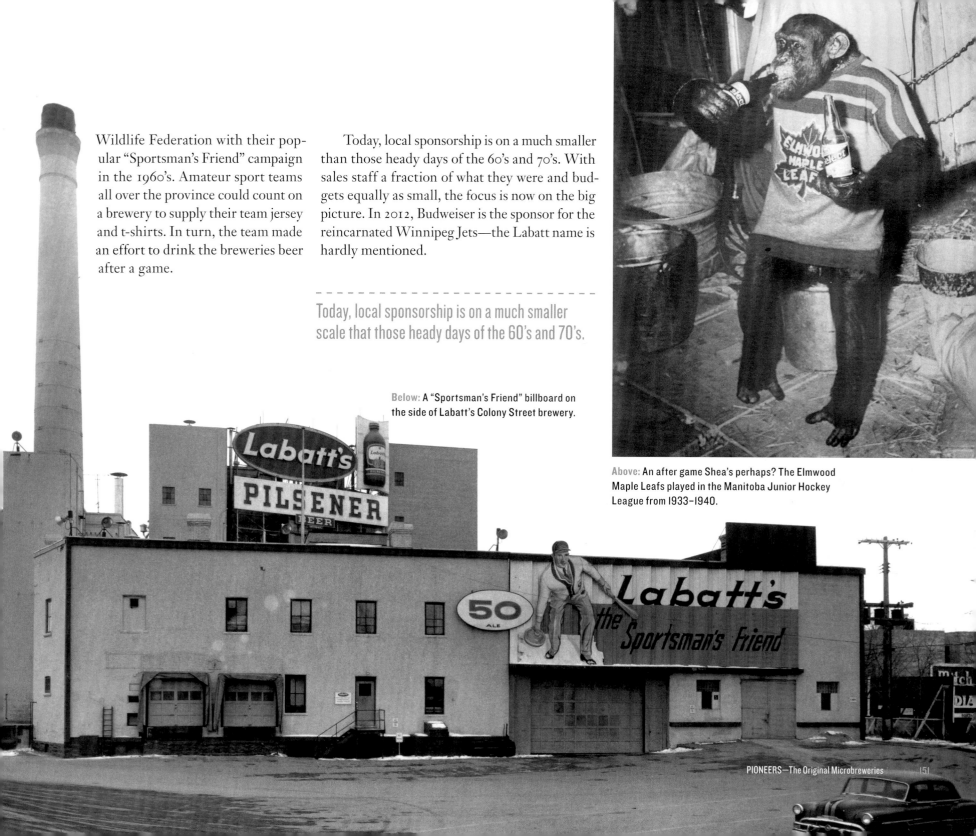

Above: An after game Shea's perhaps? The Elmwood Maple Leafs played in the Manitoba Junior Hockey League from 1933–1940.

MOLSON THREE STAR SELECTION

Molson's and the Winnipeg Jets

Much like the relationship Labatt's enjoyed with the Blue Bombers, Molson's long history with the Winnipeg Jets seemed to be made in heaven. Sharing the same colour scheme with the brewery's flagship brand, Molson Canadian sponsorship dates back to the days when the Winnipeg Jets were a Major Junior Hockey team in the late 1960's and early 1970's. By 1979, when the team was part of the struggling WHA, Molson's was sponsoring the Three Star Awards. By this time, the league was on the verge of financial collapse and had been negotiating to join the NHL. In March of 1979, Molson's found itself in the midst of a public-relations nightmare when the beloved Winnipeg Jets experienced a shut-out that had nothing to do with good goaltending.

The Montreal Canadiens had just voted against expansion to allow four WHA teams, including the Jets, from joining the NHL. The Habs were owned by Molson's and almost immediately a backlash occurred. Hockey fans across the country were outraged, but in Winnipeg and Edmonton they were especially incensed. Local media jumped on the story and soon there were calls for a boycott. Winnipeg Jets management showed their disapproval by terminating Molson's sponsorship of the Three Star selection. It even went so far that someone shot a hole in a window of the brewery on Furby Street. In hotel bars across the city patrons were asking for "anything but a Canadian" and sales began to plummet.

Morgan McCammon, president of Molson's, flew into the city to address the issue and reassure the public that it was all a misunderstanding. McCammon stressed that it wasn't expansion that Montreal was against, only the proposal that was on the table. With encouragement from the brewery, the NHL owners met again in New York and on March 22, a second vote was held. This time Montreal and Vancouver voted in favour and Winnipeg rejoiced in finally having a team in the NHL.

The boycott cost the brewery a temporary five percent loss in sales and at one point Ed Mazur, sales manager, worried his brewery was finished in Manitoba. Less than a month after the second vote, Molson's bought the promotion rights for the Jets for $3.5 million and the red white and blue were happily back together again.

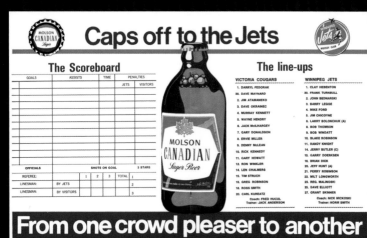

Ad from a 1971 Winnipeg Jets Western Canada Hockey League program.

CAPTAIN BLUE AND HIS BLUE BOMBER

Under Jack Labatt's leadership in Manitoba, his sales and promotion department were given much more of a free hand and indeed urged to be more creative than one would expect from the formerly conservative brewery. In that era next to "Ask for a Blue," perhaps their most visible success was Captain Blue and the Blue Bomber.

One of the most effective advertising moves Labatt's made when entering Manitoba was the sponsorship deal they signed with the Winnipeg Blue Bombers. One idea Labatt's had was to create a cannon that could be fired to celebrate touchdowns. They had it specifically made around a firing mechanism designed by an RCMP gunner in Regina. The cannon was nicknamed the "Big Blue Boomer."

They felt there was a need for a spectacular vehicle that could be used at fairs, festivals, parades and at Blue Bomber games. Labatt's proposed a World War One biplane to be piloted by Captain Blue. Jim Rempel built the

fiberglass plane which uses a Volkswagen engine. Costumes were designed to provide an exotic pilot's uniform. The real challenge was to find someone who could fill the Captain Blue role both in representing the Blue Bombers and Labatt's. The man they chose was Gary Potter, the Labatt's rep in Brandon. Part of the reason for choosing him was his past experience as a rodeo clown, (Rempel became the second Captain Blue a year later.)

Captain Blue and his plane were a smash hit at their first appearance at a Blue Bomber home game in October, 1978 against the Edmonton Eskimos. Winnipeg Tribune sports editor Jack Matheson wrote, "In over 30 years of covering football, that's the first time I saw a crowd give a standing ovation to a team mascot." Labatt's

> In that era next to "Ask for a Blue," perhaps their most visible success was Captain Blue and the Blue Bomber.

people were ecstatic as John Morgan said, "I saw 25,000 fans rise as one and give a rousing cheer for Captain Blue and the Blue Bomber. It was a proud day for everyone at Labatt's Manitoba Brewery."

Since then, besides being at every Blue Bomber home game, Captain Blue and his Blue Bomber have been in numerous fairs, Winnipeg's Santa Claus Parade, featured on the CBC and in Grey Cup Parades across Canada.

Vanishing Acts

As the industry moved into the 1970's, a few long standing traditions fell to the wayside.

NHL Cards: Contrary to the name, this item didn't have anything to do with hockey. The "Not Home, Leave Card" was hung on a customer's doorknob to notify them that they had missed their delivery. Home delivery ended in the mid 1970's.

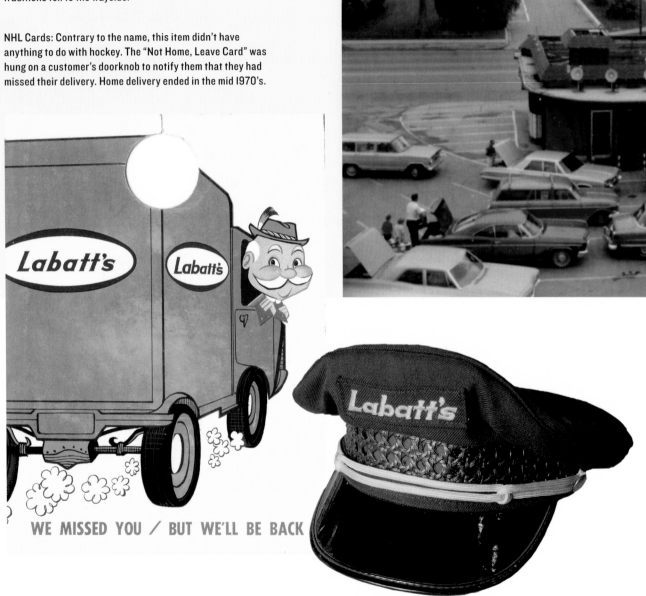

WE MISSED YOU / BUT WE'LL BE BACK

Brewery Retail Stores: Otherwise known as Cash & Carry Stores, every brewery in town had one and they served as a convenient alternative to the hotel vendor. Shea's built this store on Osborne Street in 1947 and was a precursor to the hotel beer stores we have today. Labatt's operated this outlet until 1979.

Brewery employees were some of the last to wear the military style uniforms that were customary among delivery men, service station attendants and taxi drivers. Donning jackets with the company crest, neck ties and topped up with a peaked cap, the delivery man had an official and professional look that has all but disappeared today. This type of uniform was phased out in the late 1970's.

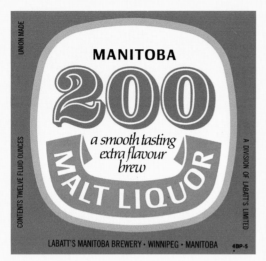

Manitoba 200 was Labatt's entry into the malt liquor category. Brewed to mark the province's entry into its second hundred years, the brand sported a higher alcohol content, as did the other malt liquors from O'Keefe and Uncle Ben's. It had a relatively short run from 1970 - 1977.

Welcome to Heidelberg

Brewed from the choicest hops and malt and pure spring water

Welcome to the taste of Heidelberg! So bright, so lively, so brimful of flavour it brings more enjoyment to your drinking pleasure.
· Welcome to the quality of Heidelberg! Heidelberg is brewed from only the best ingredients . . . the finest golden barley malt, the

choicest high prime Hallertau hops from Bavaria . . . and pure spring water.
Take your thirst to Heidelberg today. You'll get a happy welcome that will never wear out because every glass of Heidelberg is as crisp and satisfying as your first.

VB5266

So much more to enjoy

Every baby boomer will remember the Heidelberg keg shaped beer bottles of the early 1970's. When Canadian Breweries began to licence Heidelberg in Ontario in 1970, it packaged the new beer in an innovative keg shaped bottle. Sales took off, but by the time the new beer became available to Manitobans in 1971, there was pressure from the government to ban the new bottle shape. Worried that the proliferation of a variety of different bottle shapes would complicate the recycling process, the government forced the brewery to revert to the standard compact bottle in late 1971. Soon the public began devising other ways to use the defunct beer bottle. One creative use was to cut the neck off and glue it to the bottom of the bottle. The result wasn't very attractive as far as beer mugs go.

New products were introduced, but for variety of reasons, never became long lasting favourites.

Labatt's was the last of the big breweries to regularly produce a seasonal bock beer. Beginning in 1979, Super Bock appeared every spring until the mid 1980's.

LIGHT BEERS

As is always the case, when a popular phenomenon takes America by storm, Canada is soon to follow. After the success of Miller Lite in the United States, Labatt Breweries launched Cool Spring in 1973. Advertised as Canada's first light beer, the concept wasn't exactly new. Low alcohol beer had been forced upon the public during Prohibition, but now there was a new spin on the old idea. Instead of a watered down near beer, this new version was promoted as a healthy lifestyle choice. The Manitoba Liquor Control Commission certainly bought into this notion. In 1975, when Labatt's began brewing Cool Spring at its Notre Dame Avenue plant, the commission subsidized the brand by dropping the price 65 cents a dozen. The media questioned whether low ball beer was just a lower-priced novelty, but light beer quickly became a bright spot in an otherwise stagnant market. In 1978, Carling O'Keefe and Molson's entered the fray with Hi-Lite, Cascade and Crown Lager. About this same time, Labatt's came out with a new brand that raised the question of what exactly defined a light beer.

Labatt's Special Lite was promoted as a light beer with a full flavour, but the government decided Labatt's new four percent beer wasn't a light beer at all—at least not by their standards. Although light beers are considered to have fewer calories and alcohol content than regular beer, under federal food and drug regulations, light beer must be between 1.2 and 2.5 percent alcohol by volume. The government charged Labatt's couldn't legally claim their beer to be a special light or lite, no matter how it was spelled. After going all the way to the Supreme Court, the Labatt's brand was allowed to be sold despite the government's regulation and shortly after the "special" was dropped from the name. Labatt's Lite has since gone on to be a Manitoba favourite and continues to sell well in the province. As for the other brands; they would be overshadowed by the next big innovation to the market—the introduction of American beer.

The Light Beer Name Game

Carling O'Keefe's entry into the light beer category hit a snag when the Miller Brewing Company filed suit for trademark infringement. Miller believed the Highlite name was too similar to their High Life and Lite brands. The Canadian brewer compromised by changing the name to Trilight.

Molson's Crown was marketed in Western Canada until 1981, when it was replaced by Molson Light, a best seller in Ontario.

In 1981, Labatt's Special Lite became Labatt's Lite after a lengthy court case with federal regulators. The government objected to the word "special" because the brand's alcohol content was higher than than the government standard of 2.5 percent.

Associated Beer Distributors Ltd/
Brewers Distributor Ltd

Sixteen years after Brewery Products shut its doors, Manitoba's three breweries decided the idea of a central distribution system was worth another try. The obvious problems of having more than one brewery delivering their products to a customer at the same time proved to be counter-productive and costly. In April of 1976, Associated Beer Distributors Limited opened a warehouse at 1400 Saskatchewan Avenue. Jointly owned by Labatt's, Carling O'Keefes and Molson's; ABD also handled Uncle Ben's product for a short time until they went into receivership.

In August of 1995, ABD consolidated with beer distributors across Western Canada to form Brewers Distributor Ltd. From its inception, the distributor handled products from its shareholders, but since 2000 has handled imported beer as well as domestic brews from Sleemans, Big Rock and Great Western. In August of 2008, BDL moved to a bigger 193,000 square foot warehouse in order to store and ship the more than 330 different brands and package sizes combined.

Driver Mike Anthony and Charlie Trelka head out with a load of beer on the first day back to work after the beer strike of 1978.

An artist rendering of ABD's warehouse at Empress and Saskatchewan Ave: After 32 years and a few expansions, this building proved to be too small for the huge number of product lines the company was handling. Starting out with only 3 packages sizes in 1976, the consumer now has more than 10 sizes in both bottles and cans to choose from.

THE GREAT BEER STRIKE OF 1978

You don't know what you've got until it's gone. Manitoban's suffered through the summer of 1978 when the local beer supply suddenly dwindled. Brewery workers were locked-out for seven weeks, leaving beer lovers to find other ways to quench their thirst. They turned to American beer when the MLCC began importing the more expensive brands like Schmidt and Olympia. The lockout ended on July 26 and beer began to hit the streets the next day.

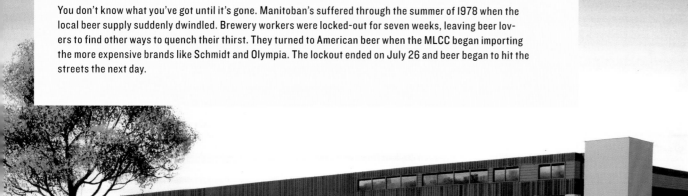

STANDARD LAGER:
A MANITOBA ORIGINAL

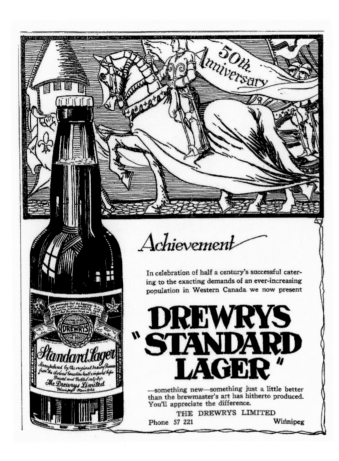

Standard Lager was introduced in 1927 to celebrate the brewery's fifty year anniversary. For a time, Standard was also brewed at Drewrys Ltd Saskatoon operation.

Some people can't believe it's still around—others couldn't live without it. No other beer sold in Manitoba today has as much local history behind it as Standard Lager. It has lived through the Dirty Thirties and World War II. It's been tossed about from one brewery to another and today is enjoying a renaissance with the younger crowd. It still lives on in a market dominated by beers born in other countries. In the 1980's, it fought its look-alike, Budweiser, in a long drawn out battle for home turf.

Standard Lager was introduced in 1927 to celebrate Drewrys fifty years in business. It was to be a "New Standard" in brewing. Along with its cousin, Pelissiers Club Beer, Standard made the cut when Winnipeg's breweries were bought out in the 1950's. Most local brands hung on for awhile, some like Select and White Seal for a quite awhile. Eventually the older brands were dropped in favour of national brands.

Introduced shortly after Edward L. Drewry retired and the Drewrys Limited was formed, Standard soon became the brewery's flagship brand until Carlings took over in the 1950's. One might say its greatest moment came in the 1980's when Labatt's secured the license to brew Budweiser in Canada but was unable to sell it in Manitoba. Carling O'Keefe threw a wrench into Labatt's plan with legal action, claiming

> Carling O'Keefe threw a wrench into Labatt's plan with legal action, claiming Budweiser's "King of Beers" slogan infringed on their KingsBeer brand; a poor-selling beer from Ontario formally brewed by Dow.

Budweiser's "King of Beers" slogan infringed on their KingsBeer brand; a poor-selling beer from Ontario formally brewed by Dow. In response to this, Anheuser-Busch countered with allegations that Standard Lager infringed on the Budweiser label. Labatt's was ordered to remove the "King of Beers" from their Budweiser bottles but the Standard Lager case went all the way to the Federal Court of Appeal. The judge ruled that indeed the Standard label was similar to Budweiser but Anheuser-Busch had waited too long to file a complaint. According to evidence, Carlings had used the label since the 1950's with Budweiser's knowledge and without objection. The court ruled the two brands could co-exist in Manitoba.

Beer drinkers across the country were downing Labatt's version of Budweiser since the beginning of the decade but in May of 1988, almost eight years later, Manitobans could finally get a taste of what would eventually become Canada's best-selling beer. Little old Standard Lager had managed to hold off the King of Beers and keep some cash in Carling O'Keefe's pocket—at least for a time!

Enjoyed by a loyal following throughout the generations, the brand eventually fell into the category called "Grandpa's beer." Since the older generation tends not to be the target audience for beer advertisers, you won't find ads with scantily clad women in Standard Lager tank tops. It's the anti-Bud and perhaps that's why it has a new following among the 18 to 24 set. It's off the cultural radar and that's just what appeals to the kind of people who like to go against the beer grain. A few young hipsters have gone so far as to get Standard tattoos and let's hope their taste in beer lasts as long as those "tat's" will. In 2009 Molson's decided to de-list the 24 carton case and a few drinkers went into an absolute panic not realizing that 12 pack bottles were still available.

An ink blotter from the 1940's.

OLD STOCK ALE · REFINED ALE · EXTRA STOUT

ESTABLISHED 1877

With this new group of drinkers and the people who have always called it their own, Standard doesn't seem to be going away anytime soon. The irony in this story is that Standard is only available in Manitoba but it is now brewed by Molson in Toronto.

Standard had been available in every type of bottle the local market produced since its inception.

Miller was an instant hit when Carling O'Keefe began brewing the popular American beer in Canada. In Winnipeg, the brewery couldn't keep up with the demand and ran this ad apologizing for the shortages.

"THIS BUD'S NOT FOR YOU"

Despite the many changes in the local brewing scene, the 1970's proved to be a slow growth period for the big three. The decade began with a bang. The province lowered the drinking age to 18 in 1970 and that same year beer was allowed at sporting events. Brewery expansions were taking place when both Labatt's and Molson's increased capacity. But by 1974, when the industry suffered its first strike of the decade, beer companies were complaining the market was flat. Government rules, they also charged, were stifling competition. Every place of retail was forced to carry every major brand of beer from each brewery. When Uncle Ben's arrived, the market was instantly split between four breweries instead of three. Prices were on the rise and every increase had to be approved by the MLCC and Manitoba's

---

In the spring of 1980, after losing market share to Molson's, Labatt's announced a licensing agreement with Anheuser-Busch to brew their famous Budweiser brand for the Canadian market.

Public Utilities Board. This type of red tape was always difficult for the breweries to accept. At one point, after losing $200,000 in revenue, the four breweries ganged up and successfully sued the board for delaying their request by a month, leaving the liquor commission to foot the bill.

By the end of the decade, Canada's beer consumption had levelled off. The tail end of the thirsty baby boomer generation had arrived. High taxes, beer strikes and inflation battered

the bottom line and a shake-up was in order. The beginning of the 1980's proved to be another defining moment for Canada's brewing industry.

In the spring of 1980, after losing market share to Molson's, Labatt's announced a licensing agreement with Anheuser-Busch to brew their famous Budweiser brand for the Canadian market. It was a bold move considering the public's biased attitude towards American beer. Canadians have always felt our beer was superior to what most thought were lighter-tasting American brews. It was a rude awakening when Budweiser captured almost seven percent of market share. More remarkable is the fact that Manitoba wasn't included in those figures. The province was shut out from the Bud phenomenon due to the lawsuit involving Standard Lager. When another American beer came to the province, beer drinkers gobbled it up faster than the brewery could make it.

After the success of Budweiser's introduction in Canada, Carling O'Keefe was not about to sit back and watch their profits dwindle. Having sunk to third place from their heyday in the 1960's, the brewery countered by securing the Canadian rights to Miller High Life in 1983. Miller took the province by storm with its American-style tall bottle. In the hot summer of 1983 beer sales soared and Carling O'Keefe couldn't keep up with the demand. Full pallets of Miller flew off trucks from the brewery and straight onto a delivery truck headed for the hotels. Production problems with the cross-shaped neck label put the brewery further behind. In what was most likely a first, the brewery ran ads apologizing for the delays. The "Champagne of Beers" became the most successful launch in the province's brewing history. Of course there were naysayers claiming the locally brewed product didn't taste like the real thing. Free Press columnist Gordon Sinclair ran a casual taste test which only proved one thing; not everyone's tastes are the same.

Miller's introduction sealed the fate of the stubby bottle. Gradually, breweries shifted to a variety of taller bottles in different shapes and sizes. The great beer war of the 1980's was in full swing as new package sizes, canned beer and twist-off caps hit the market. By the time Manitoban's were finally able to sip a northern Bud in 1988, another threat to Canada's identity was about to occur. Manitoba's brewing industry was about to get hit hard.

WINNIPEG

THIS BUD'S FOR YOU.

Breakthrough!

**Molson Canadian.
Molson Light.
Now in aluminum cans!**

Labatt's took the industry by surprise when they introduced the Swift-Off cap. The innovation was a well kept secret until the caps were matched with the new private mold bottles in 1984. Later to be known as the twist-off cap, they soon became the standard for the industry. Private mold bottles came in different shapes depending on the brewery and many had the brewery name embossed on them. All the different bottle types proved to be too costly for the breweries. Associated Beer Distributors opened a separate facility for bottle sorting which ran for a number of years before the breweries switched to an industry standard long neck bottle in 1992.

In 1988, after an eight year lawsuit, Budweiser was finally made available to beer drinkers in Manitoba. Today the brand is not only a best seller in the province but is the number one beer in Canada.

Beer Bottle Battle

The beer wars of the 80's and 90's pushed aside the beloved stubby in favour of long neck and private mould bottles. Here are a few of the other events of that era.

- Labatt's held a mock funeral at the St. Boniface Hotel for White Seal in May of 1990. The venerable brand was discontinued after 65 years of service.

- In 1985, Molson introduces Coors and Coors Light to the Canadian market. After declining sales in Manitoba, Molson Canadian gets a new taste in 1988. Consumer taste tests revealed Canadian was too bitter for Manitoba beer drinkers. The brewery claimed the "new" Molson Canadian was an upgrading of the Manitoba version to national standards.

- Molson Special Dry was introduced in April of 1990. With this entry into the "Dry" beer category, Molson Dry soon helped rejuvenate the breweries lackluster sales in Manitoba. It came in a new painted label design, as did Labatt's Dry and Black Label.

BBO · BOTTOM BOTTLE OPENER

The Bottom Bottle Opener was devised as a better solution to Labatt's early version of the twist-off cap, which was difficult to open. It did nothing for Miller's slumping sales and was eventually dropped.

After Labatt's shocked the industry by introducing the twist-off cap, Carling O'Keefe countered with their own innovations. In 1985, the rip-cap was used on Old Stock stubbys before this bottle type was discontinued. Uncle Ben's had used a rip cap in the 1970's.

CLOSURE

In the midst of the battle between Canada's brewing giants in the 1980's, another important event was taking place. Brian Mulroney's Progressive Conservative government was negotiating a free trade agreement with the United States that would have a devastating impact for breweries across the country. For decades the provinces imposed inter-provincial trade barriers to protect local breweries from outside competition. Breweries were required to have a plant in each province where their beer was sold

> Before the breweries could compete on even ground with the Americans, the Canadian companies would have to become leaner and meaner.

while imported beer was subjected to price mark-ups. This policy had worked to the advantage of the big three in the past, but it also made for an inefficient industry.

When the trade agreement between the two countries came into effect on January 1, 1989, there was a sigh of relief in breweries across the land. The Canadian brewers had lobbied for an exclusion from the agreement, claiming their inefficiencies would doom them to the big mega breweries to the south. Before the breweries could compete on even ground with the Americans, the Canadian companies would have to become leaner and meaner. It happened sooner than anyone would have thought. On January 18, 1989, in an announcement that stunned the industry, Molson's merged with Carling O'Keefe to become the largest brewery in the country.

Although the new company took the Molson name, no one was sure which brewery plant in Winnipeg would survive. Most speculated the older Redwood location would be axed, so it was a surprise when news came of the Furby Street's plant pending closure within the year. The decision was based on Redwood's potential for expansion. At the time it was estimated that 50 workers would lose their jobs while others would be integrated into the Redwood plant.

Now known as the Big Two, Molson's and Labatt's were determined to continue their war

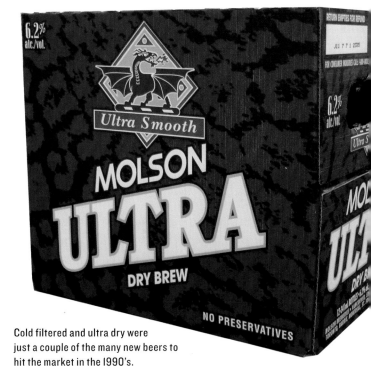

Cold filtered and ultra dry were just a couple of the many new beers to hit the market in the 1990's.

for top spot. By the early 1990's, sales were slumping again and so the public was inundated with new terms like Dry, Ice, Cold Filtered and Draft Beer in bottles. It was a game of one-upmanship. When one brewery introduced a new beer, the other was sure to follow. While the consumer was left in a state of confusion from all these different choices, it also left the breweries with huge costs for promotion and advertising. While this new phase of the war was going on, the issue of free trade hadn't gone away.

In 1991, officials of the General Agreement on Tariffs and Trade (GATT) ruled that the exemption from the free trade agreement that Canada's brewing industry had enjoyed for the last three years was in violation of the GATT and that the trade of beer between the provinces must be open. In 1995, with the ruling in place, Molsons and Labatt's could now shed the excess capacity that was spread over the country. That same year, John Labatt Limited was bought by Belgian brewing giant Interbrew and the axe began to fall.

Back in 1970, with the flair of a Hollywood pageant, Premier Ed Schreyer climbed into a helicopter parked at the Legislative Building and flew to the sod turning for Labatt's new brewhouse on Notre Dame and Keewatin Street. It

Labatt brewhouse employees stand among the silent equipment, 1996.

was the final stage for the breweries' expansion into the province and no one there could have thought that a mere 26 years later the brewery would close its doors. In May of 1996, the brewery fell silent having run out of beer the week before. Most of the company's products would now come from Edmonton. It was a tough blow for the 121 workers who either lost their jobs or were forced to

In 1995, with the ruling in place, Molsons and Labatt's could now shed the excess capacity that was spread over the country.

retire. Most considered working for a brewery a lifetime job and looked upon their co-workers as family.

There was a bit of a backlash among consumers but it didn't last. Drinkers thought they would boycott Labatt's by drinking Kokanee—not realizing it's a Labatt's product too. Molson's, on the other hand, took advantage of the situation with their "Brewed with Pride" campaign. After injecting $1.3 million worth of upgrades to the Winnipeg plant in 1996, which helped extinguish fears of more closures, the Proudly Brewed in Manitoba motto failed to sway Labatt's loyal customers. A year later Labatt's had maintained their 65 percent market share and with Molson operating at 50 percent capacity, the inevitable happened.

On January 28, 1997 Molson announced the Redwood plant would close in August. Disillusioned, many of the 91 workers felt betrayed by Manitoba beer drinkers and thought they should have had more support. Winnipeg beer drinkers proved to be too loyal to their brands, but in the end brewery shutdowns were bound to happen. The industry was changing, as it always does, and rationalization could not be held back. Fortunately, there was a quiet revolution happening all over the country. Beer drinkers were given an alternative to what the Big Two were offering. In Manitoba, a young brewer named Richard Hoeschen decided to introduce microbrewing to the local market. Regardless of the big guys leaving us behind, Manitoba's brewing industry wasn't going to die.

Molson employees in front of the 120 year old Redwood plant.

In 1999 these three men revitalized the local brewing industry
after Molson and Labatt's shut down their Manitoba plants.

Left to right: Gary De Pape, Richard Hoeschen, and Doug Saville

CHAPTER 12

SMALL BREWERY, BIG FLAVOUR

MICRO AND CRAFT BREWING

In the spring of 2009, the Labatt Brewing Company introduced Bud Light Lime to the Canadian market. It was wildly successful and they sold boatloads of the stuff. Quite literally in fact because Labatt's imported the bottled versions of the sweet tasting brew all the way from the United Kingdom. The brewery couldn't keep up with the demand and of course when the consumer can't buy what they want— they want it even more. Soon, other companies were jumping on the bandwagon with their own versions of the beer with a hint of lime.

Fort Garry's Orest Horechko (left), Roger Palmer and brewmaster Matthew Wolff.

The Russell Brewing Company's Fort Garry plant rushed in to fill the void with Cactus Lime Lager. Orest Horechko, general manager at Fort Garry was quoted as saying, "When you're small and the big boys throw you a bone, you take it." On the other side of town Dave Rudge, brewmaster at Half Pints Brewing Company, was asked by Free Press reporter Geoff Kirbyson if he would market a lime beer and his response was typical of the rebellious craft brewer; "It's a microbreweries

job to set trends, not follow them. If you really want a lime taste in your beer that badly, pick up a good beer and cut up some actual limes. It's really not that difficult."

The onslaught of Bud Light Lime proved to be another in a long line of challenges small breweries face when living in the shadows of the big multinational companies. The fashion in which these two breweries handled the situation illustrates just how different they are from

each other. For Dave Rudge and other craft brewers, Bud Light Lime is a perfect example of the light tasting, mass marketed beers that spawned the creation of the microbrewery industry in the first place. Small craft brewers like Half Pints aren't interested in competing toe to toe with the big boys and so Dave Rudge shrugged it off as just another fad. Fort Garry took a different path. Ever since Richard Hoeschen

Microbrewing pioneer John Mitchell at work draining the mash tun.

built his 24,000 square-foot, 40,000 hectolitre plant in 1999, the brewery has always set its sights on the larger market. Through mergers, buyouts, and the popularity of the specialty beers, Fort Garry has slugged it out every step of the way.

As the craft brewing industry flourishes in other provinces, Manitoba has proven to be a tough beer nut to crack. It's been that way from the very beginning. The trials and tribulation of microbrewing in Manitoba started not with

In 1978, Frank wrote a scathing article on the state of the brewing industry for Harrowsmith magazine. The article condemned Canada's brewing giants for making generic tasteless beer aimed at the common denominator.

Richard Hoeschen, but ten years before in 1984. The seed was planted in British Columbia, the epicentre of microbrewing in Canada.

Craft beer lovers in Canada owe a great deal of gratitude to Frank Appleton and John Mitchell. The two British expatriates are considered to be the founding fathers of microbrewing in Canada. In 1972, Appleton was a microbiologist and quality control supervisor with Carling O'Keefe's when he turned his back on the ruling beer establishment to become a brewing consultant and freelance writer. He combined his skill as a brewer with a sharp sense of wit. This talent proved to be potent. In 1978, Frank wrote a scathing article on the state of the brewing industry for Harrowsmith magazine. The article condemned Canada's brewing giants for making generic tasteless beer aimed at the common denominator. Writer Ian Coutts called Appleton's commentary, "the Canadian beer drinkers' declaration of independence." Three years later when the article was brought to the attention of John Mitchell, it sparked the beginning of a new era for brewing in Canada.

John Mitchell was co-owner and manager of the Troller Pub on Horseshoe Bay and had an affinity for the ales he enjoyed while living in England. During a trip back to Britain in 1981, Mitchell was influenced by a new movement called the Campaign for Real Ale. When he returned, he was determined his Troller Pub should brew its own beer. He also knew Frank Appleton could help make it happen.

The first challenge Mitchell was forced to deal with concerned B.C.'s liquor laws. One old law from the days after Prohibition stated brewery owners could not own an establishment with a liquor license. After securing an amendment to the law governing brewery licenses, Mitchell was able to build his brewery across the street from his pub. In 1982, the Horseshoe Bay Brewery and Troller Pub became an instant success. A year later, Mitchell was invited to help found Spinnakers in Victoria. Again, Frank Appleton's expertise was put to use. After a few regulatory changes were made, Spinnakers became the first in-house brewpub in Canada.

John Mitchell and Frank Appleton paved the way for others. The Granville Island Brewing Company became Canada's first microbrewery in 1984 and soon other small breweries were sprouting up across the country. Frank Appleton went on to a successful career as a brewery consultant and designer. He served as a mentor and builder for many of British Columbia's most successful microbreweries and in his long career has had many awards bestowed upon him. But there is one venture in Manitoba that didn't pan out as well as Frank would have liked.

NOBLEMAN BREWING FRIDAYS AT THE TRAVELODGE

In 1984, the newspapers described it as Canada's first federally licensed brewpub. Colin Noble, owner of the Niakwa Travelodge Hotel, said his mini brewery at the hotel would make real British style beers with no chemical preservatives. The brewpub was called "Fridays" and it was a brand new concept for Manitoba. Up to this point, the only local beers with a full bodied taste were Country Club Stout and Velvet Cream Stout, both produced by Labatt's. Unfortunately, Friday's failed to find a following. In a letter to Dave Craig, Frank Appleton described what happened at the Niakwa.

What was the real story behind the rapid opening/closure of this brewpub, you ask? I would say it was an idea before its time in Winnipeg, foisted on an unsuspecting and unappreciative pub crowd in an unsuitable area. Having products that were somewhat variable in the beginning didn't help.

I got my education in microbiology and brewing in England. I worked eight years for Carling O'Keefe in Vancouver before leaving in disgust at the products and politics of the majors in 1972. I then became a freelance writer, and through seeing one of my articles, The Underground Brewmaster, in Harrowsmith magazine in 1981, the now-legendary John Mitchell came to see me, and asked if I would help him design and build a brewery to supply his pub, The Troller Pub, with "real ale" in the British tradition.

The result was Canada's first brewpub, opened in 1982.

By 1984, Mitchell was working on another brewpub in Victoria, B.C. – Spinnakers. Once again, I was his technical help. The plant was built by SPR in England. Colin Noble came out to see the great success Mitchell was enjoying with his fine line of British beers, and decided the same idea would work just as well in his Travelodge beer parlour (what a fatal assumption!) He also ordered a plant from SPR, and SPR asked me if I would oversee the startup, which I did.

When I arrived in Winnipeg, I was a bit surprised at the pub crowd we thought to delight and amaze with our British beers. To say it was schizophrenic was putting it mildly. The daytime scene reminded me of the typical beer parlour crowd of Vancouver in the sixties – blue collar, baseball caps, raised on a steady diet of Canadian corn adjunct lager and distrustful of anything new. After the obligatory supper closing from 6 - 7 p.m. the bar was transformed into a Disco, with 90 decibel music, swirling coloured lights and a crowd who were barely into their twenties! The drink of choice for these folks was light beers and wine coolers. Neither set looked like the Anglophile drinkers of West Vancouver and Victoria who had welcomed our ales with glee.

The brewing plant was a showpiece of polished stainless steel, and beautifully displayed

CANADA'S FIRST IN HOUSE MINI BREWERY

Fridays

AT THE TravelLodge

WINNIPEG

JULY 1984

Fridays beer mat (coaster)

behind glass along one side of the pub, in a setting of red tile. However, the floor plan had been laid out by SPR and Noble with no input from me. The behind-the-scenes operation left much to be desired; for example there were no drains in the conditioning cellar, and the brewhouse and two cellar areas were so far apart we had to wear walkie-talkie headsets when transferring beer! There were also no water filters

> The daytime scene reminded me of the typical beer parlour crowd of Vancouver in the sixties – blue collar, baseball caps, raised on a steady diet of Canadian corn adjunct lager and distrustful of anything new.

whatever for filtering the product water, and when I tasted (and smelled the chlorine) in the local water supply, I started to get concerned. I'd fill the brew kettle with "clean" cold water and noted I could not see the bottom, the water was so murky. Spring in Winnipeg! The startup of the plant went without a hitch, but there were other concerns. It was an article of faith with Mitchell and myself that we would produce better beers by not filtering them, but achieving clarity by fining and aging. This leaves beer much superior in body and flavour. But Noble had not purchased nearly enough tanks to treat his beers this way, so filtration was the only alternative.

The first beers were off as a result, not what I had hoped for, but one wonders if the reception would have been different if they had been; the daytime crowd were reluctant to even try something if it was called an ale, and the disco crowd found our products too heavy. "Well, brew a lager," was Colin Noble's reaction to this. I spent a farcical few days trying to get some lager yeast from the Carlings plant in Winnipeg, (they turned us down) before ordering and culturing my own strain. We tried, but the plant (with open fermenters and minimal aging tank space) was not designed for lagers, especially all-malt lagers, and they were not a success. The two products we did best were a light blonde ale and a brown ale.

The brewer I trained, Peter Wong, took a lot of flak, a lot of pressure, and even some behind-the-back snide comments about "the Chinese brewmaster." Poor Peter! He tried his best, but had no previous knowledge of brewing, being one of the bar staff who Noble seconded to me to learn brewing – all in the space of a couple of weeks. It was a steep learning curve for Peter, and more than most people could have managed. When it looked like things were running okay, Noble would send me home to B.C. – then a few weeks later I would be getting desperate phone

Frank Appleton in front of Fridays' brewing equipment.

calls from Peter that something had gone wrong with the beer. Trying to figure out just what had gone wrong from a distance of a thousand miles over the phone when talking to a guy with an Asian accent and no real knowledge of brewing terminology! It was more in the realm of clairvoyant than brewmaster.

Frank Appleton's experience at Fridays served him well in later years. He wouldn't make the same mistakes again and was resolved to have a significant input regarding floor plans, and plant designs before accepting any future jobs.

Fridays at the Travelodge closed in less than a year. Perhaps Colin Noble was ahead of his time

in this province. In an interview with the Free Press in 1992 he said, "Quite often the guy who pioneers these things isn't the guy who makes money on it." With a view that was slightly different than Frank Appleton's, Noble went on to say government regulations, advertising restrictions and a lack of publicity killed his business. "I made marvelous ales, I just couldn't sell them." Had he opened in a more suitable location and with a bit more planning, Winnipeg's first brewpub might have had a better future. It was ten years later before someone else thought Manitoba was ready to join the micro-beer phenomenon.

RICHARD HOESCHEN AND THE FORT GARRY BREWING COMPANY

Back in 1960, when Molson's bought out the little brewery on Furby Street, no one would have predicted the Fort Garry name would still be in use a half century later. That Molson's gave back the name to a young man with brewing in his heritage and a dream in his heart was a miracle in itself; never mind the fact his brewery was still in business years after Molson's left town. Richard Hoeschen's dream lives on, but it hasn't been easy.

Hoeschen was supposed to follow in his father's footsteps and go into medicine. Before dropping out of pre-med studies he had taken courses in microbiology and bio-chemistry, and never imagined he would use the knowledge again. Brewing wasn't his goal in life, but adventure was. He worked on the D.E.W. Line at Cambridge Bay, NWT, laid track for the railroad and was a roughneck in Alberta's oil patch. He lived in Ecuador, France and England and during those

> Believing the time was right to start his own brewery, Hoeschen moved back to Winnipeg in 1991 and began lining up investors.

travels he developed a taste for fine ales and full-bodied beers.

Once back in Canada he learned the art of brewing at the Vancouver Island Brewing Co. in Victoria, BC. He completed a Quality Control program at the Davis Campus of the University of California and now had a solid background for his next adventure.

In the early 1990's there were about 25 microbreweries in Canada, but none in Manitoba. Believing the time was right to start his own brewery, Hoeschen moved back to Winnipeg in 1991 and began lining up investors.

Confident he could brew quality ale, Richard convinced nineteen investors to contribute $180,000. With a business plan in hand, he secured a loan from the CIBC for an additional $250,000. His intention was to call the new brewery, The Mid Continental Brewing Company, but after talking with his father and being reminded of the family's brewing tradition, he was convinced the Fort Garry name should be resurrected. As Molson owned the name it was thought they would never give it up. Ever confident, Richard flew to Montreal, met with the Molson lawyers and flew home the same day with permission to use the name.

Hoeschen hoped to have his brewery set up in a light-industrial area much like a bakery so

A Frontier label from the original Fort Garry Brewery, 1934.

Richard Hoeschen resurrected the Fort Garry brand in 1995 and a new era of brewing in Manitoba began.

his business would have a storefront public profile. The city changed its zoning by-law to allow for this—not a great idea if you happen to be a tenant next door to a brewery. As good as beer tastes, the smell during the brewing process can't compare to the aroma of freshly baked bread.

After a 3,000 square foot location was found in a strip mall at 1249 Clarence Avenue, Hoeschen began the task of building his new brewery. He purchased equipment from all over the world.

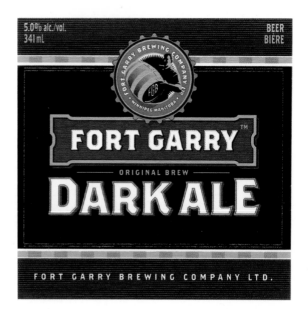

When Richard Hoeschen and Gary De Pape were experimenting with their Dark Ale recipe they rejected the first batch because it wasn't dark enough. Richard wanted his beer to be instantly recognizable across a room. At the time there were no other dark beers widely available in Manitoba.

The stainless steel fermenting tanks came from Victoria. A yeast filter was bought from Italy and his computerized keg filler came from California. With the help from friends, all this complicated equipment was pieced together. Future Agassiz Brewery founder Gary De Pape joined him and the first batch of Fort Garry Draught Ale was rolled out on January 13, 1995.

Hoeschen's plan was to start small and only sell draught beer until he built up his business. Packaged beer would come later when he could afford the huge outlay for bottling equipment. It seemed like a solid business plan, but immediately industry insiders became sceptical. They didn't believe he could survive by just selling draught in a market dominated by "Mobatt's,"

the nick-name Frank Appleton had impudently given the Big Two. One such insider that needed convincing was G.R. "Jeep" Woolley.

Jeep Woolley knew a thing or two about the beer business. During his long marketing and sales career he served for over twenty years with Kiewel/Pelissier and Labatt's Brewery. When Richard approached Woolley on the idea of opening a brewery, the marketing man's first reaction was less than enthusiastic. Quite simply he thought the idea was nuts. But after a trip to Denver to see his son, Jeep dropped by a few liquor stores and a beer distributor. What he discovered opened his eyes to the potential of craft brewing. In Denver customers were paying extra for premium craft brews and the distributor in Fort Collins told him, "Miller pays my bills, but the micros make me money."

With Woolley on board as VP of marketing, Fort Garry's sales went from three accounts to 70 in six months. In the first year of operation they shipped 3,000 kegs of beer. Fort Garry Pale Ale was added in early 1996 and along with Albino Rhino, a recipe brewed exclusively for the Earl's Restaurant chain, Hoeschen's brewery was near full capacity. It wasn't long before the dream got bigger.

In May of 1996, with the closing of Labatt's, Fort Garry became the second largest brewery in town. Not much to boast about since there were only two breweries left in the province, but it was completely home grown—an angle Jeep

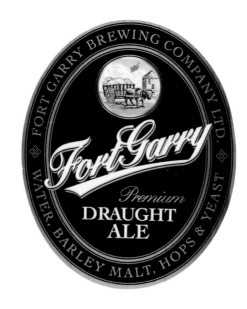

Fort Garry Pale Ale was added in early 1996 and along with Albino Rhino, a recipe brewed exclusively for the Earl's Restaurant chain, Hoeschen's brewery was near full capacity.

Woolley used to full advantage. Two years later, Fort Garry's sales had grabbed 12 percent of the local draught market, selling in 150 hotels and restaurants with sales of $500,000. Molson's had closed the year before and sales were increasing, due partly to a backlash against the big breweries. Hoeschen began a plan to build a new "state of the art" brewery with a bottling line, bottle washer and a completely computerized brewing system. His intention was to become a regional brewery and ship his beers as far Saskatchewan, Northern Ontario, Minnesota and North Dakota.

Fermenting and Aging room.

It was an ambitious undertaking at a time when the market was rapidly changing. Molson's and Labatt's were now large multinational companies with ties to United States and Europe. Speciality beers from other provinces and countries would soon flood the market. By the time Hoeschen built his new brewery there was more competition in town. The River City Brewing Company, Agassiz and Two Rivers were the new upstarts and suddenly the game had changed.

On September 16, 1999, Fort Garry's gleaming new brewery opened at 130 Lowson Crescent. Overlooking Kenaston Boulevard, the plant had a capacity of 40,000 hectolitres a year. With a crowd of well-wishers, Premier Gary Filmon praised Richard as he cut the ribbon for the first

ceremonial beer coming down the line. That first beer was a new recipe with an old name. Frontier Pilsner dates back to 1930 when Richard's great grandfather opened the original Fort Garry Brewery. Frontier took first prize later that year in a competition of new products hosted by the Western Canada Food Industry.

His new brewery was an amazing achievement, but it came with a huge price tag. Before construction began Hoeschen raised $4.75 million in a public offering at $1.00 a share. In spite of increased sales, in June 2000, the brewery announced a loss due mainly to the construction costs and the introduction of Frontier. And then the challenges deepened. The move to markets in Alberta, Saskatchewan, North-West Ontario and

Below: Fort Garry's brewhouse uses a computer controlled brewing system.

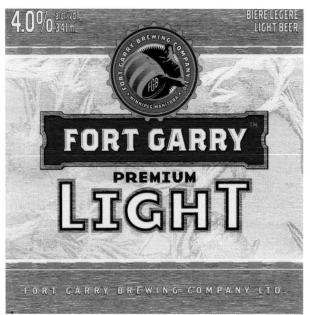

even as far as Chicago were rife with red tape and sales were only boosted by two percent.

The next year the company's bread and butter—draught sales—fell by 25 percent. A change in government policy meant that draught beer could not be served at the lower price Manitobans had known for decades. There was to be no more "Happy Hour."

In March of 2001, Fort Garry entered the light beer category with Fort Garry Premium Light. Light beer represented 34 percent of the market and the competition was fierce. The big players were busy duking it out amongst themselves by offering price incentives and free T-shirts, leaving a small brewery like Fort Garry out in the cold. But it never deterred Hoeschen from trying. In a Free Press interview he said,

"There's got to be people who are tired of drinking Labatt's Lite and Coors Light all the time. I've got a new one for them." The brewery ended up borrowing another $1 million from the Ensis Growth Fund for working capital and a portion was spent on much-needed promotion and advertising in an effort to hike their tiny share of the market. If 2001 proved to be difficult, the next year was disastrous.

The breweries poor performance was the main focus at the company's annual meeting in August of 2002. Gary Coopland, company chairman, was forced to deal with an irate crowd of shareholders who were demanding answers. They had every right to be concerned. In sixteen

months, shares of Fort Garry stock had fallen from 70 cents to an almost worthless six cents. Fort Garry's bottom line wasn't the only reason shares in the company had fallen so far. The one man who might have eased the apprehensions of everyone that night was lying in a hospital bed. In May of 2002, after battling a series of health scares, Hoeschen had been diagnosed with Hodgkin's Disease, a type of lymphoma. On September 16, 2002, exactly one month after the company's annual meeting, Richard Hoeschen died.

Hoeschen dared to dream big in a business that is not kind to newcomers. He came along at a time when brewing in this province was on its last legs and there was a perfect opportunity to fill the void. Unfortunately Hoeschen bet the farm when he could have held back and slowly grown his business. It's a lesson others would soon learn.

- -

"There's got to be people who are tired of drinking Labatt's Lite and Coors Light all the time. I've got a new one for them."—HOESCHEN

THE PUMPHOUSE RESTAURANT AND BREWING CO. THE BREWERY THAT NEVER WAS – PART TWO

Twelve years after the failure of Friday's, the brewpub concept had still not yet taken hold in Manitoba. It wasn't for a lack of trying. City councillor Glen Murray was touting the idea of a brewpub for the exchange district as one of many ways to revitalize the area. By 1997, a number of proposals were floating around to convert the district's empty buildings into brewpubs. There were talks of a brewpub for the Bank of North America at 436 Main Street and a second proposal by a company called the Brewski Brewing Co involved the old Ashdown Hardware store, also on Main Street. But the proposal that garnered the most press was from Leon Moryl, owner of Hands on Design, a local interior and building renovation company. Along with Vancouver businessman Keith Budd, they planned to renovate the old James Avenue Pumping Station. Built in 1906, the station provided a high pressure water system for fighting fires and served the city for almost eight decades before it was closed in 1986.

Adorned with two large arched windows looking out towards the river, the aging building contained massive pumping equipment with giant gears, sunken pits and wrenches so big a crane was needed to lift them. Inspired by a Victoria, B.C. brewpub, Leon Moryl imagined this building transformed into a uniquely decorated gathering place, part restaurant, part museum; a one of a kind building that would draw people downtown. He thought the project was bullet proof. It was close to the theatre district and the city's

Leon Moryl (right), partner Keith Budd (middle) and German brewmaster Stephan Lieftuechter inside the James Avenue Pumping Station, 1999.

brand new ball park. Moryl believed it was a great idea whose time had finally come to Winnipeg. As passionate as he was, it would take more than imagination to get the project off the ground.

In 1997, the Manitoba Liquor Control Commission was woefully behind the times in regards to brewpubs. Colin Noble's Travelodge mini brewery had been federally licensed and was in an established beverage room. Ten years later provincial liquor laws still had no proper category for brewpubs. Neither cabaret nor restaurant licences were suitable for the brewpub concept. A cabaret is required to have four hours of live entertainment daily, while restaurants must have 40 percent of their receipts from food sales. Having said that, the liquor commission seemed to be open the idea and so licensing was the least

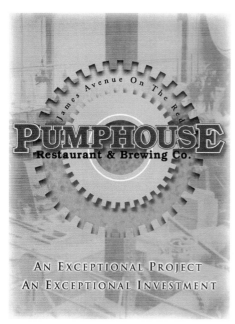

The boarded up pumping station in 2012.

of Moryl's problems. Buying the property was another matter.

Moryl and Budd planned to invest almost $2.5 million to convert the building into a 100 seat brewpub and restaurant for 200 diners. They also wanted to retain the highly prized antique machinery that filled the building as part of a glassed-in museum. In September of 1998, Moryl was granted an option to buy the building from the City of Winnipeg for $310,000. This was less than half of the assessed value of the structure that had been vacant since 1986.

In the following months of planning, Moryl spent $175,000 on the project. Construction estimates were done, which included a detailed inventory of all the assorted pumping equipment. He even went so far as to hire a German brewmaster from Munich. In the process of securing investors, Brenda Andre, owner of nine Perkin's restaurants was brought on board and helped craft a business plan. Government grants were secured and with backing from the newly formed Centre Venture and the Exchange Business Improvement Zone (BIZ) everything seemed in place. And then the city turned it down.

All this preparation had taken time and money. When the proposal was finally put before the city's property and development committee in the fall of 1999, the option to buy the building had expired and Moryl was now offering one dollar for the property. That was the same amount Red River College had paid for an entire block of buildings on Princess Street. Moryl was adamant that for his project to get off the ground, he should get the same kind of deal. The city turned down the proposal because they believed the business plan was weak and doubted Moryl could raise the $2.5 million needed for the project. Moryl was furious and wanted to appeal the decision but felt the cards were stacked against him. By then others were jumping on the bandwagon with their own ideas for the pumping station. With growing interest in the property, the city undoubtedly felt they could get more than one dollar for the building.

After rejecting Moryl's project, the city's property and development committee put out a request for proposals and the next year Jeff Cleven came forward with a plan to spend $3.25 million to convert the pumping station to, of all things, a museum and brewpub. Finally, in November of 2000, the property was sold to the Pony Corral Restaurant chain and was to be renamed the Pumphouse; another 'borrowed' idea from Moryl's original plan. Four years later, the building was still not refurbished. Now known as Waterfront Drive, the area was slated for condominium development and Centre Venture felt a noisy bar on the street was no longer conducive to the area. After buying the property for $150,000, business partners Peter Ginakes and Bob Harris sold the building back to the Centre Venture Development Corporation for over $700,000, but not before donating a valuable Crossley gas engine to the Manitoba Agricultural Museum. The irony of it all is not lost on Leon Moryl. Ignoring the old proverb, "a bird in the hand is worth two in the bush," the city instead held out for a better deal that never materialized and in the process lost half a million bucks.

As of 2012, the building sits empty and boarded up; an eyesore among the row of upscale condominiums that now line the street. With no new development in sight, the building waits for the next visionary to rescue it from decay. In 2012 dollars, Leon Moryl and Keith Budd's dream would cost over $8 million. Whatever happens, its future as a brewpub seems very unlikely.

As of 2012, the building sits empty and boarded up; an eyesore among the row of upscale condominiums that now line the street.

RIVER CITY BREWING CO.

British Columbia's vibrant microbrewing industry has been the inspiration for many entrepreneurs across the country. For the founders of the River City Brewing Co., it was no different.

David Leb and Jason Guralnick had been friends for most of their lives. After graduating from university, Jason went into the family garment business while David moved to Vancouver, where he worked in the restaurant and hospitality industry. While there, he noticed the popularity of the city's many brewpubs. Another friend happened to be the owner of the Horseshoe Bay Brewing Co., in West Vancouver and David was able to see firsthand how beer was brewed. While visiting Winnipeg in April, 1997 the idea of creating a brewpub in a city that had none, was too good to ignore.

After months of planning and research that included visits to brewpubs in Canada and the U.S., the River City Brewing Co., opened in September, 1998 on the corner of Osborne and Stradbrook Avenue. The two 28-year-old businessmen strived to include all the attractive features found in most brewpubs at the time. One unique feature was a giant grain silo. Decorated with the River City logo, the silo was installed in front of the building and filled with over nine metric tons of Western Canadian malted barley.

While most brewpubs offer standard fare, like burgers and fries, River City planned on a higher end menu that included a wide range of American and global dishes. Chef Keith Hosien's menu was extensive and many dishes were cooked with beer brewed on the premises.

Nova Scotia born brewmaster Greg Nash brought a wealth of experience from working at a half dozen brewpubs in the U.S. and his beers were concoctions local drinkers had never seen the likes of. Brews such as Golden Jet Honey Ale, Prairie Dog Ale and Colony Creek Stout, were not only full flavoured, they also had locally flavoured names. Colony Creek Stout was a nod to Patrick Shea's Winnipeg Brewery and the owners were keen on educating patrons on the city's brewing heritage. In the first year, Nash made 16 different beers and the business seemed to be doing well.

The challenges of a brewpub are two-fold. Operating a successful restaurant is difficult enough without the extra responsibility of brewing good beer. When Greg Nash left in the summer of 1999 his expertise was sorely missed. He was replaced by Jason Wagnitz, but his tenure was also short. By 2003, River City had been without a professional brewmaster for some time and business dropped off. In February of that year River City, the city's only brewpub closed its doors.

Please return for deposit to **RIVER CITY BREWING CO.**, 437 Stradbrook Ave., Winnipeg, MB. R3L 0J7

The long tradition of brewing on Osborne Street came to an end when River City closed in 2003. The owners of Regina's Bushwakker Brewpub planned on brewing beer on the premises when they opened the Osborne Village Freehouse but decided it was more cost effective to ship their beer in from Saskatchewan.

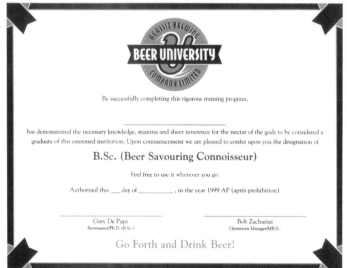

By successfully completing this rigorous training program,

_____

has demonstrated the necessary knowledge, stamina and sheer reverence for the nectar of the gods to be considered a graduate of this esteemed institution. Upon commencement we are pleased to confer upon you the designation of

B.Sc. (Beer Savouring Connoisseur)

Feel free to use it wherever you go.

Authorized this ____ day of _____ , in the year 1999 AP (après prohibition).

_____   _____
Gary De Pape   Bob Zacharias
Brewmaster/Ph.D. (B.Sc.)   Operations Manager/MB.Sc.

Go Forth and Drink Beer!

Top Right: Gary De Pape at the launch of Harvest Haze Hefeweizen. Agassiz held a huge party for 3000 people to celebrate the wheat beer's introduction. Harvest Haze had a pale golden colour and so the Agassiz staff dyed their hair blonde for the occasion.

Left: Agassiz offered tours of the brewery and every participant was given a certificate claiming to have graduated from Beer University.

Top Left: After the departure of Gary De Pape in 2000 Don Harms became general manager.

AGASSIZ BREWING CO.
1999–2002

Gary De Pape found his way into brewing by accident. His interest in quality beers began while playing professional hockey in Germany when he was 19 years old. A few of his teammates were brewers and they introduced him to beers with different styles and tastes. Drinking beer was OK, but as he soon found out, the fun was in making it. Later on, while working as a news reporter in Nanaimo, B.C. he tried a bottle of Herman's Dark Lager from the Vancouver Island Brewery. The fresh, new taste rekindled his love for all malt beers and sparked the idea to start his own brewery.

Back home in Winnipeg a mutual friend introduced De Pape to Richard Hoeschen when Richard was still building his brewery on Clarence Avenue. The two men shared a passion for the art of brewing and became fast friends. De Pape hung out at the brewery every day and while not getting paid, he eventually learned enough to become the brewer at Fort Garry. He worked with Richard on the brewery's first brand, Fort Garry Dark Ale, and later created the recipe for another popular brand, Fort Garry Pale Ale.

As much as De Pape loved working for the brewery, his ambition was stirring. He believed, with his connections from working as a bartender, he could better serve the company working in sales. Hoeschen disagreed. He appreciated De Pape's ability to brew the same beer, batch after a batch, and was cool to the idea of having to find another brewer. But De Pape couldn't be

Above: Gary De Pape hoisting a beer at Fort Garry's Clarence Avenue brewery. Gary was brewmaster at Fort Garry before forming Agassiz in 1998.

held back and soon joined the ranks of the rapidly growing, but crowded microbrewing scene.

So how does a young man of 30 years raise $2 million to start his own brewery? A born salesman, De Pape believed in his dream and as he tells it, "after raising the first $100,000, the rest jumped on board!" Gary wanted to make and market his beers as full bodied with lots of flavour and character, similar to beers brewed in Europe. In essence it would be Winnipeg's first craft brewery—different from Fort Garry or the more mainstream Two Rivers. In fact Agassiz and Two Rivers began bottling beer at virtually the same time—March of 1999.

Most Winnipeg beer drinkers of the 1990's grew up drinking the same beer their fathers did; lagers like Old Vienna, Blue and Canadian.

Bock beer had not been made in Manitoba since the 1980's. Agassiz Bock Beer was available on a limited basis—as per tradition.

When it came to promoting his beer, De Pape had to win over the beer drinking public, the hotel establishment, and even a few people at the liquor commission. His Harvest Haze Hefeweizen was not only difficult to say, most people had never even heard of it before. Hefeweizen, a wheat beer, is unfiltered and cloudy in appearance. De Pape occasionally had to explain to people, "no there is nothing wrong with the beer, that's the way it's supposed to be."

By following the lead from British Columbia's microbrewery industry, which was so much more mature than Manitoba's, De Pape began

MANITOBA CRAFTED
AGASSIZ
Beer/Bière 5% alc./vol.
355 ml
DARK LAGER
Available here.
MANITOBA MADE

Agassiz product line for 1999:
Catfish Cream Ale, Premium
Pilsner, Harvest Haze Hefeweizen,
Bock and Dark Lager.

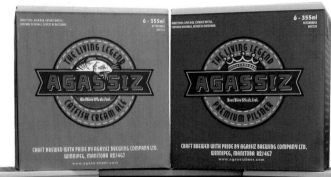

selling his draft in 20 litre kegs to serve lower volume bars and restaurants. By claiming two of the smaller kegs would fit into the same space as a standard 59 litre keg, he won over many sceptical licensees. These kegs allowed bars to offer a greater variety of tapped draught.

Retail space was also at a premium. The national breweries were constantly introducing new brands and package sizes. Breweries like Agassiz and Two Rivers would never have the same clout as Molson's and Labatt's and so acquiring cooler space was always an uphill battle.

De Pape was finally in his element, marketing his beers as "The Living Legend." Each case was embellished with phrases such as, "Congratulations! You've just purchased really good beer.' Or, "Store contents in cool, secret place" The brewery name was also a marketing angle. Lake Agassiz, a glacial lake formed after the last ice age, covered most of Manitoba, parts of Saskatchewan and Northwest Ontario and stretched as far as Minnesota and North Dakota. It was a familiar, refreshing name, even if the beer wasn't made from cold melted glacial ice.

In what has been a common occurrence with many breweries in Manitoba's past, De Pape's vision for Agassiz differed from those who also held an interest in the company.

The CBC Television series "Venture" spent a better part of a year filming the growing pains the brewery experienced in its first year of production. When it aired in November of 1999 the public and microbrewing wannabe's found out just how hard it was to build a brewery from scratch. Among his problems; setting up a bottling line from Germany with missing parts and instructions that didn't make sense, long gruelling days, and dealing with shareholders demands. The latter proved to be too much for De Pape.

In what has been a common occurrence with many breweries in Manitoba's past, De Pape's vision for Agassiz differed from those who also held an interest in the company. After attempts to increase sales, cut costs and restructure the company were met with limited success, De Pape became so stressed he resigned from the brewery on May 11, 2000. "It all came back to the fact we built a bigger brewery than we should have," said De Pape. "Looking back, I should have just focused on the Winnipeg market. You have to get strong in your own backyard first before the business will thrive. But I was excited, a go-getter."

Don Harms became the new general manager in late 2000. Although Agassiz had used distinctive bottles from the beginning they were not

The award winning
Bison Blonde Lager.

Not only did Gary De Pape want his beer to taste different than everyone else's, he also gave it a distinct bottle shape. After his departure the company changed to the industry standard bottle.

Bison Blonde won gold in the European Light Lager category, besting 15 other entrants including Big Rock and the Belgian-based Interbrew.

re-useable and had to be crushed and recycled. Proving to be too costly, the unique bottles were scrapped and the brewery adopted the industry standard bottle in 2001.

In the following year sales increased and new brands came on line. In July 2001, Agassiz won a gold medal for their Bison Blonde Lager. The event was the Microbrewery Stampede Beer Festival and was held during the Calgary Stampede. Bison Blonde won gold in the European Light Lager category, besting 15 other entrants including Big Rock and the Belgian-based Interbrew. This brand accounted for half of all sales and was a bright spot in an otherwise cloudy outlook.

The hot summer of 2001 was a blessing to Winnipeg's microbreweries. As Orest Horechko of Fort Garry is fond of saying, "The best beer salesman is the big guy in the sky." All three breweries in town recorded record breaking sales, but not one had made a profit. In a Winnipeg Free Press interview Doug Saville explained "We've stemmed the bleeding. We are very close to having a positive cash flow, but by no stretch of the imagination are we making money. It just goes to show how much volume you need in this province to make a dime." By the end of the year Agassiz was filing for creditor protection and looking for ways to stay afloat. In early 2002, Don Harms announced the 9,400 square foot brewing facility in St. Boniface would shut down and three of its brands contracted out to Northern Breweries Ltd. of Sault Ste. Marie, Ontario.

Maple Leaf Distillers' Costas Ataliotis had an ambitious plan to build a regional brewery using the equipment from the former Agassiz brewery.

Under the name New Manitoba Brewing Ltd, Catfish Cream Ale was the last surviving Agassiz brand until it was discontinued in 2010.

It was thought that out of the ashes of Agassiz, a new company would brew beer for the Manitoba market and beyond. After a friendly takeover of the struggling Fort Garry Brewing Company failed to materialize, Maple Leaf Distillers president Costas Ataliotis purchased Agassiz' brewing equipment with a plan to sell beer across the country using the company's liquor distribution network. With the purchase of Phoenix-based Tommy Knockers brewpub equipment and it's recipes, he believed he had enough capacity to market his product in the same fashion as regional breweries like Sleeman and Alberta's Big Rock. Ataliotis was confident he would succeed where others had failed by catering to wider beer drinking market. In the end, Maple Leaf's brewery never got off the ground.

Why, after so much effort, did the brewery fail to materialize? One possible reason was the difficulty with brewing beer in a distillery. Apparently, there is a cross-contamination problem with the fermenting of beers in the same facility were spirits are distilled. Ataliotis considered a different location for his brewhouse and even thought of adding a brewpub to the plans. Had he followed through with the scheme it would have all been in vain. In 2006, Maple Leaf Distillers and its parent company, Protos International was put into receivership under the weight of more than $23 million of debt.

As for Agassiz, they weren't finished yet. Later in 2002, Don Harms and eight of the original shareholders acquired the rights to the Agassiz name and brands and formed a company called the New Manitoba Brewing Ltd. A warehousing and distribution agreement for Manitoba was signed with Fort Garry Brewing and with the beer now being produced in Ontario, the company was able to break into the lucrative Toronto market. The 2006 closure of Northern Breweries Ltd. in Sault Ste. Marie prompted them to move back to Manitoba and a production agreement was signed with the Fort Garry Brewing Co.

Finally in 2010, Catfish Cream Ale, the last surviving brand from the Agassiz stable of beers, disappeared from the market. Fort Garry ended its contract agreement to produce Catfish for the simple reason of over-capacity—a problem Richard Hoeschen would loved to have had ten years earlier. Busy brewing for parent company Russell Brewing Inc, Fort Garry was short of tank space. Catfish was no longer a priority in an ever expanding product line.

Gary De Pape is philosophical about the demise of the brewery once considered to be part a brewing renaissance in the city. He feels his efforts opened the door for craft brewers like Dave Rudge and that may be true to a certain extent. While Agassiz was leaning towards the craft brewing end of the market there was another brewery in town that took a different approach.

TWO RIVERS BREWING COMPANY

When Molson's Redwood Avenue plant ceased production in 1997, most of the 91 employees were left in shock wondering what they would do with the rest of their lives. Doug Saville was not one of them. He was the last in a long line of brewmasters at the 125 year old plant and wasn't ready to pack it in. When visiting microbreweries and brewpubs in other cities, Saville was always fascinated by these smaller plants. The closure of Molson gave the journeyman brewer a chance to start over. Before Molson's shut the doors Saville, along with plant manager Peter Walker and a handful of other brewery employees got together to form a business plan. There were a number of important steps involved before a drop of beer could be made. First on the list; what would they call their new brewery?

In the basement of Doug Saville's North Kildonan home the group mulled over a variety of names. Coincidently, Agassiz and River City were considered. "Northern Lights" was another option before the group finally picked an appropriate name for a Winnipeg brewery— Two Rivers Brewing Co.

By the fall of 1998, there were eight partners and 65 investors involved. Support from the Caisse Populaire de Saint Boniface brought the total to $1.2 million in capital. Although planning for the brewery was done in Saville's basement, it was by no means a "basement operation" as Saville had publicly stated in the newspapers. He noted the partners held a combined 125 years of experience in making beer.

Demolition of the 125 year old Redwood brewery. The chimney was the last structure to be torn down.

As president and general manager, it was Saville's job to find a suitable building for the new brewery. Having worked at the Redwood Avenue brewery for almost 25 years, Doug Saville knew every inch of the Molson plant. Before the old brewery was torn down he tried to buy the newest buildings in the complex. He also wanted various pieces of brewing equipment, but his attempts were in vain. Predictably, Molson's wasn't interested in selling anything to a competitor—no matter how small. Before demolition, Molson's high speed bottling equipment was moved to the Brick Brewing Company's plant in Formosa, Ontario. In 1997, Molson had previously acquired a stake in the Waterloo-based brewery.

Saville also made an offer to buy the old Pic-a-Pop plant with the idea of producing soft drinks and beer—just like the breweries did in the old days. When negotiations fell through the plants equipment went up for auction. Saville managed to buy various pieces of equipment for the brewery and one of them was a bottle-filler for only 500 bucks. The owner was so incensed that his equipment was going for such little cash, he shut the auction down. This $500 filler wasn't just a good deal; it played a key role in the breweries early success.

Two Rivers finally found a home in an existing building at 551 Ferry Road in St. James and the process of putting a brewery together began in earnest. A stroke of luck happened when

Below: Two Rivers president and general manager Doug Saville.

Two Rivers Red was a move towards the specialty beer segment the company wanted to tap into before it merged with Fort Garry.

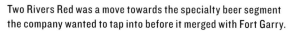

partner Armand Bedard heard about a Quebec brewery, Brasse Monde, closing. They were able to purchase nearly new equipment for $170,000, which included a bottling line and a bottle washer. This was a fraction of the $1 million Fort Garry had laid out for their new bottling line.

One of the most important decisions any brewery makes is the development of a product line. Two Rivers initial plan was to go with a mainstream product instead of entering the speciality beer market most microbreweries target. A marketing survey was done to back up what Saville already knew; the majority of beer drinkers prefer a lager with no taste. But there was no point in trying to compete head on with the

Taste alone wasn't going to set the brewery apart from the majors. They needed another angle and that came in the form of packaging.

nationals and make a Budweiser clone. Instead the brewery developed Two Rivers Lager. Saville described the recipe as a "clean, crisp, clear lager" but with a "little more" taste. Taste alone wasn't going to set the brewery apart from the majors. They needed another angle and that came in the form of packaging.

It had been over two years since beer lovers could twist the cap off a beer bottled in Manitoba. In March of 1999, both Agassiz Brewing and the Two Rivers Brewing Company ramped up their bottling lines to compete in the ever-crowded beer market. Besides bottles, Saville had another weapon up his sleeve. A large supply of 19 litre pressurized soft drink containers he had purchased from the Pic-a-Pop auction would now be used for restaurants, and bars. More importantly, with a deposit, the newly christened "Peg Keg" could be enjoyed at home.

By far the most popular product the brewery hit upon was a bottle different than anything else offered in the province. Stone Cold was a 6.2 percent draught and came in a 2 litre plastic bottle; the same type of soft drink bottle consumers had known since Pepsi first introduced it in the early 1970's. When Stone Cold was introduced in August of 2000, it quickly became their best seller and eventually took 60 percent of their business. Beer purists were horrified by the thought of beer in plastic, but the product was never intended for the connoisseur. Purchased as individual bottles, Stone Cold was marketed as a discount brand and as such quickly boosted the company's bottom line. Following the success of Stone Cold the brewery introduced "The Cold One" a new recipe in a one litre bottle.

Doug Saville showing off the company's products in 2001: Two Rivers was on pace to almost double its annual production due in large part from the sales of its popular Stone Cold and Cold One draught beers.

In early 2002 Two Rivers added a second bottling line to keep up with demand, but after three years in business, the company was still not making money. By this time the brewery held two percent of the market and in order to keep growing Two Rivers needed to expand. Across town Fort Garry was also at a crossroads. After the death of founder Richard Hoeschen the company continued to bleed red ink and was about to go under. A merger was the best option.

AND THEN THERE WAS ONE –
MERGERS, CLOSURES AND BUYOUTS

At the end of the 1990's Manitoba's brewing industry was re-inventing itself. After the closure of the two big breweries in town, a rebirth was in the works. In 1999, the city sported three breweries and one brewpub. A mere four years later the brewpub was closed and Agassiz, now brewing in Ontario, could no longer claim to be homegrown. So, with the merger of Fort Garry and Two Rivers in February of 2003, the province's only brewery could now pool their resources, save money on overhead and hopefully reach profitability.

The deal took seven months to finalize and with the company retaining the Fort Garry name, all ten brands of beer would now be produced under one roof. As president of the newly merged company, Doug Saville faced an uphill battle as he tried to maneuver the company into the black.

The hot summer of 2003 was a blessing for

Under the Minhas Creek banner, the company introduced five recipes to the Manitoba market in the December of 2004.

---

the company, but the two nationals weren't making it easy for Fort Garry. Both Molson's and Labatt's countered the success of Fort Garry's money making Stone Cold by dropping the price of their 750 ml cans by a third.

Good news finally came in 2004 when the company announced its first profit since going public in 1999. It was a small victory because that same year new competition was about to enter the field.

Mountain Crest was a discount brand owned by Ravinder and Manjit Minhas, a brother and sister duo based in Calgary, Alberta. By brewing their beer in Wisconsin on a contract basis, they were able to sell their product at huge mark downs. This would never have been possible in the days when provincial and international trade barriers were still in place. It wasn't long before the two siblings were stirring things up in Manitoba.

Under the Minhas Creek banner, the company introduced five recipes to the Manitoba market in the December of 2004. Four of these new brands were offered in six packs at a whopping $3.00 discount. This immediately ignited a price war in the canned beer segment when the nationals matched that price with their Lucky Lager, Molson Dry and Black Ice six pack cans.

Fort Garry was left in the dust since they weren't canning beer at the time. Saville was quick to point out the commercials Minhas were running advertised a price that didn't include GST, PST or deposit costs. He told Geoff Kirbyson of the Free Press, "People shouldn't get fooled by the smoke and mirrors." Saville wasn't the only one to criticize the creative marketing style Minhas was employing. Labatt took out full page ads accusing the company of misleading the public by posing as a domestic beer company when their product was made in the USA. Manjit Minhas reacted to the ads by saying their company was 100 percent Canadian and had more

of a right to use the maple leaf than the foreign-owned Labatt Breweries. If the public hadn't known there was a beer war going on, they certainly did now!

In 2004, Doug Saville had been reluctant to enter the canned beer segment of the market because of the additional costs of installing a canning line. A year later he couldn't ignore the fact canned beer was gaining momentum and would soon over-take bottles for their share of the market. Then, after shelling out $200,000 for a canning line in the spring of 2005, the brewery faced an additional threat to their bottom line.

After merging with Two Rivers in 2003 Fort Garry's product line carried 10 different brands of beer.

If Fort Garry hadn't had enough to deal with in the summer of 2005, they also had to keep an eye on a regional brewery from Saskatchewan that was nipping at its heels. Much like Two Rivers, the Great Western Brewing Co. was formed when a group of employees took over the old Carling O'Keefe plant in Saskatoon after that company merged with Molson's in 1989. It wasn't the only thing they had in common. Great Western also sold beer in two litre bottles and their product line was very similar to Fort Garry's. It got to the point where there were so many choices it was easy to get lost in the crowd.

In 2007, even though Fort Garry was battle-scarred from joining the previous year's price wars, the company managed to produce two profitable quarters in 2006. Doug Saville was confident the brewery could finally celebrate its first-ever profitable year. The plant was efficiently run but only operating at about 65 percent capacity. Because of this fact, it began to attract interest from a smaller brewery in British Columbia.

The Russell Brewing Co. was struggling to keep up with demand after it inked a deal to replace Molson Breweries as the official beer at B.C. Place, home of the CFL's B.C. Lions. Its Surrey facility was capable of producing almost two million litres a year while Fort Garry's capacity was closer to five million litres. Russell CEO, Brian Harris, saw an opportunity to grow his company by using the strength of both breweries and in the process expand into the Alberta and Saskatchewan market.

Fort Garry was cautious at first, but after going over the proposal, shareholders voted in favour of the deal and the brewery was officially sold to Russell Brewing Inc. in October of 2007. Saville's new role was as vice-president of operations and he continued on as brewmaster for the Fort Garry plant.

In 2004, Alberta's Minhas Creek sparked a price war when they began importing their discounted beer into the Manitoba market. Seven years later Minhas demolished the Regal Furniture building on Logan Avenue and announced they might build a brewery on the site. Since then the company has opened a micro brewery in Calgary, but as of 2013 the project in Manitoba is on hold.

Kona Imperial Stout won a silver medal at the Canadian Brewing Awards in June of 2012. This isn't the first time Fort Garry has taken home an award from the CBA. During Doug Saville's tenure Fort Garry Dark took a gold medal in 2005 and in 2008 Two Rivers Red earned silver.

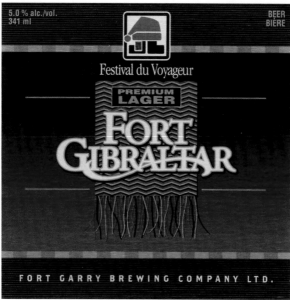

It had been a crazy ten years since Doug Saville lost his job at Molson's. He championed the cause for microbrewing in Manitoba and was instrumental in bringing Fort Garry back from the brink. With hard work and sacrifice from its employees, the brewery seemed to be on stable ground. It came then as a total shock when he was fired in November of 2008.

Sometimes people are a victim of their own success. Brian Harris stated that it was a change in corporate philosophy and not a reflection of Saville's skill as a brewmaster that led to his departure. It had not been Saville's decision alone to sell the brewery but by doing so, his fate had been sealed.

In 2012 Fort Garry continues to brew the popular brands from the Richard Hoeschen era as well as products from Russell. The Two Rivers name has fallen off, but Stone Cold remains a stalwart brand for the brewery. The company has kept a strong local presence by producing special beers for festivals such as Folklorama and Festival du Voyageur. Fort Garry has also managed to break into an area usually reserved for the nationals when it partnered with the Winnipeg Goldeyes and introduced the limited edition Angry Fish Pilsner in May of 2012. And finally, by taking a cue from its sister brewery in B.C., Fort Garry began to produce a Brewmaster Series of specialty beers.

Winnipeg's Secret Brewery:
The Canadian Malting Barley Technical Centre

You can't ask for their beer at your favourite watering hole or buy it at the local vendor. People walk by it every day, oblivious to the fact that one of the city's best-kept secret lies hidden in an office tower in downtown Winnipeg. Beer made at this little brewery is not for public consumption, but for research.

The Canadian Malting Barley Technical Centre isn't some sort of clandestine government organization. It's a non-profit agency set up to provide technical assistance to the malting and brewing industries. One of the major goals of the CMBTC is to promote Canadian malting barley internationally by offering their expertise to breweries all over the world. Located in the Grain Commission building at 303 Main Street, CMBTC has two state of the art pilot breweries as well as a malting facility.

Funding is provided by its members which include barley producers, breweries, malting companies and government agencies such as the Canadian Grain Commission. It also offers its services to non-members for malting and brewing trials. Rob McCaig, managing director and director of brewing has often worked with local breweries offering advice from his experience at CMBTC and as a former brewmaster for Molson Breweries. The breweries two pilot facilities can brew as little as II litres or up to 300 litres of finished beer in a controlled environment without being tainted by other brews; a problem larger breweries sometimes have when experimenting with new recipes. With all these resources at hand it's no wonder CMBTC has been an important asset to the local and national brewing industry since its inception in 2000.

So next time you're having a cold one brewed with Canadian barley, think of all the research that goes into making sure it's made with the best ingredients this country has to offer.

CMBTC's 3 hectolitre pilot brewery: The research facility is unique as there is no other organization quite like it the world.

The centre's malting facilities include drying kilns and germinators.

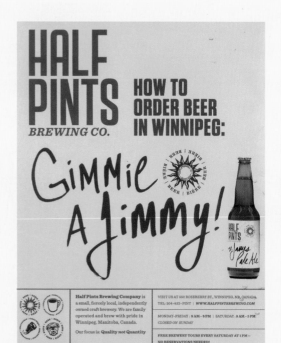

300 YEARS OF BEER—AN ILLUSTRATED HISTORY OF BREWING IN MANITOBA

HALF PINTS
BREWING COMPANY

When visiting Half Pints' St. James brewery patrons are greeted with a parking sign that says "For Beer Lovers Only! Lite Beer Drinkers Will Be Towed." This cheeky remark was written by brewmaster Dave Rudge and it perfectly sums up what his brewery is all about. Since bursting onto the local scene in 2006, Half Pints has steadily grown by following the craft brewing philosophy of making high-end specialty beers and ignoring the mainstream market. But that alone doesn't guarantee success. Co-owners Dave Rudge and Nicole Barry have managed to navigate the murky waters of Manitoba's brewing industry by being true to themselves, brewing beer with personality and setting realistic business goals. However, none of this was planned when Dave Rudge bought his first home brewing kit in the late 1990's.

In charge of 45 different brews with 12 being on tap at any one time, he was given creative freedom to develop new recipes and with winning results.

It's a little odd that the man regarded to be a local craft brewing guru didn't drink until he was 20 years old. When he took his first sip of a Guinness, Rudge easily singled out the subtle qualities of the dark stout and liked what it had to offer. The Winnipeg native honed his taste buds from working as a cook and brewing beer was a natural progression of this. After a few years of slaving in the kitchen Rudge had become, by his own admission, an "angry cook" from working

long hours in restaurants and at Winnipeg's Pyramid Cabaret. While working for the Hop and Vine, one of Winnipeg's original wine and beer making stores, he began experimenting with traditional recipes and it wasn't long before his wife Nicole was encouraging him to make brewing his profession.

He immersed himself in the art of brewing and eventually found himself on a first name basis with local microbrewing pioneers like Richard Hoeschen, Gary De Pape and Greg Nash. Rudge applied for a job at Fort Garry before deciding to take the Craft Brewing Science and Engineering course offered by the American Brewers Guild. When he finished the course it was off to British Columbia to work as an assistant brewer at the Backwoods Brewing Company, now known as the Dead Frog Brewery.

In 2002, Dave and Nicole moved closer to home when he took a job as Head Brewer at Regina's Bushwakker Brewing Company. The Bushwakker is considered to be one of Canada's best brewpubs and it was here that Dave really began to sharpen his skill as a brewer. In charge of 45 different brews with 12 being on tap at any one time, he was given creative freedom to develop new recipes and with winning results. At the 2004 and 2005 Canadian Brewing Awards he took home no less than 10 medals—including seven gold medals in a wide variety of categories.

With so many different beers to choose from he began to form an idea, a philosophy

Half Pints Brewing Company is a small, fiercely local, independently owned craft brewery. We are family operated and brew with pride in Winnipeg, Manitoba, Canada. Our focus is quality not quantity.

Unlike other breweries, we specifically set out to brew small batches of beer packed with big flavours. We cater to true beer lovers who care more about what's actually in their glass than what trinkets came in the case.

We hope you enjoy - cheers!

perhaps, on drinking and trying new beers. By drinking a half pint of beer (ten oz.) and then moving on to a different beer, one could enjoy a wide variety of beers without getting drunk. The phrase he soon began to use was, "A half pint of good beer is better than six pints of lousy beer any day." With this mantra, the Half Pints credo was formed.

Most Winnipeg beer drinkers were new to the style of craft beer Half Pints was making. To educate patrons each label gave a descriptive tutorial on what type of beer it was, how it made and even offered advice on what foods went best with it.

unfiltered   unpasteurized   unadulterated

small brewery BIG FLAVOUR
HALF PINTS
BREWING COMPANY

Half Pints Brewing Company is a small, fiercely local, independently owned craft brewery. We are family operated and brew with pride in Winnipeg, Manitoba, Canada. Our focus is quality not quantity.

Unlike other breweries, we specifically set out to brew small batches of beer packed with big flavours. We cater to true beer lovers who care more about what's actually in their glass than what trinkets came in the case.

We hope you enjoy - cheers!

334 Keewatin Street
Winnipeg, MB
R2X 2R9
Tel: (204) 832-PINT

Hekla Ave.
Keewatin St.
Park Lane Ave.

halfpintsbrewing.com

craft brewed in winnipeg mb canada

strong beer
little scrapper ipa
bière forte

To admit that the brewer at Half Pints is a bit of a hophead is an understatement. This India Pale Ale is unabashedly hoppy, not only from the Amarillo hops we add to the brew kettle, but also from the northwest U.S. variety called Cascade that we add directly to the final tank (a process called "dry hopping"). A firm, toasted malt presence forms the background for all these hops, and we're confident our Little Scrapper IPA could take other so-called IPA's to the mat if called upon to do so. Try it with a curry or a basket of beer battered fish & chips. Serve in a glass at 8°C. Bottle may contain sediment.

6 93314 01031 7

50 IBU   6.0% alc./vol.   660ml   keep refrigerated

Zach Mesman fills a 660ml bottle of beer. Over 200,000 bottles were hand filled and labelled before the brewery automated the process and switched to the 341 ml industry standard bottle.

"I'm not going to go the cheap beer route; I wouldn't be able to look at myself in the morning."

The Half Pints Brewing Company was born out of necessity. After being downsized out of her job in Regina, Nicole and Dave moved back home to Winnipeg in 2005 where, by this time, there was one surviving brewery in town. Now confident of their skills—Dave's brewing experience and Nicole's business acumen—the couple decided their only option was to open their own brewery. The question remained—was Winnipeg ready for real craft beer?

The new brewery was launched in the late summer of 2006. The previous year's beer war continued as both Fort Garry and Minhas lowered prices on select brands, but Half Pints was unconcerned. The discount beer market was as far away from their target audience as you could get. Instead, they would offer small batch, full-flavoured brews made with high quality ingredients. Always good for a colourful quote, Rudge commented when asked about discount beers, "I'm not going to go the cheap beer route; I wouldn't be able to look at myself in the morning."

That first year Dave and Nicole hardly had time to look at themselves at all. One thing was for sure; they wouldn't make the same mistakes others had made. Instead of laying out huge amounts of cash for expensive bottling lines and automatic labelers, everything was done by hand at their 3,000 square foot brewery. Although this savings in start-up costs was practical, it was also labour intensive. In addition to sales in kegs and 2 litre plastic bottles, they sold nearly 100,000 of the hand-filled 660 ml bottles in the first year of operation.

The Latin name for hops is Humulus Lupulus so it was only natural to call the ultra hoppy Double IPA, "Humulus Ludicrous."

Starting small was crucial to the company's future success. The brewery was built in a strip mall at 334 Keewatin Street and funding came from the Business Development Bank of Canada as well as family and friends. With Dave concentrating solely on the creative side of brewing, Nicole ran the business end while earning her degree as a Certified General Accountant.

Half Pints began offering Saturday afternoon brewery tours where patrons could see for themselves how Bulldog Amber Ale, Little Scrapper IPA and Stir Stick Stout were made. These popular outings demystified the brewing process that was normally hidden away behind brewhouse walls. They were, in a small part, responsible for converting the uninitiated.

Another advantage to small batch brewing is the ability to brew seasonal beers and different types of "one off's" used for promotions. This creates a certain buzz when beer is in limited supply. When Half Pints launched their "Humulus Ludicrous" the first batch sold out in four days. This was an eight percent, extremely hoppy concoction and not for the faint of heart. It proved once and for all that Winnipeg was finally embracing the craft beer movement.

Dave Rudge kept busy introducing new recipes for his growing fan base. During the first year of operation Half Pints products were only available inside the confines of the city's Perimeter Highway. And then a remarkable thing began to happen. Local fans began sending bottles to friends in far off places and soon Half Pints beers were collecting rave reviews on websites and blogs from around the world. In less than two years Half Pints sales grew to the point where filling bottles by hand just wasn't going to cut it. An automatic bottling line was installed in March of 2008 and at the same time they switched to the industry standard 341 ml bottle. With this smaller bottle they were now open to a wider market and sales exploded.

It's only fitting when Half Pints moved to their new St. James location at 550 Roseberry Street in November of 2008 they would name a new beer after the Winnipeg suburb. St. James Pale Ale was a response to a request from customers for a beer that was a little more attractive to people who liked conventional beers. The idea of brewing a light beer was tantamount to treason so Dave Rudge came up with a recipe that

Although she isn't the first women to head a brewery in Manitoba, (Natalie Riedle takes that distinction) Nicole Barry is a rarity in the male dominated brewing industry. As part owner and CEO of Half Pints she has kept the company on firm ground throughout the early years of its growth.

Brewed by

HALF PINTS
BREWING COMPANY

Winnipeg, MB
(204)832-7468

STRONG BEER
BIER FORTE

8.4 % Alc/Vol
75 IBU
650ml

$ELLOUT $TOUT

Brewed with heaps of roasted barley, crystal malts, and flaked oats, and then hopped up with Willamette and Centennials. During the fermentation, Jaggery (a sugar derived from palm tree sap in India) is added, and when finished, the brew is aged in whisky barrels for six months.

The result is a beer of unquestionable character and complexity, much like the folks at Half Pints.

Serve at 12 C. in a brandy snifter.

WWW.HALFPINTSBREWING.CO

$ellout $tout was a nose thumbing to those that might have thought Half Pints had gone mainstream with their St. James Pale Ale. The brewery has always had a punk rock attitude and for good reason; Dave Rudge spent his youth playing in punk bands and the brewery is an avid supporter of the local music scene.

under one license. More importantly, brewpubs will be able to sell their beer off premise to the general public and to liquor stores. This might be the catalyst that's needed to kick start another brewpub venture. Or how about an idea that harkens back to the early days of brewing when all the ingredients were grown locally?

There is nothing better than free publicity. Queer Beer was an instant hit when Half Pints first brewed a limited supply for the Pride Winnipeg Festival in 2011. With the tag line "Impeccable Taste, A Little Fruity and 100% Fabulous" the beer was an innovative and somewhat daring way to celebrate the festival and it gave the brewery more publicity than money can buy.

341
4.8
11

Soft and smooth with a floral finish

HALF PINTS
BREWING CO.
St. James Pale Ale

CRAFT BREWED & BOTTLED BY HALF PINTS BREWING COMPANY LTD., WINNIPEG, MB, CANADA. 204-832-PINT | WWW.HALFPINTSBREWING.COM

KEEP REFRIGERATED RETURN FOR REFUND WHERE APPLICABLE

In 2009, two of Half Pints beers appeared in a book called "The World's Best Beers" by British-based writer Ben MacFarland.

was user friendly, but definitely in the Half Pints tradition. When St. James Pale Ale became the company's bestselling brand, a question was pondered. Would the beer nerds accuse Half Pints of selling out to the masses? Rudge and his crew answered that query with "$ell Out $tout" another in a long line of specialty beers the company was making. The punk rock themed beer lived up to its name and sold out in no time.

And so it goes. In 2009, two of Half Pints beers appeared in a book called "The World's Best Beers" by British-based writer Ben MacFarland. A year later, Humulus Ludicrous landed a spot in "1001 Beers You Must Taste Before You Die." Half Pints motto of "quality not quantity" has taken it a long way since it opened in 2006 and its future seems intact.

What of the future? Will the success of Half Pints inspire more development in the industry? In 2011, long overdue changes to Manitoba's liquor laws finally allowed brewpubs to operate

CREATED BY HALF PINTS BREWING COMPANY FOR PRIDE WINNIPEG

PRIDE
WINNIPEG
Queer BEER
IMPECCABLE TASTE, A LITTLE FRUITY, AND 100% FABULOUS!

HALF PINTS
BREWING CO.
Brewed by Half Pints Brewing Company Ltd., Winnipeg, Canada

4.8% alc./vol.

WWW.HALFPINTSBREWING.COM   341ml   KEEP REFRIGERATED   10 IBU   WWW.PRIDEWI

BACK TO BASICS
THE FARMERY
ESTATE BREWERY

Rob McCaig of the Canadian Malting Barley Technical Centre (middle) with Chris and Lawrence Warwaruk. Rob worked with the brothers developing the recipe for their first beer.

Breweries come and go, leaving broken dreams in their wake. But don't tell brothers Lawrence and Chris Warwaruk not to dream. In 2011, the owners of Winnipeg's Luxalune Gastropub announced they were planning to build Canada's first estate brewery. What sets this concept apart from other breweries is that the brothers will grow all the ingredients for their beer on their own farm. Combining the two words farm and brewery, the Farmery will be located east of Neepawa, Manitoba in an area that hasn't had a brewery for over one hundred years.

Raised on a farm, the brothers are up to the challenge of growing hops and malting their own barley. And they're no strangers to beer either. The Luxalune Gastropub offers 150 different brands of beer. Now the Warwaruks can add the Farmery Estate's beer to their list.

As of 2012, Chris and Lawrence haven't set a firm date for construction, but they are busy growing hops and barley. With the help of Rob McCaig from the CMBTC they developed a sample recipe and on December 7, 2012 the Farmery Premium Lager finally became available to the general public. Sold in bright orange six packs the brewing is contracted out to an Ontario brewery. If all goes well and there is enough a demand for the product Chris and Lawrence will take their dream to the next step and build their Farmery.

What sets this concept apart from other breweries is that the brothers will grow all the ingredients for their beer on their own farm.

In the mean time patrons at the Luxalune can sample the light lager served in mason jars, just like back on the farm!

1836—The Council of Assiniboia passes a resolution banning the sale and traffic of beer to Aboriginals under a penalty of 20 shillings. In 1847 it becomes unlawful to sell or barter beer to be drunk on an individual's premise without a licence. (Source: The House of Shea, page 90)

1878—Manitoba's first provincial liquor commission is established. The commission allows one bar for every 300 people in the province. (Source: Manitoba Gaming Control Commission)

1906—In Beausejour, MB, the Manitoba Glass Works Company is established. They produced embossed glass bottles for Edward L. Drewry for a period of time until the closure of the factory in 1913.

1911—Manitoba's first beer strike occurred when employees from E. L. Drewry and McDonagh & Shea walk off the job. The short 30 hour strike ended after the brewery workers demands were met. The brewery dropped the work day in the winter months from ten hours to nine. (Source: *Manitoba Free Press*, July 10, 1911)

1916—Prohibition grips Manitoba forcing breweries to export their beer to other provinces, a loophole not available to U.S. breweries when that country goes dry in 1920. Breweries survive by making temperance beer and soft drinks.

1923—Prohibition ends in Manitoba and the Government Liquor Control Act introduces strict regulations for pricing, advertising, sales quotas and personal purchasing limits. (Source: Manitoba Gaming Control Commission)

1920's—Manitoba's breweries keep busy supplying beer to thirsty Americans. In 1925 Canadian beer exports are close to the 3 million gallon mark. Manitoba Government bans the exportation of liquor into the United States in 1926 on the grounds that it was in contravention of the liquor control act. (Source: *Manitoba Free Press*, March 25, 1930)

1928—Beer parlours can now be licenced to sell beer by the glass. However, all rules are strictly prescribed in an attempt to establish a moral and respectable public space for drinking.

Manitoba's only women's beer parlour opens at Winnipeg Beach in 1928, but is shut down after a few hours because it has not obtained the necessary licence.

The Liquor Control Licensing Board (the Board) is established to control which establishments will be granted permits to sell or serve beer. The Board works with the LCC as part of a larger government-sponsored agency. The following year, the Office of the Chief Inspector is created to enforce liquor laws. (Source: Manitoba Gaming Control Commission)

1934—Beer vendors appear in Manitoba. Hotels can now become licensed to sell beer for off-site consumption. (Source: Manitoba Gaming Control Commission)

1936—The beginning of interprovincial trade barriers. A bottle of beer manufactured outside Manitoba must be sold for five cents more than locally produced beer. (Source: Manitoba Gaming Control Commission)

1946—In spite of the holdover of wartime beer rationing, Manitobans consume 8,808,744 imperial gallons of beer. (Source: Dominion Brewers Association, 1948)

1955—During a provincial review of Manitoba's liquor laws (the Bracken Report), local breweries came under fire for a number of issues. From excessive profits, hotel ownership, and political donations, brewery representatives found themselves defending their employers in front of commission inquiries.

1956—*The Liquor Control Act* replaces the *Government Liquor Control Act*. The new act relaxes many of the restrictive laws put in place after Prohibition. Manitobans no longer need to apply for a permit to buy alcohol. Beer parlours are now required to serve food and non-alcoholic beverages. They must also close during the supper hour. The next year mixed gender drinking is allowed in cocktail lounges, beverage rooms and restaurants. In 1960 Aboriginal people can purchase liquor for off-premises consumption. However, they are still unable to consume liquor in licenced establishments, and sales are not allowed on reserves. (Source: Manitoba Gaming Control Commission)

1956—Wooden barrels are phased out in favour of steel-aluminum kegs.

1965—Games are permitted for the first time. Bars are allowed to add games like darts and shuffleboard, adding the air of an English pub to many establishments. (Source: Manitoba Gaming Control Commission)

1967—Banned since the Second World War liquor advertising is now permitted with some restrictions on when ads can be aired. Beer ads return to local newspapers and magazines.

1970—The legal drinking age is lowered to 18. Manitoba becomes one of the first provinces to reduce the eligible age to buy liquor from 21 years of age. During the next decade, all provinces will lower the minimum age to 18 or 19. (Source: Manitoba Gaming Control Commission)

1975—Women are permitted to handle, serve and sell beer in a beer parlour, but by this time the antiquated establishments are beginning to disappear. (Source: Manitoba Gaming Control Commission)

1974—Labatt's Manitoba Breweries, Kiewel-Pelissier Breweries Ltd and Uncle Ben's go on strike.

1975—Canned beer sales cease until the idea is revived in the 1980's.

1977—Waiters and waitresses no longer need to be licensed by MLCC.

1980—Individuals can bring alcohol into Manitoba from other provinces. They no longer need to leave liquor at the border when entering Manitoba. (Source: Manitoba Gaming Control Commission)

1982—Unavailable to the general public since the mid 1970's, the 24 case of beer returns. The 18 pack, a first for Manitoba, is introduced. This is the beginning of the package wars that are still being waged in 2013.

1984—Beverage rooms and beer parlours no longer need to close during the supper hour.

1985—Aboriginal people can consume liquor, both on and off reserve as Manitoba acts on provisions put in place by the federal government in 1951. (Source: Manitoba Gaming Control Commission)

1991—New Beer Distributor. Started in 1991 by Bill Gould and Todd Thurston as a beer distributorship, WETT Sales & Distribution has grown from a two man operation in Manitoba to a full service beer distributor in Manitoba and a beer, wine, and spirits agency in Manitoba and Saskatchewan. (Source: Wett Sales & Distribution)

1993—Vendors have more price and product options. They can now sell imported beer, as well as domestic. They are no longer required to carry beer from each brewery in the province, and can charge different prices for different domestic beers. They can also conduct

beer sampling. (Source: Manitoba Gaming Control Commission)

2011—Licencing improvements are implemented. Manitoba begins offering a new class of licence for brew pubs. (Source: Manitoba Gaming Control Commission)

2013—Canada, with an average tax rate of 50% on beer, is the second highest taxed country in the world. (Source: Brewers Association of Canada)

The price of beer in Manitoba continues to rise.

Here is the average cost of a 12 pack case of domestic beer over the ages.

1928 – $1.65

1959 – $2.60

1967 – $2.93

1986 – $9.75

2013 – $23.75

INDEX

CREDITS

Every effort has been made to correctly identify and credit copyright holders of the illustrations used in 300 Years of Beer. Any oversights or errors will be corrected in subsequent editions.

Contributors from the Great White North Brewerianists Club wish to remain anonymous. These credits will be listed as GWN.

Studio Photography – Bill Wright.

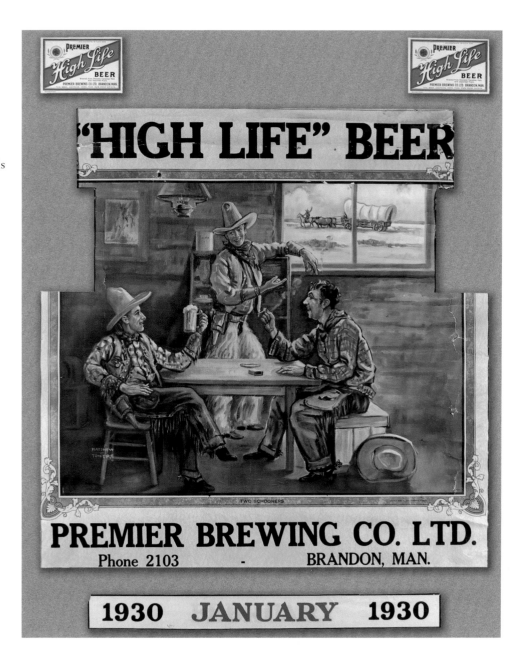